Monstrous No. 1

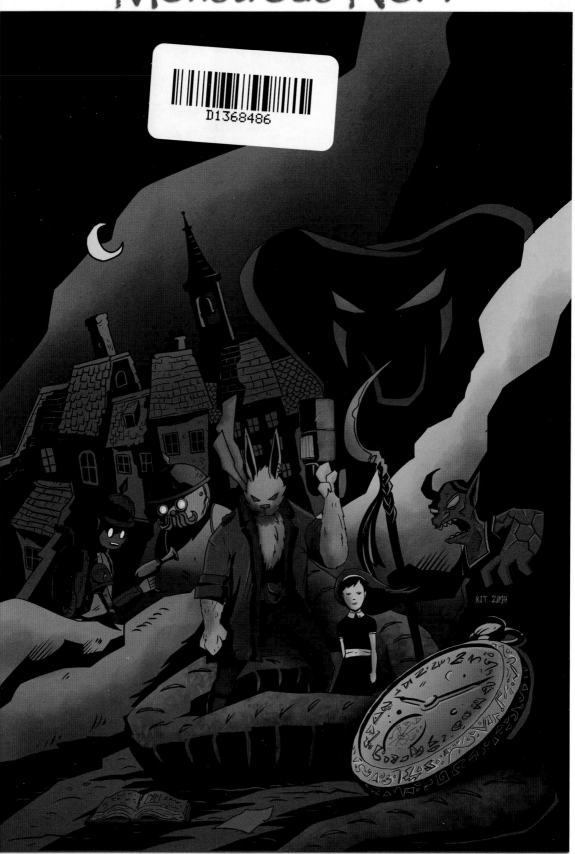

Hire Power

MONSTROUS

Journal Entry: C3941

Journal Entry: C3941

The story of **Frankenstein** *and his creation has been told many times: a tale of a man who cobbled together corpses and made a* **monster**...

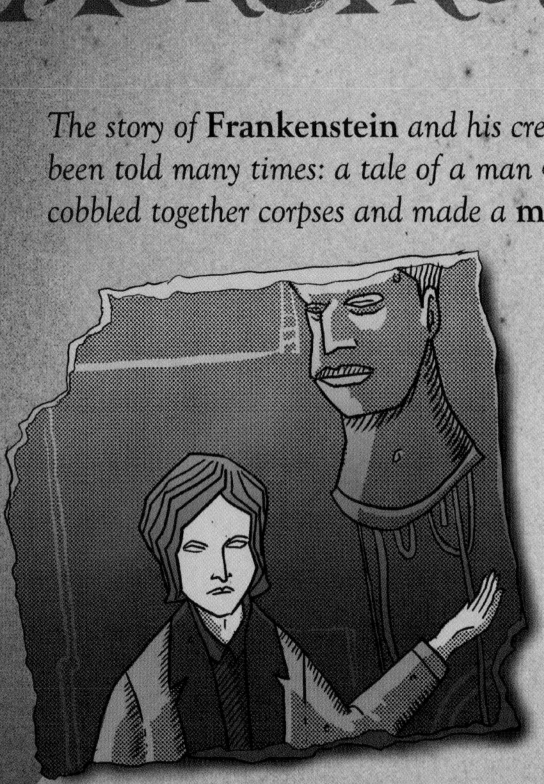

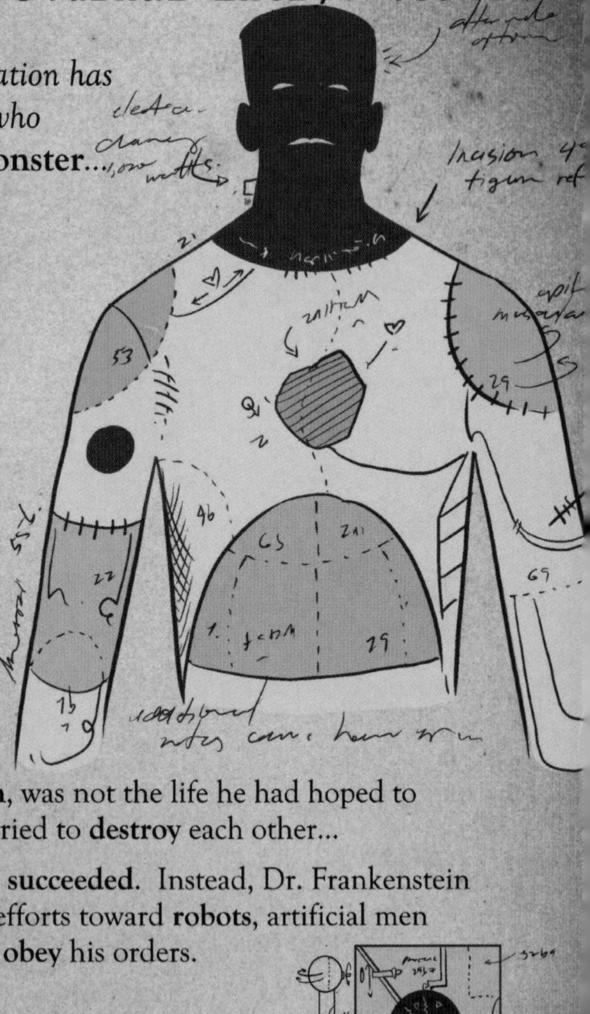

Frankenstein's creature, his new **Adam**, was not the life he had hoped to construct. The two **hated** each other, tried to **destroy** each other...

But neither **succeeded**. Instead, Dr. Frankenstein turned his efforts toward **robots**, artificial men who would **obey** his orders.

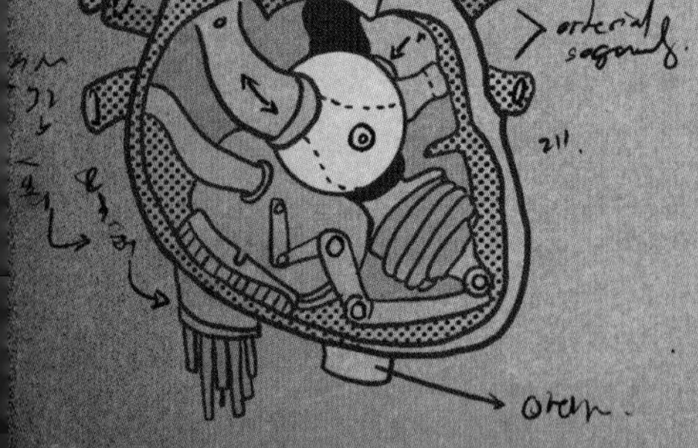

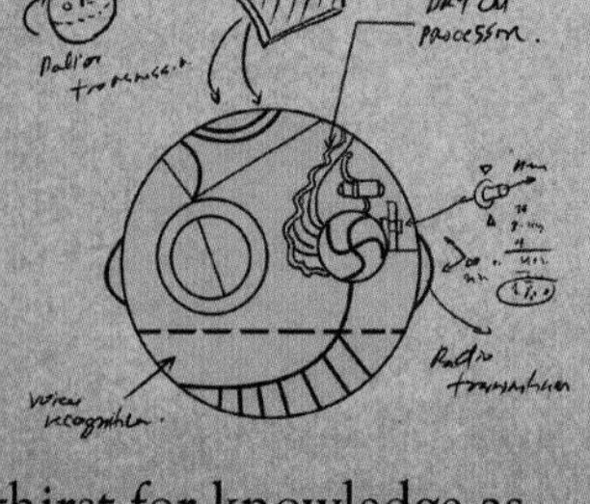

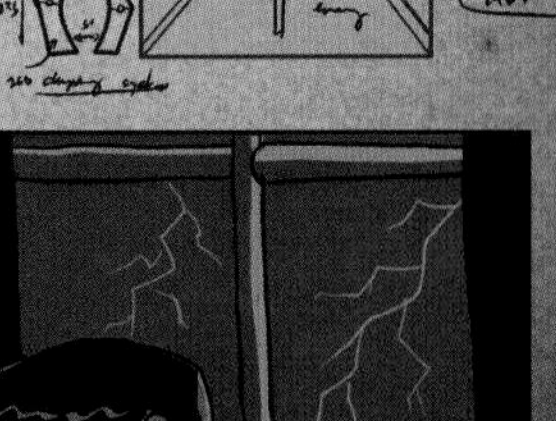

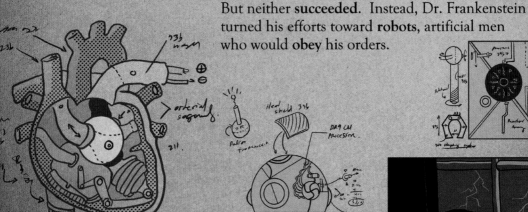

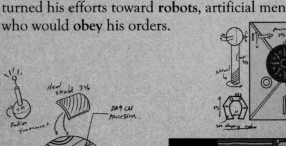

The creature, spurred by a thirst for knowledge as much as **hate**, sought out Frankenstein's secrets of life and death to manufacture more **monsters** like himself...

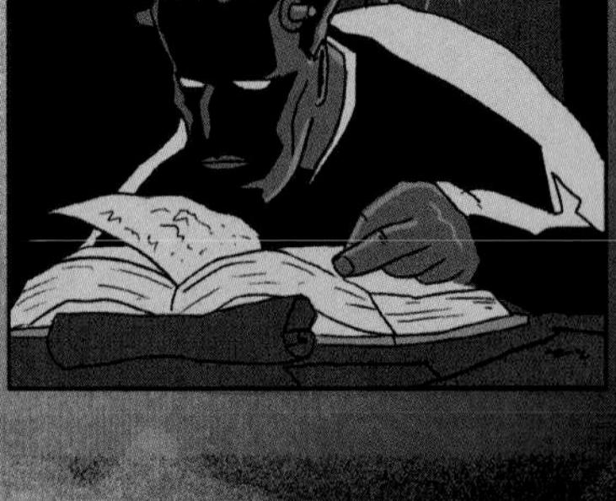

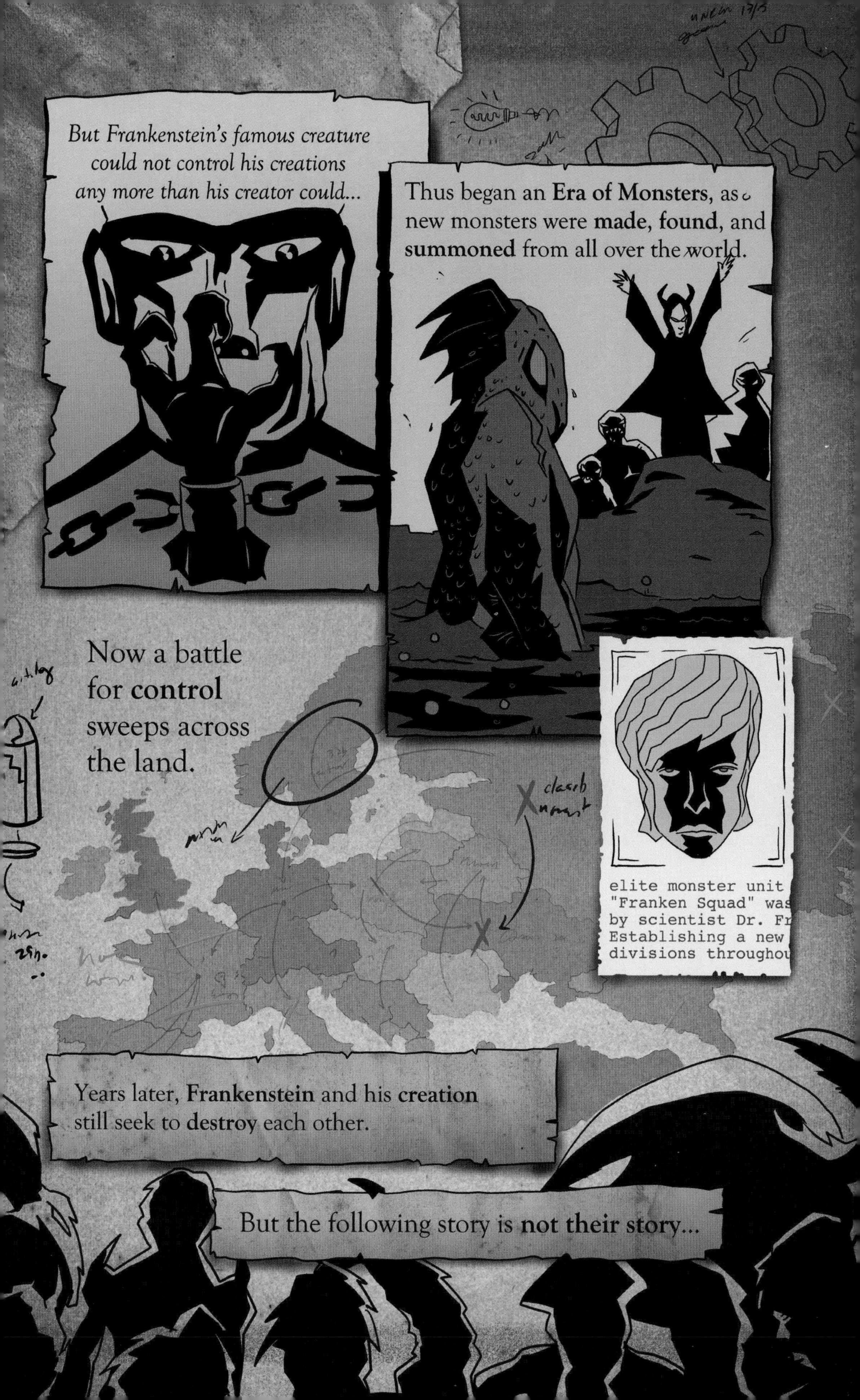
But Frankenstein's famous creature could not control his creations any more than his creator could...
Thus began an Era of Monsters, as new monsters were made, found, and summoned from all over the world.
Now a battle for control sweeps across the land.
elite monster unit
"Franken Squad" was
by scientist Dr. Fr
Establishing a new
divisions throughou
Years later, Frankenstein and his creation still seek to destroy each other.
But the following story is not their story...

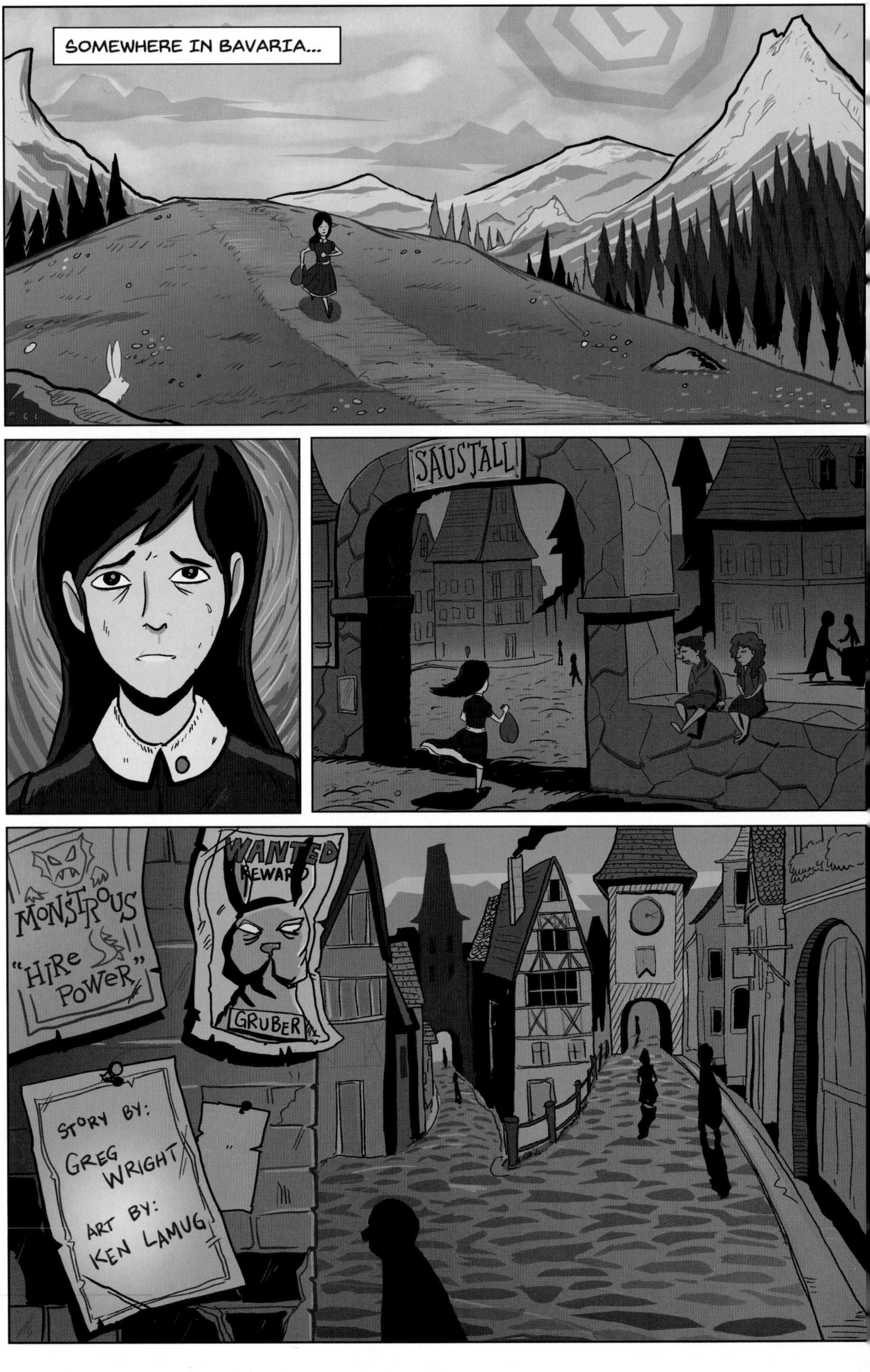
SOMEWHERE IN BAVARIA...
SAUSTALL
MONSTROUS
"HIRE POWER"
WANTED
REWARD
GRUBER
STORY BY:
GREG WRIGHT
ART BY:
KEN LAMUG

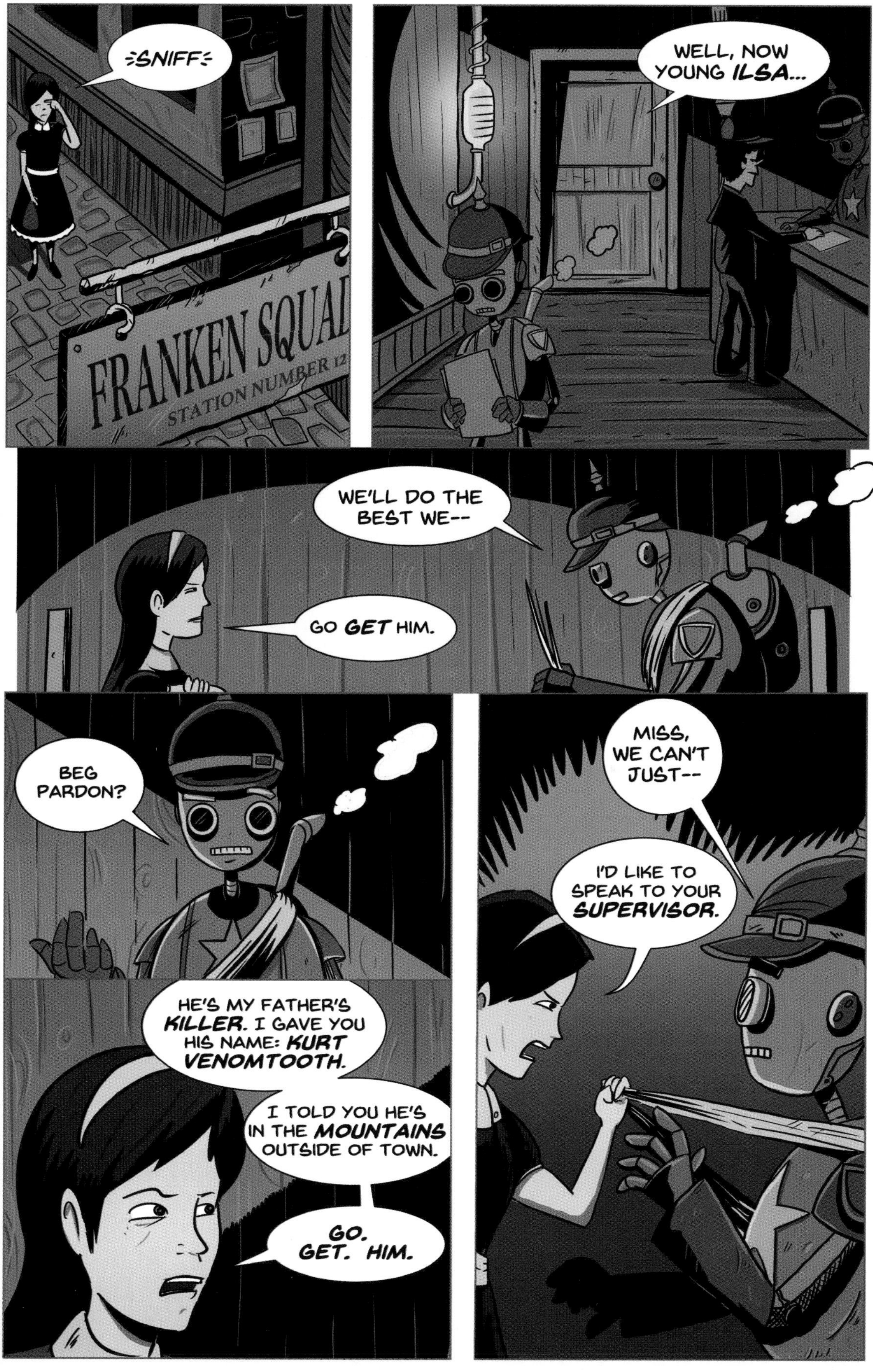
SNIFF
FRANKEN SQUAD
STATION NUMBER 12
WELL, NOW YOUNG ILSA...
WE'LL DO THE BEST WE--
GO GET HIM.
BEG PARDON?
HE'S MY FATHER'S KILLER. I GAVE YOU HIS NAME: KURT VENOMTOOTH.
I TOLD YOU HE'S IN THE MOUNTAINS OUTSIDE OF TOWN.
GO. GET. HIM.
MISS, WE CAN'T JUST--
I'D LIKE TO SPEAK TO YOUR SUPERVISOR.

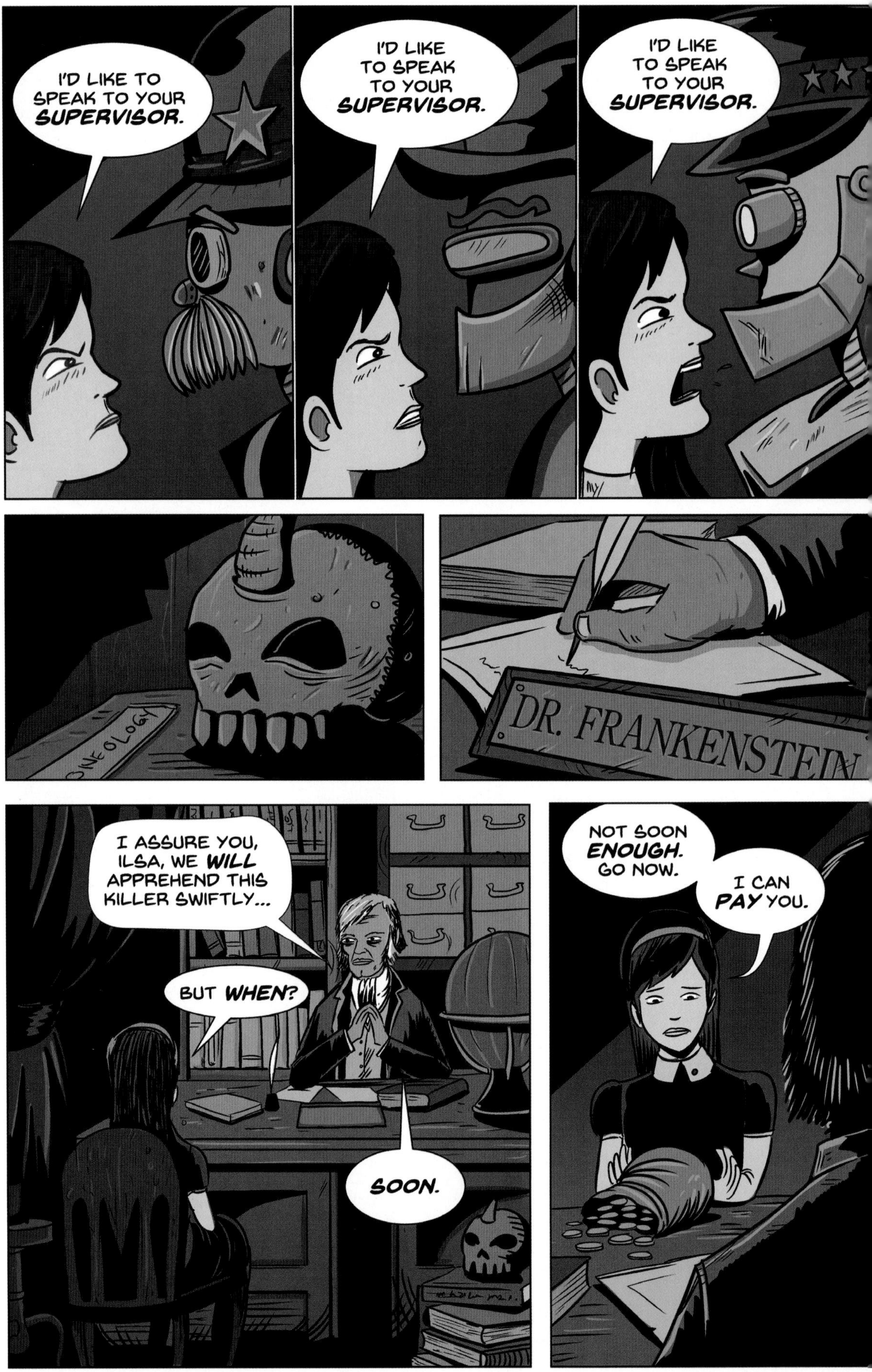
I'D LIKE TO SPEAK TO YOUR **SUPERVISOR.**
I'D LIKE TO SPEAK TO YOUR **SUPERVISOR.**
I'D LIKE TO SPEAK TO YOUR **SUPERVISOR.**
DR. FRANKENSTEIN
I ASSURE YOU, ILSA, WE **WILL** APPREHEND THIS KILLER SWIFTLY...
BUT **WHEN?**
SOON.
I CAN **PAY** YOU.
NOT SOON **ENOUGH.** GO NOW.

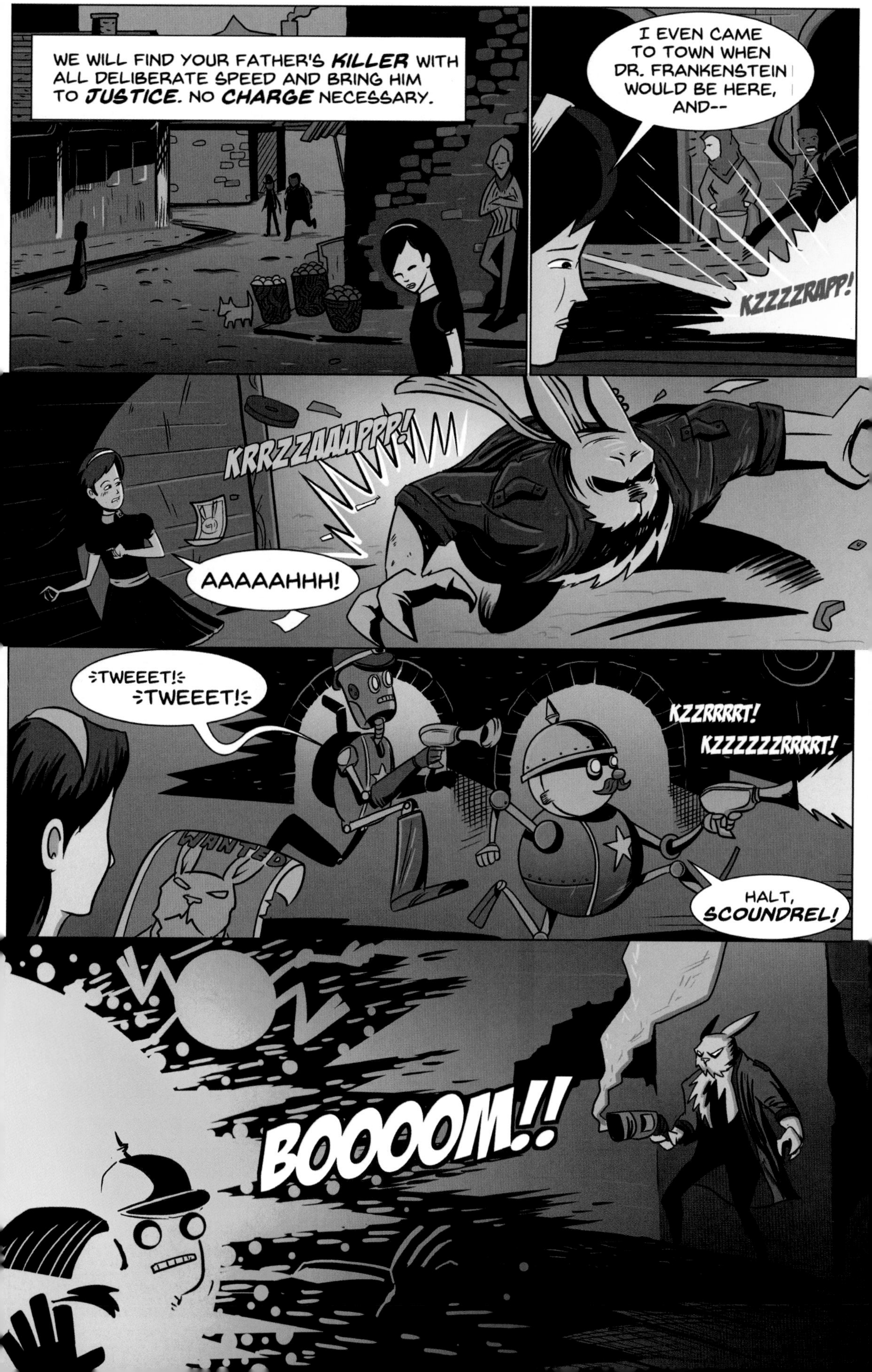
WE WILL FIND YOUR FATHER'S KILLER WITH ALL DELIBERATE SPEED AND BRING HIM TO JUSTICE. NO CHARGE NECESSARY.
I EVEN CAME TO TOWN WHEN DR. FRANKENSTEIN WOULD BE HERE, AND--
KZZZZRAPP!
KRRZZAAAPPP!
AAAAAHHH!
TWEEET!
TWEEET!
WANTED
KZZRRRRT!
KZZZZZZRRRRT!
HALT, SCOUNDREL!
BOOOOM!!

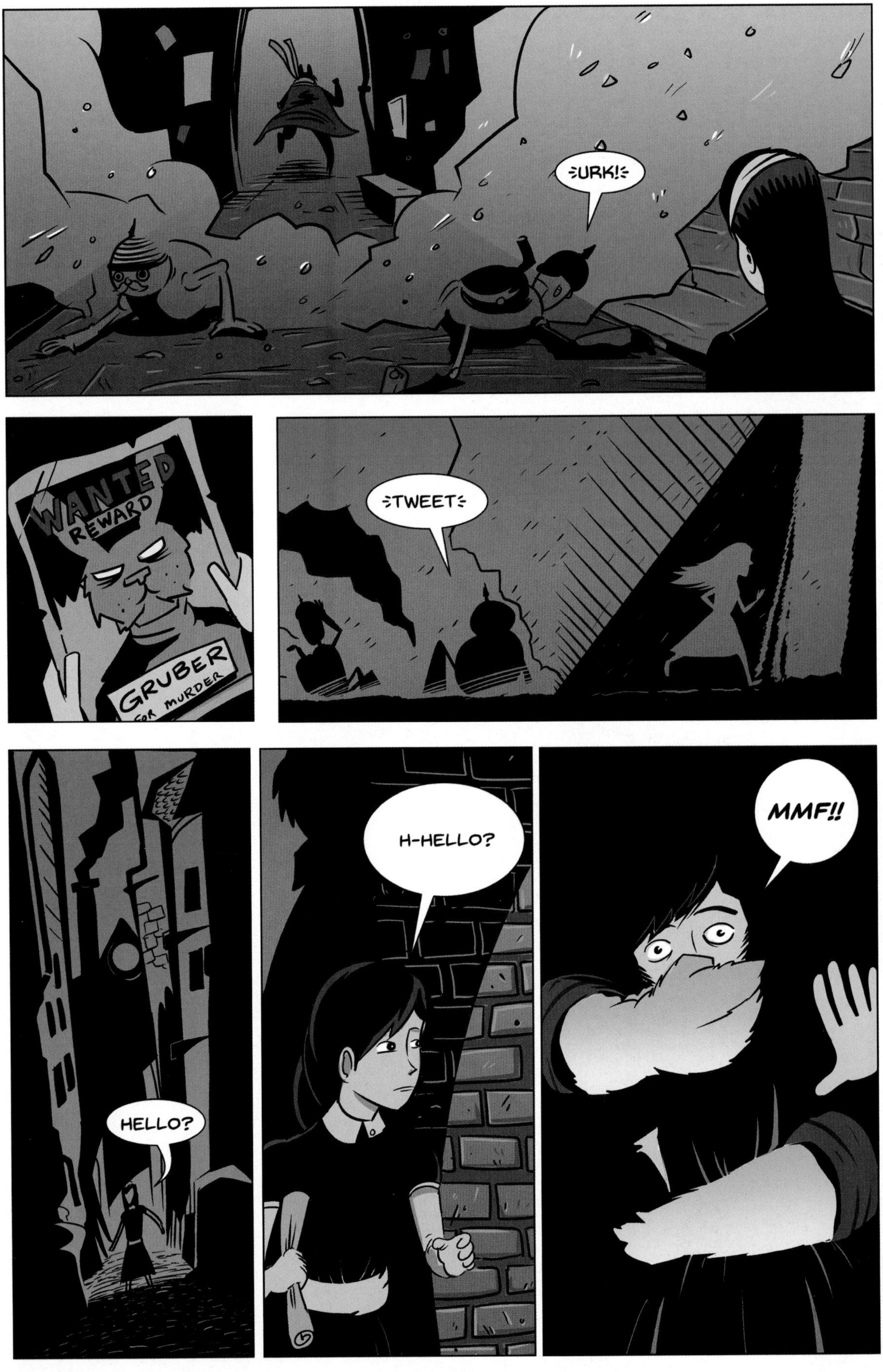
URK!
WANTED
REWARD
GRUBER
FOR MURDER
TWEET
HELLO?
H-HELLO?
MMF!!

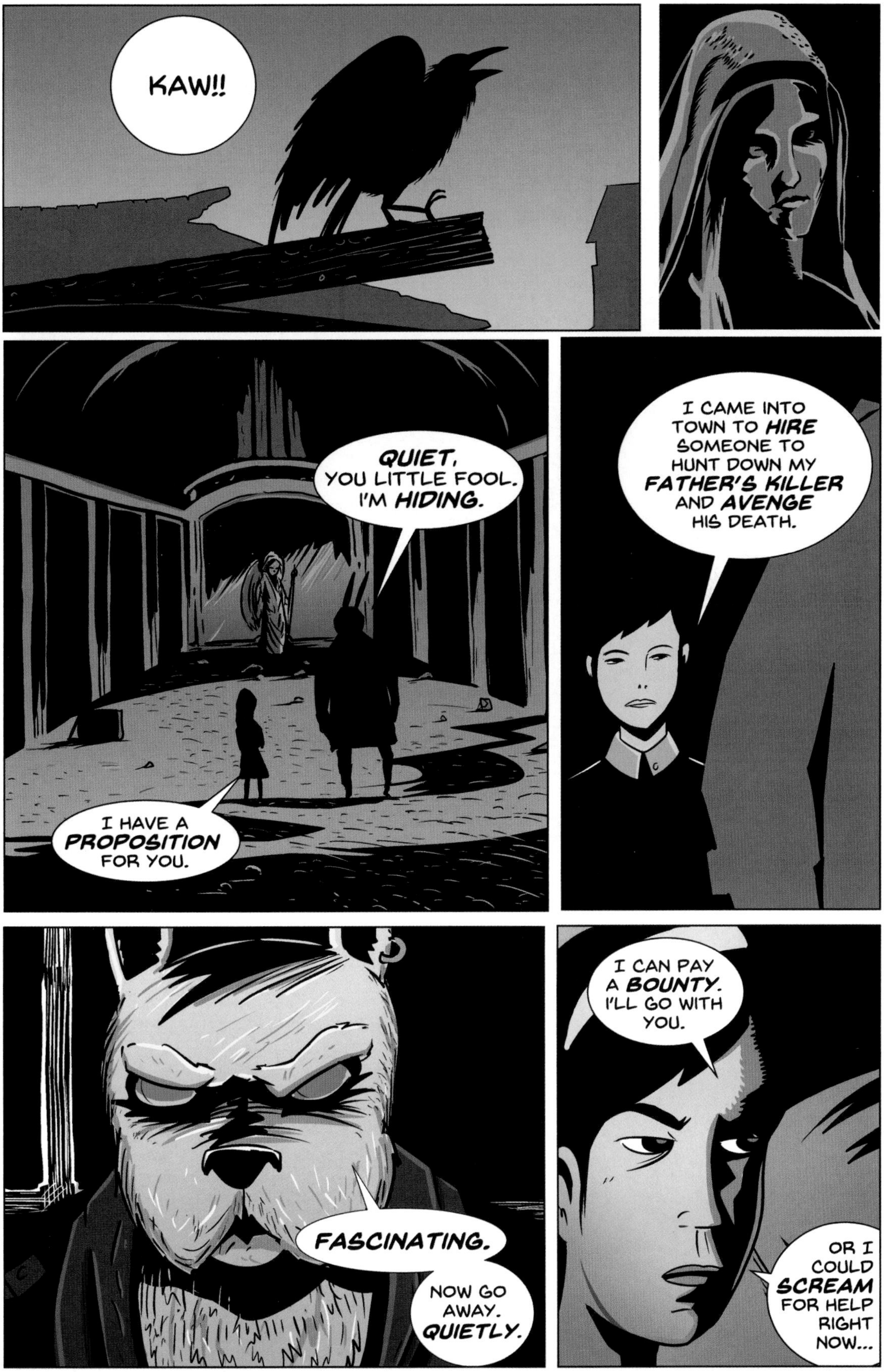
KAW!!
QUIET, YOU LITTLE FOOL. I'M HIDING.
I HAVE A PROPOSITION FOR YOU.
I CAME INTO TOWN TO HIRE SOMEONE TO HUNT DOWN MY FATHER'S KILLER AND AVENGE HIS DEATH.
FASCINATING.
NOW GO AWAY. QUIETLY.
I CAN PAY A BOUNTY. I'LL GO WITH YOU.
OR I COULD SCREAM FOR HELP RIGHT NOW...

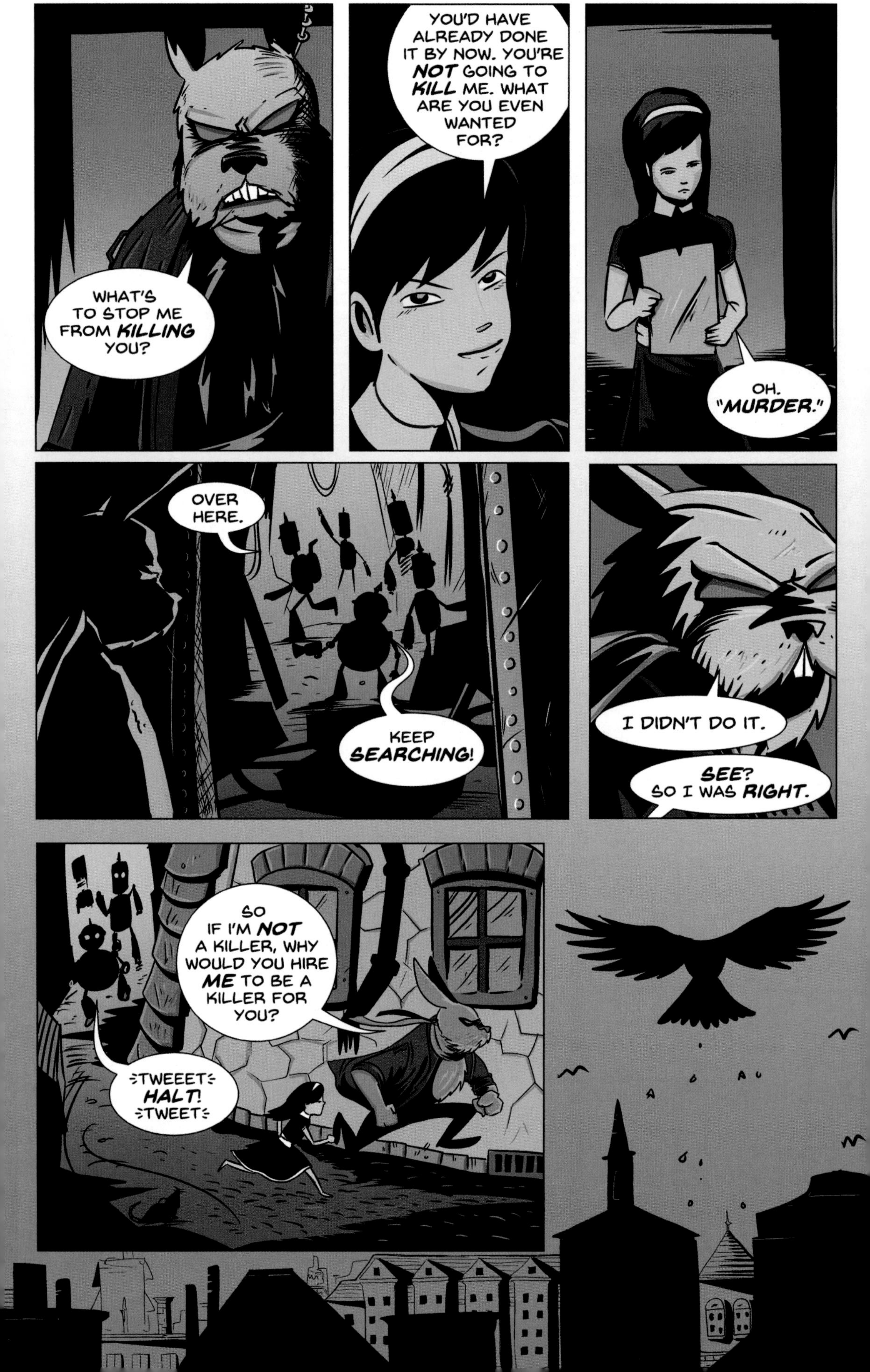
WHAT'S TO STOP ME FROM KILLING YOU?
YOU'D HAVE ALREADY DONE IT BY NOW. YOU'RE NOT GOING TO KILL ME. WHAT ARE YOU EVEN WANTED FOR?
OH. "MURDER."
OVER HERE.
KEEP SEARCHING!
I DIDN'T DO IT.
SEE? SO I WAS RIGHT.
SO IF I'M NOT A KILLER, WHY WOULD YOU HIRE ME TO BE A KILLER FOR YOU?
TWEEET HALT! TWEET

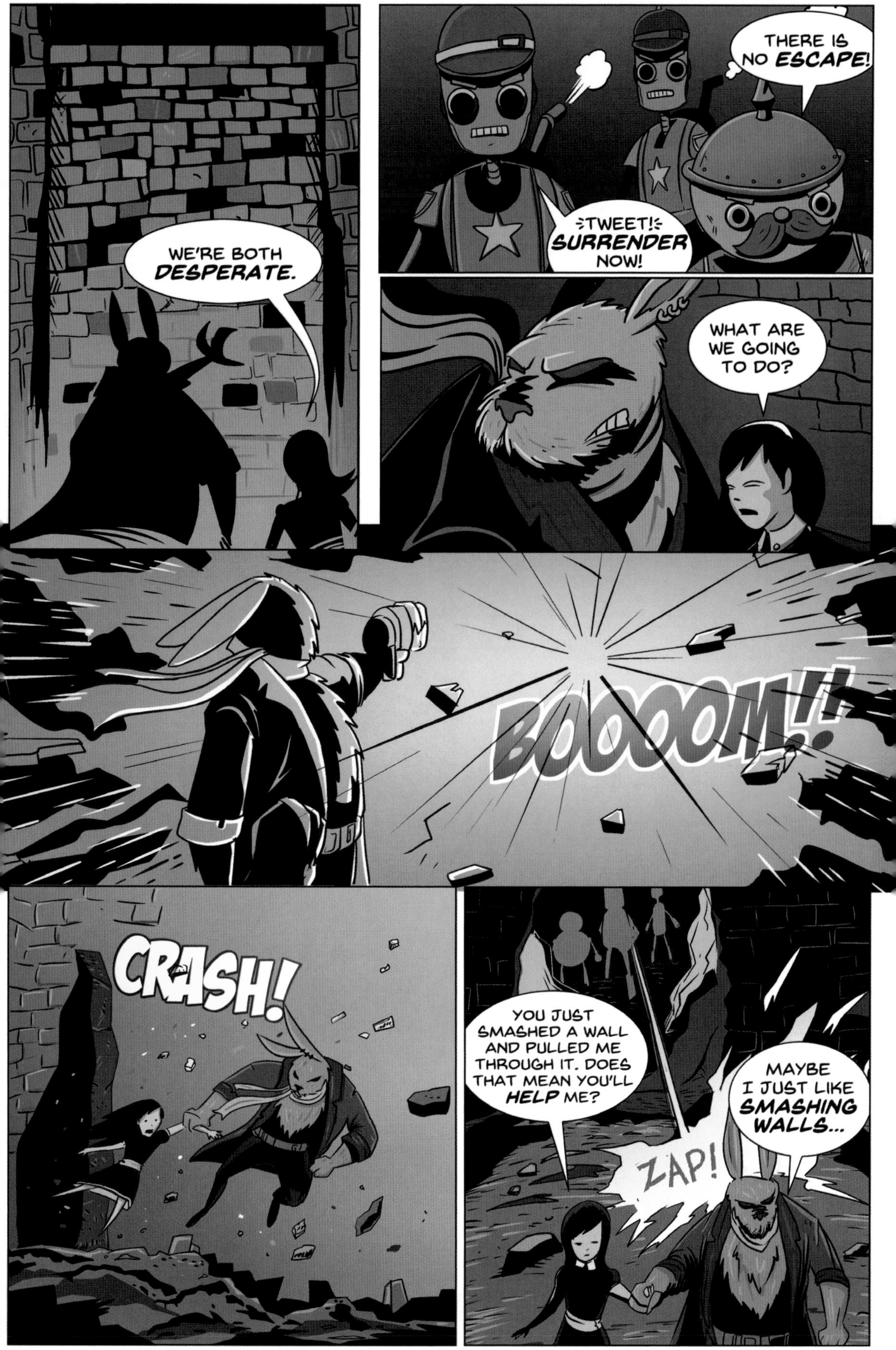
WE'RE BOTH DESPERATE.
THERE IS NO ESCAPE!
TWEET! SURRENDER NOW!
WHAT ARE WE GOING TO DO?
BOOOOM!!
CRASH!
YOU JUST SMASHED A WALL AND PULLED ME THROUGH IT. DOES THAT MEAN YOU'LL HELP ME?
MAYBE I JUST LIKE SMASHING WALLS...
ZAP!

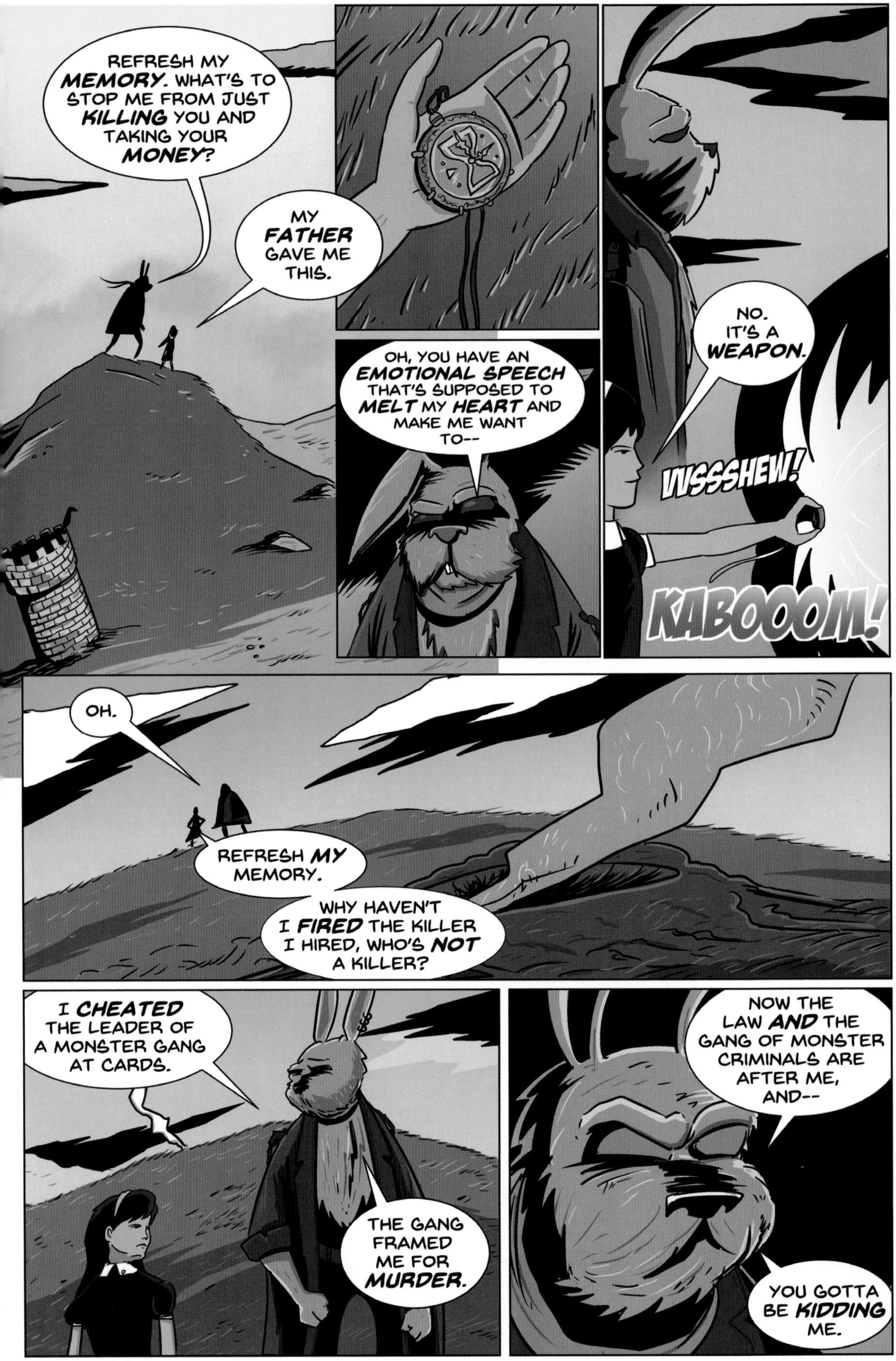
REFRESH MY MEMORY. WHAT'S TO STOP ME FROM JUST KILLING YOU AND TAKING YOUR MONEY?
MY FATHER GAVE ME THIS.
OH, YOU HAVE AN EMOTIONAL SPEECH THAT'S SUPPOSED TO MELT MY HEART AND MAKE ME WANT TO--
NO. IT'S A WEAPON.
VVSSSHEW!
KABOOOM!
OH.
REFRESH MY MEMORY.
WHY HAVEN'T I FIRED THE KILLER I HIRED, WHO'S NOT A KILLER?
I CHEATED THE LEADER OF A MONSTER GANG AT CARDS.
THE GANG FRAMED ME FOR MURDER.
NOW THE LAW AND THE GANG OF MONSTER CRIMINALS ARE AFTER ME, AND--
YOU GOTTA BE KIDDING ME.

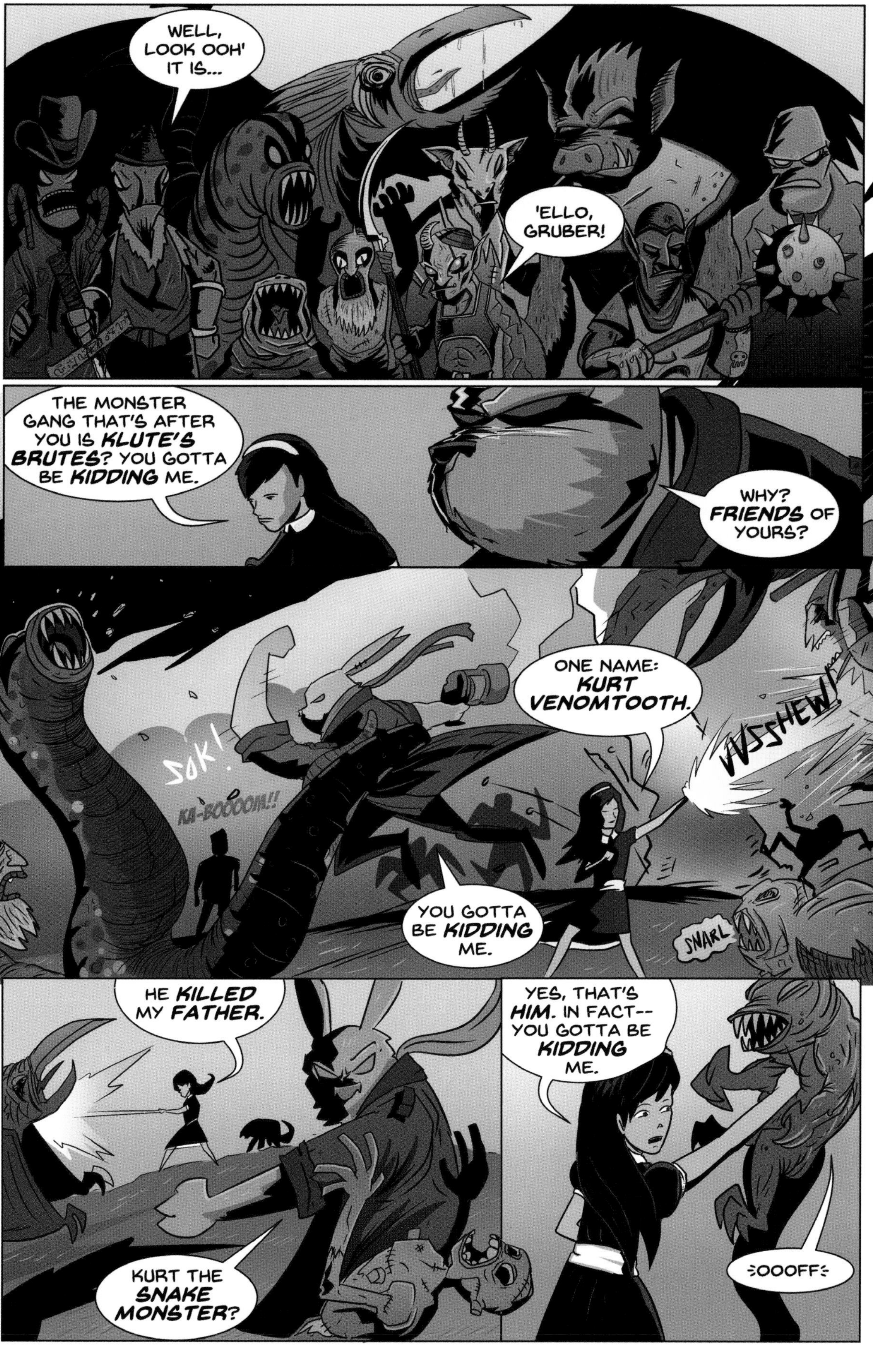
WELL, LOOK OOH' IT IS...
'ELLO, GRUBER!
THE MONSTER GANG THAT'S AFTER YOU IS KLUTE'S BRUTES? YOU GOTTA BE KIDDING ME.
WHY? FRIENDS OF YOURS?
ONE NAME: KURT VENOMTOOTH.
VVSSHEW!
SOK!
KA-BOOOOM!!
YOU GOTTA BE KIDDING ME.
SNARL
HE KILLED MY FATHER.
KURT THE SNAKE MONSTER?
YES, THAT'S HIM. IN FACT-- YOU GOTTA BE KIDDING ME.
OOOFF

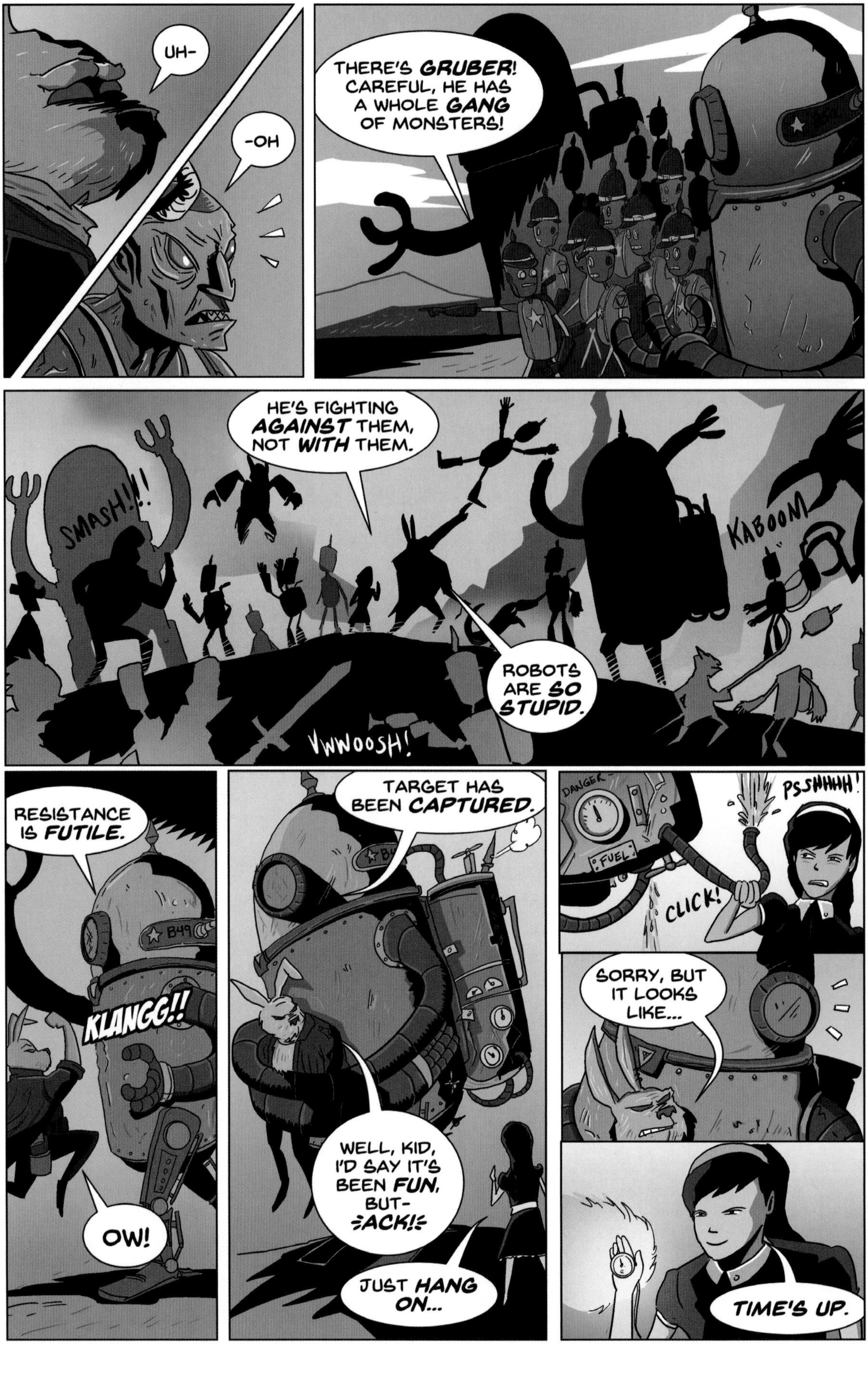
UH-
-OH
THERE'S GRUBER! CAREFUL, HE HAS A WHOLE GANG OF MONSTERS!
HE'S FIGHTING AGAINST THEM, NOT WITH THEM.
SMASH!!!
KABOOM
ROBOTS ARE SO STUPID.
VWWOOSH!
RESISTANCE IS FUTILE.
B49
KLANGG!!
OW!
TARGET HAS BEEN CAPTURED.
WELL, KID, I'D SAY IT'S BEEN FUN, BUT- ACK!
JUST HANG ON...
DANGER
FUEL
PSSHHHH!
CLICK!
SORRY, BUT IT LOOKS LIKE...
TIME'S UP.

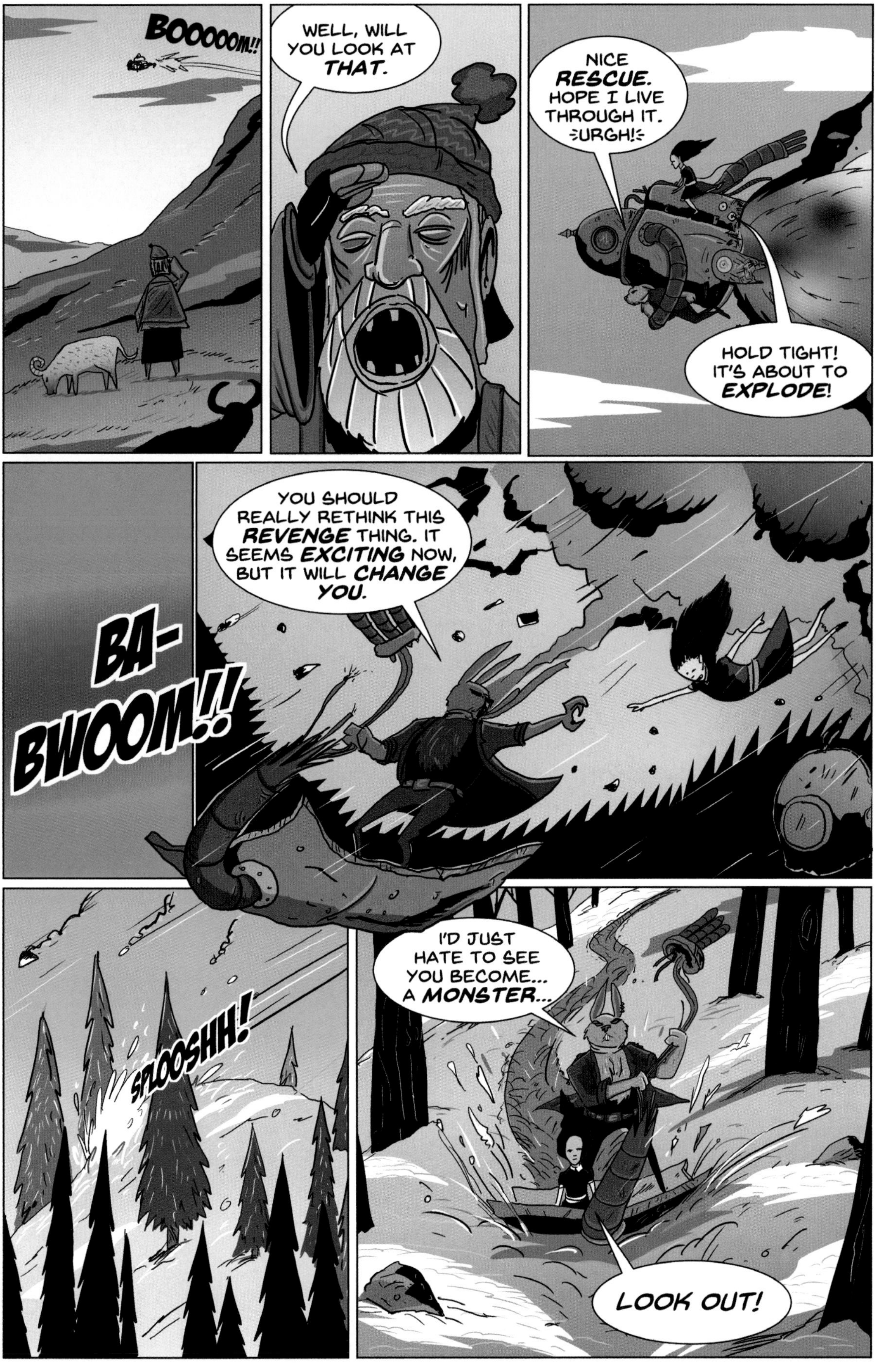
BOOOOOM!!
WELL, WILL YOU LOOK AT THAT.
NICE RESCUE. HOPE I LIVE THROUGH IT. URGH!
HOLD TIGHT! IT'S ABOUT TO EXPLODE!
BA-BWOOM!!
YOU SHOULD REALLY RETHINK THIS REVENGE THING. IT SEEMS EXCITING NOW, BUT IT WILL CHANGE YOU.
SPLOOSHH!
I'D JUST HATE TO SEE YOU BECOME... A MONSTER...
LOOK OUT!

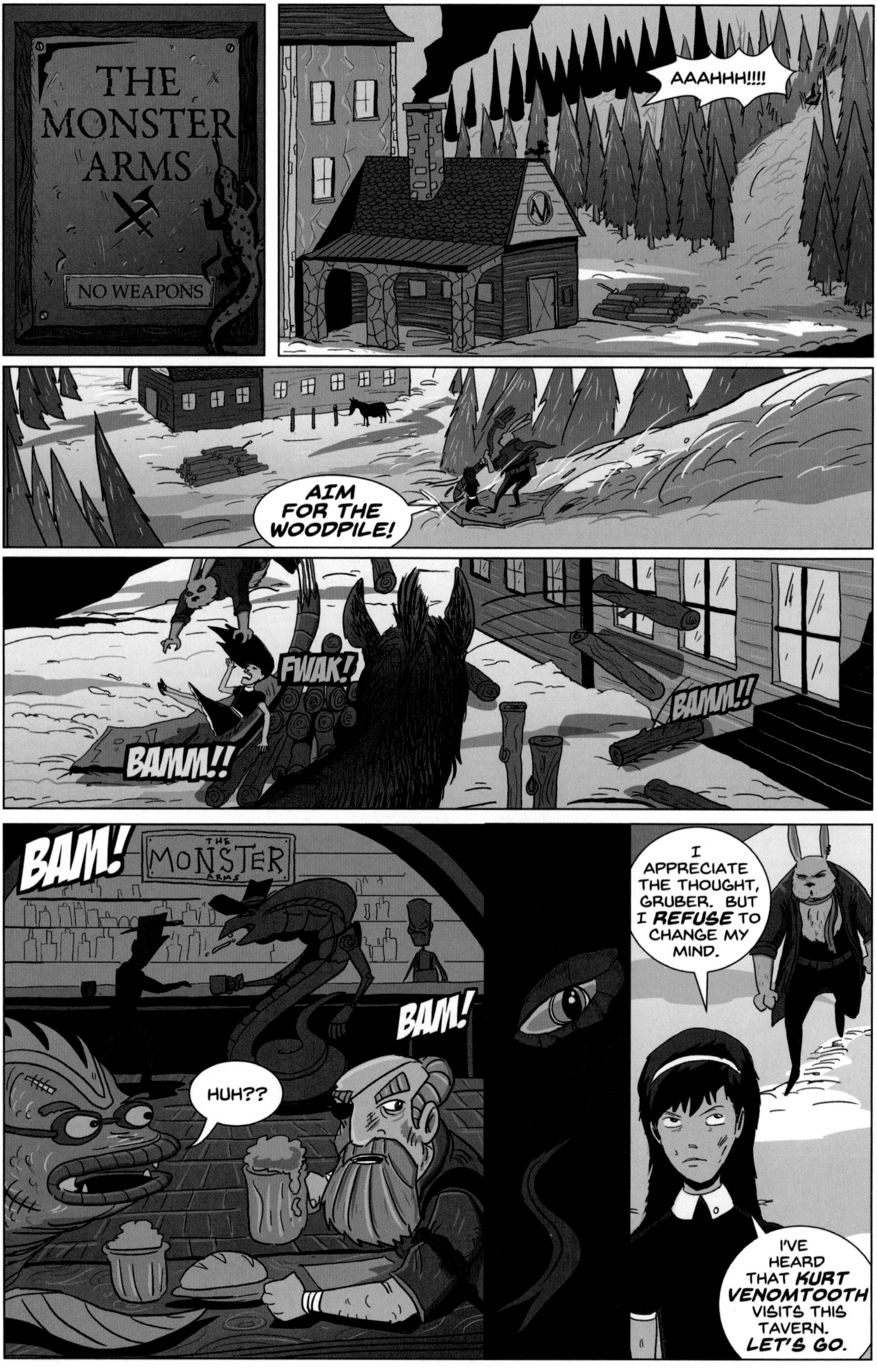
THE MONSTER ARMS
NO WEAPONS
AAAHHH!!!!
AIM FOR THE WOODPILE!
FWAK!
BAMM!!
BAMM!!
BAM!
THE MONSTER ARMS
BAM!
HUH??
I APPRECIATE THE THOUGHT, GRUBER. BUT I REFUSE TO CHANGE MY MIND.
I'VE HEARD THAT KURT VENOMTOOTH VISITS THIS TAVERN. LET'S GO.

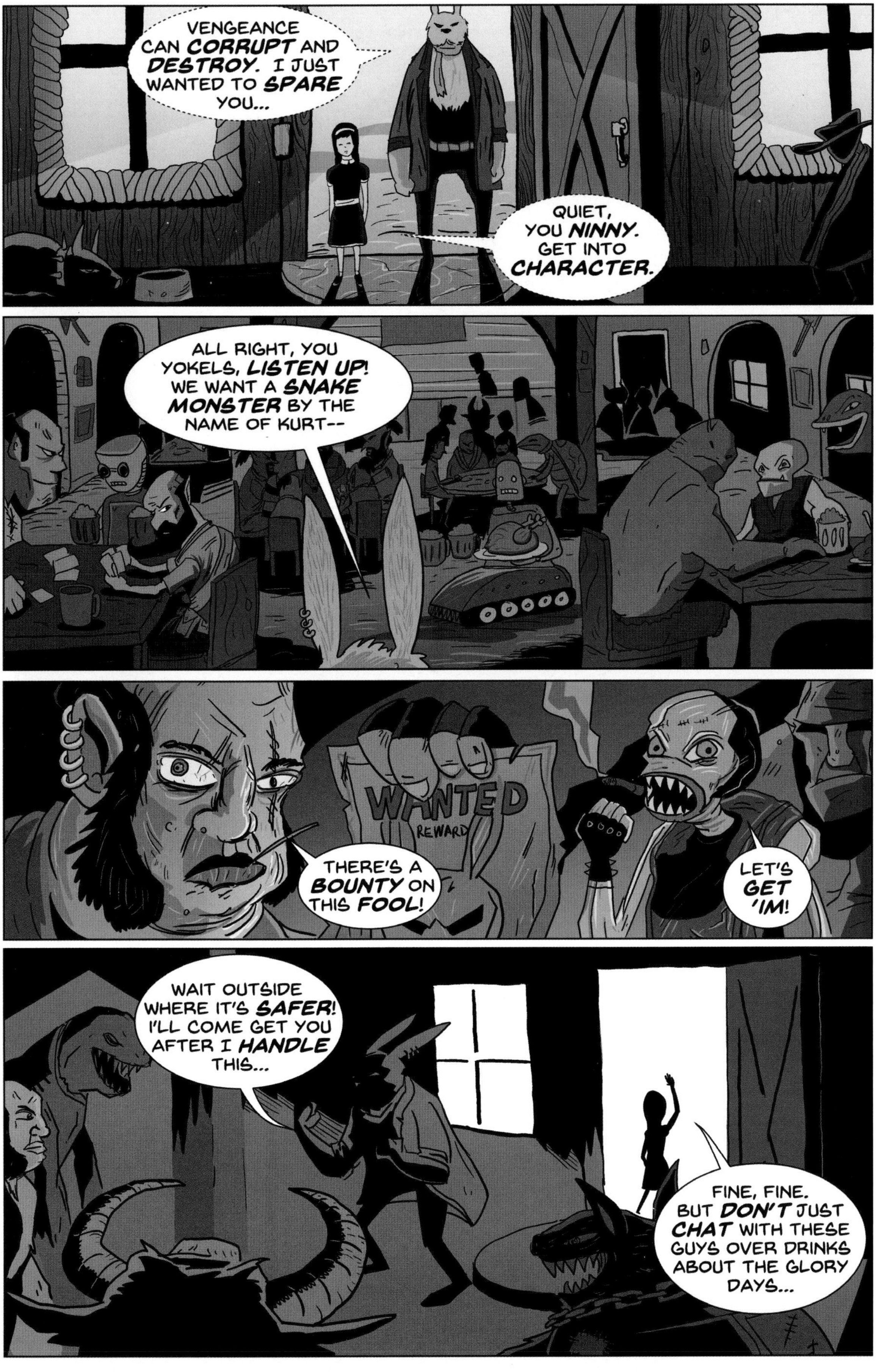
VENGEANCE CAN CORRUPT AND DESTROY. I JUST WANTED TO SPARE YOU...
QUIET, YOU NINNY. GET INTO CHARACTER.
ALL RIGHT, YOU YOKELS, LISTEN UP! WE WANT A SNAKE MONSTER BY THE NAME OF KURT--
WANTED
REWARD
THERE'S A BOUNTY ON THIS FOOL!
LET'S GET 'IM!
WAIT OUTSIDE WHERE IT'S SAFER! I'LL COME GET YOU AFTER I HANDLE THIS...
FINE, FINE. BUT DON'T JUST CHAT WITH THESE GUYS OVER DRINKS ABOUT THE GLORY DAYS...

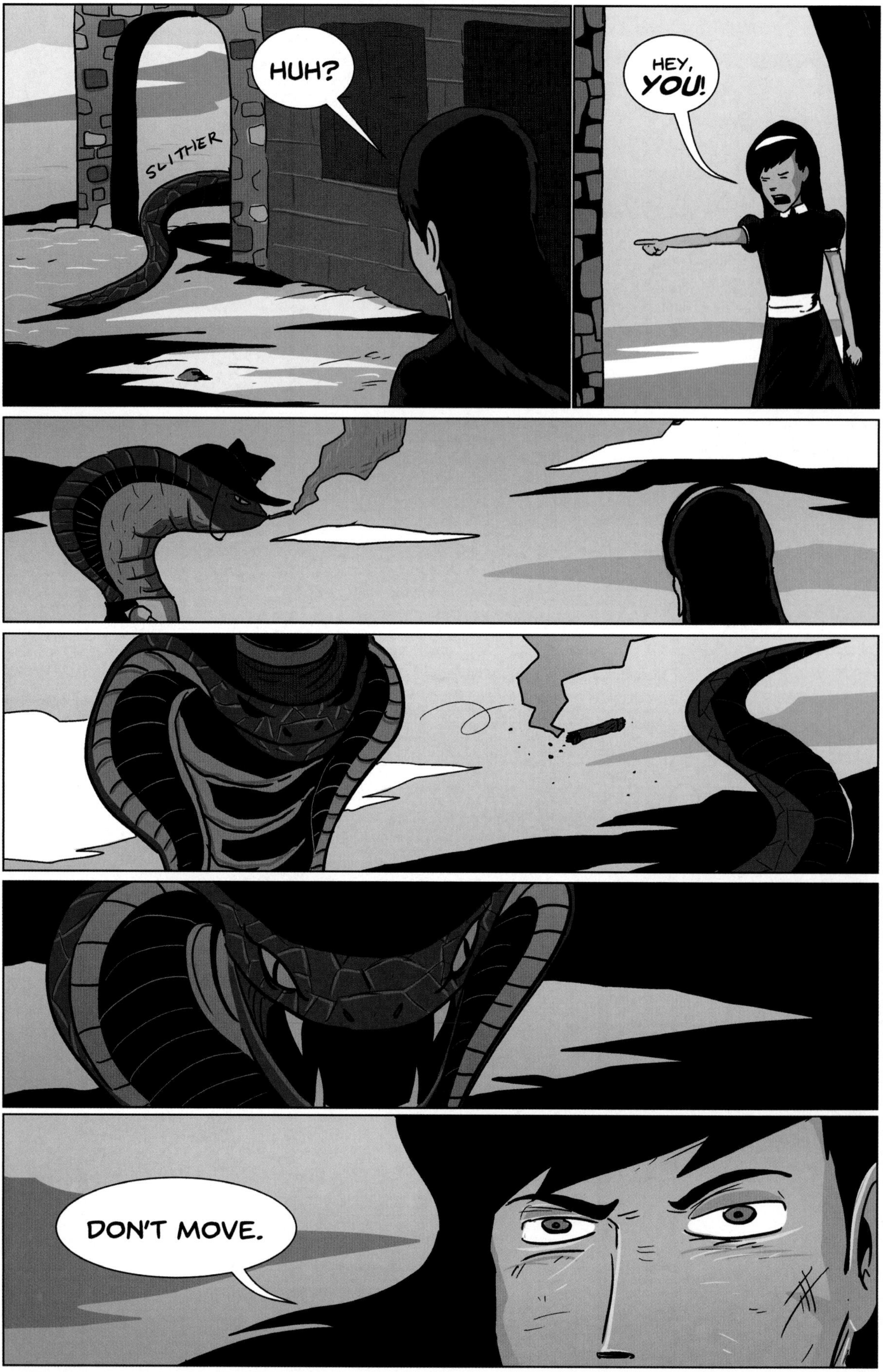
SLITHER
HUH?
HEY, YOU!
DON'T MOVE.

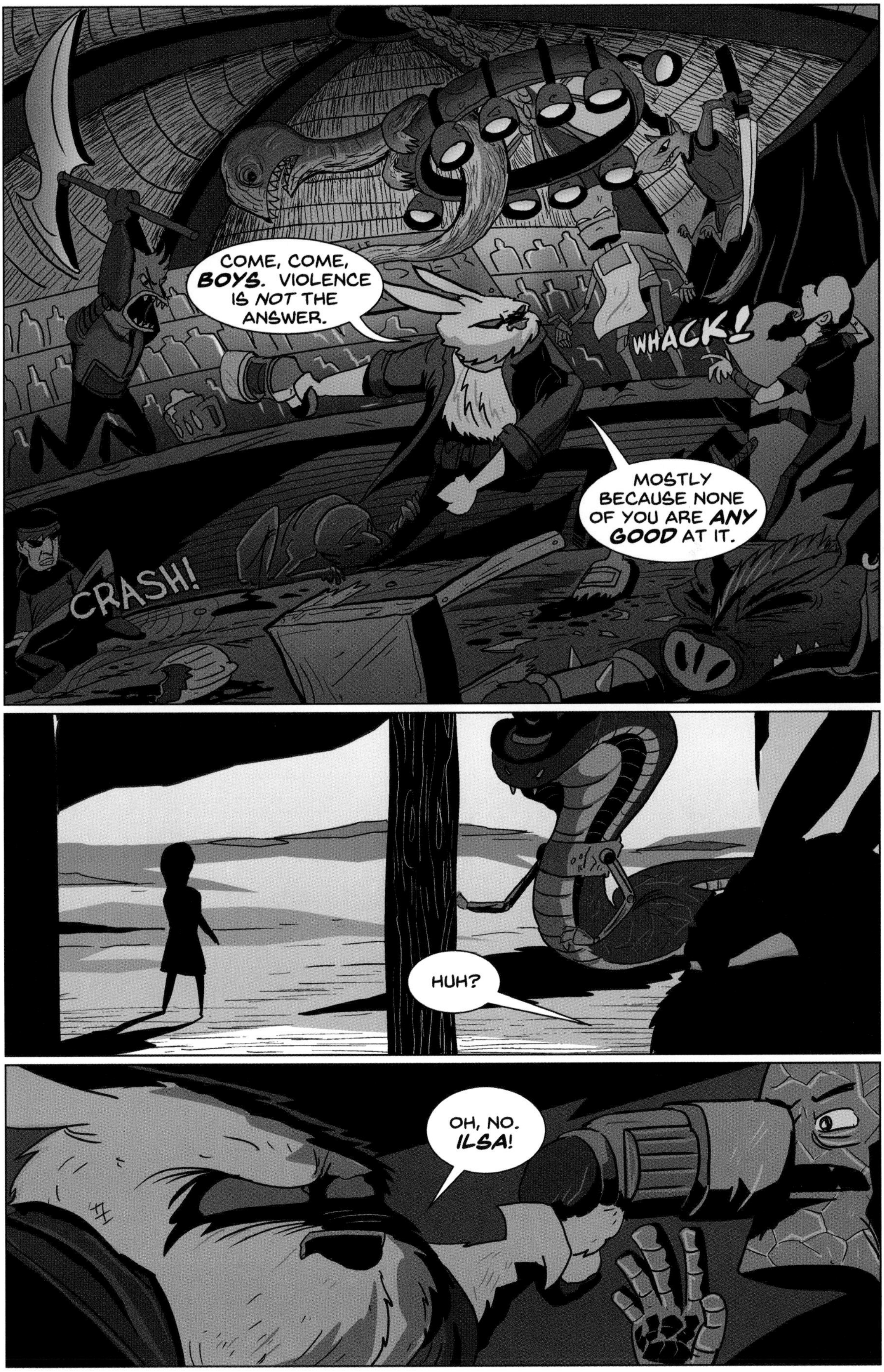
COME, COME, BOYS. VIOLENCE IS NOT THE ANSWER.
WHACK!
MOSTLY BECAUSE NONE OF YOU ARE ANY GOOD AT IT.
CRASH!
HUH?
OH, NO. ILSA!

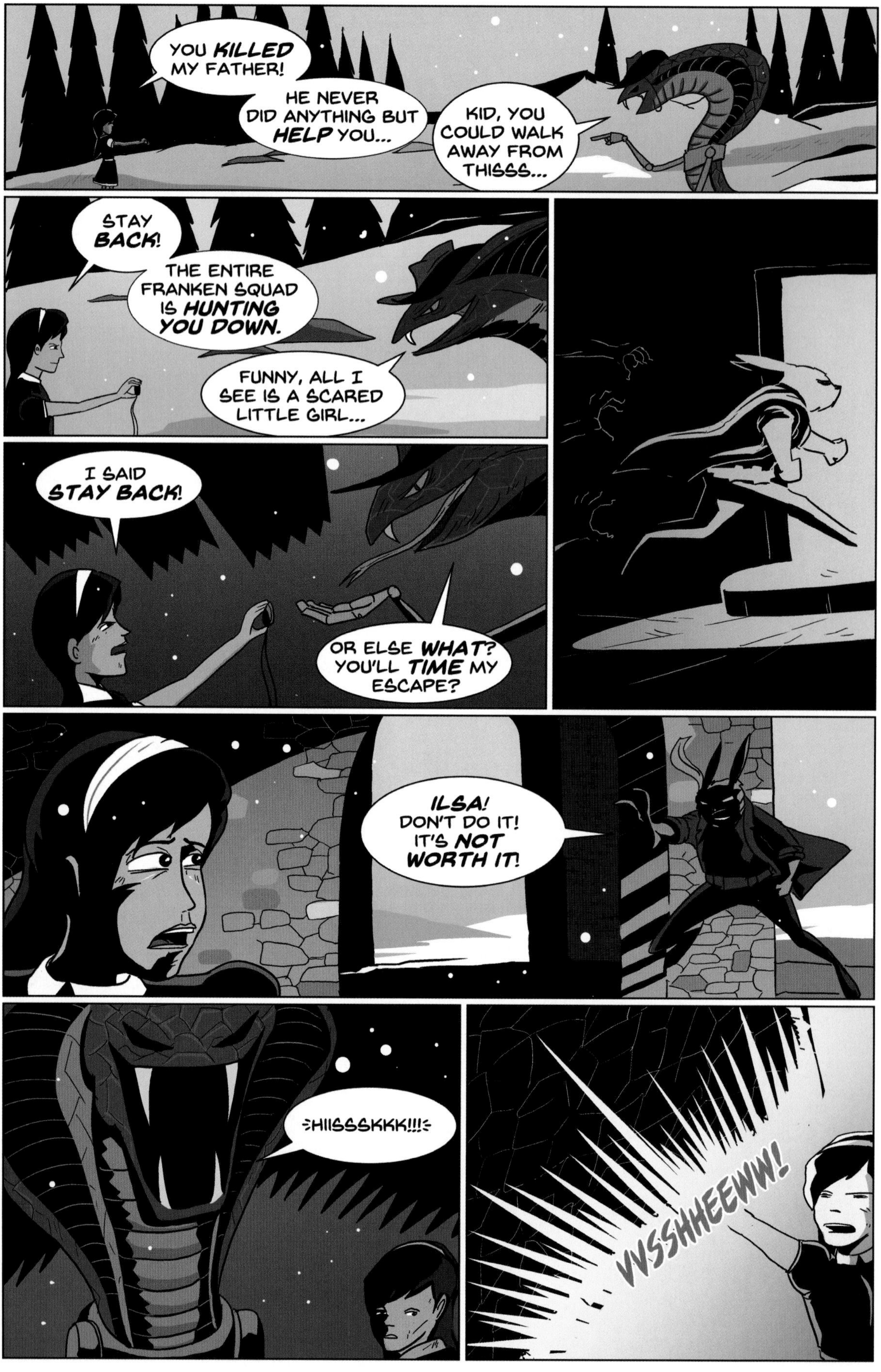
YOU KILLED MY FATHER!
HE NEVER DID ANYTHING BUT HELP YOU...
KID, YOU COULD WALK AWAY FROM THISSS...
STAY BACK!
THE ENTIRE FRANKEN SQUAD IS HUNTING YOU DOWN.
FUNNY, ALL I SEE IS A SCARED LITTLE GIRL...
I SAID STAY BACK!
OR ELSE WHAT? YOU'LL TIME MY ESCAPE?
ILSA! DON'T DO IT! IT'S NOT WORTH IT!
HIISSSKKK!!!
VVSSHHEEWW!

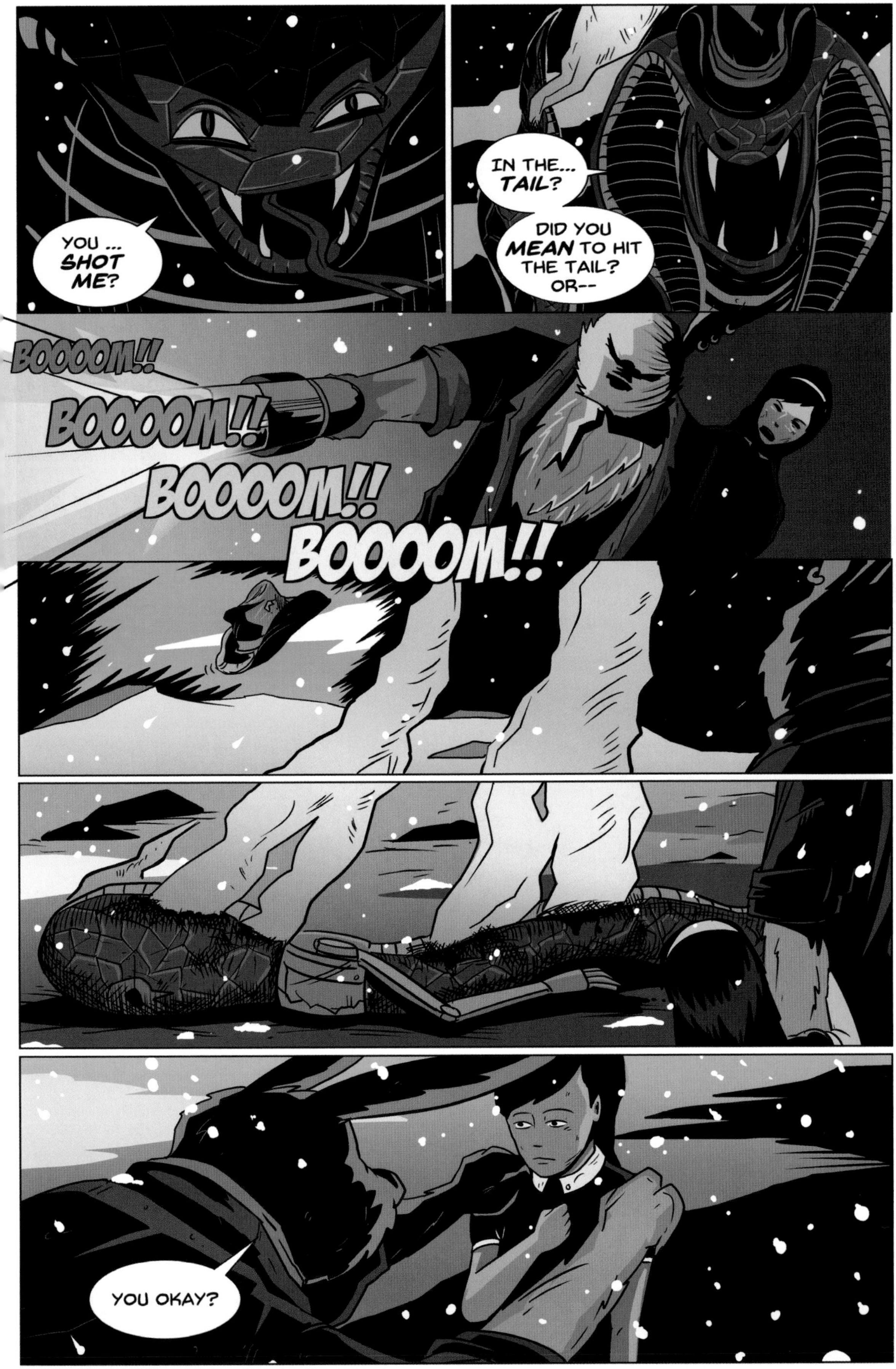
YOU ... SHOT ME?
IN THE... TAIL?
DID YOU MEAN TO HIT THE TAIL? OR--
BOOOOM!!
BOOOOM!!
BOOOOM!!
BOOOOM!!
YOU OKAY?

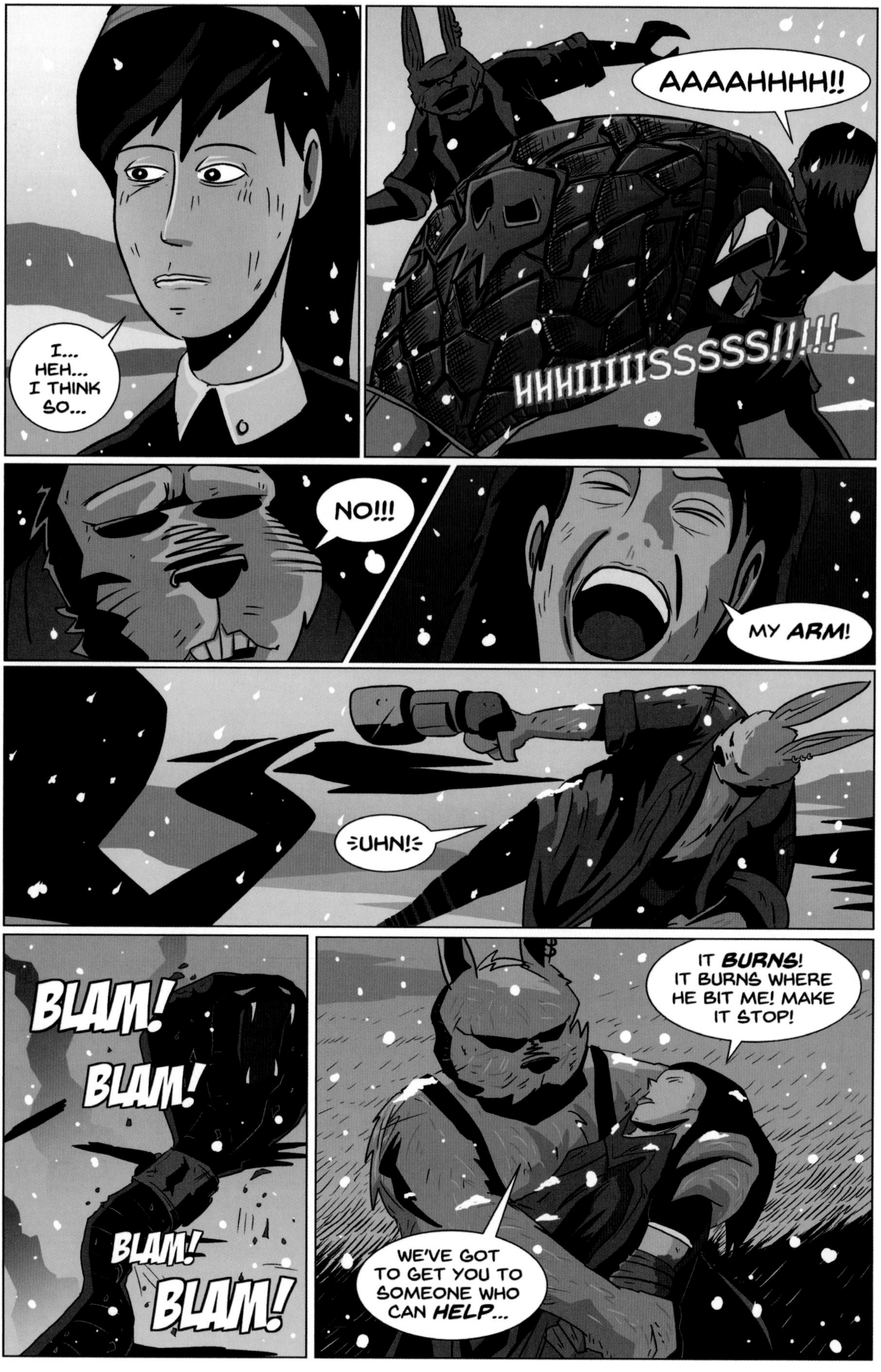
I... HEH... I THINK SO...
AAAAHHHH!!
HHHIIIIISSSSS!!!!!
NO!!!
MY ARM!
UHN!
BLAM!
BLAM!
BLAM!
BLAM!
IT BURNS! IT BURNS WHERE HE BIT ME! MAKE IT STOP!
WE'VE GOT TO GET YOU TO SOMEONE WHO CAN HELP...

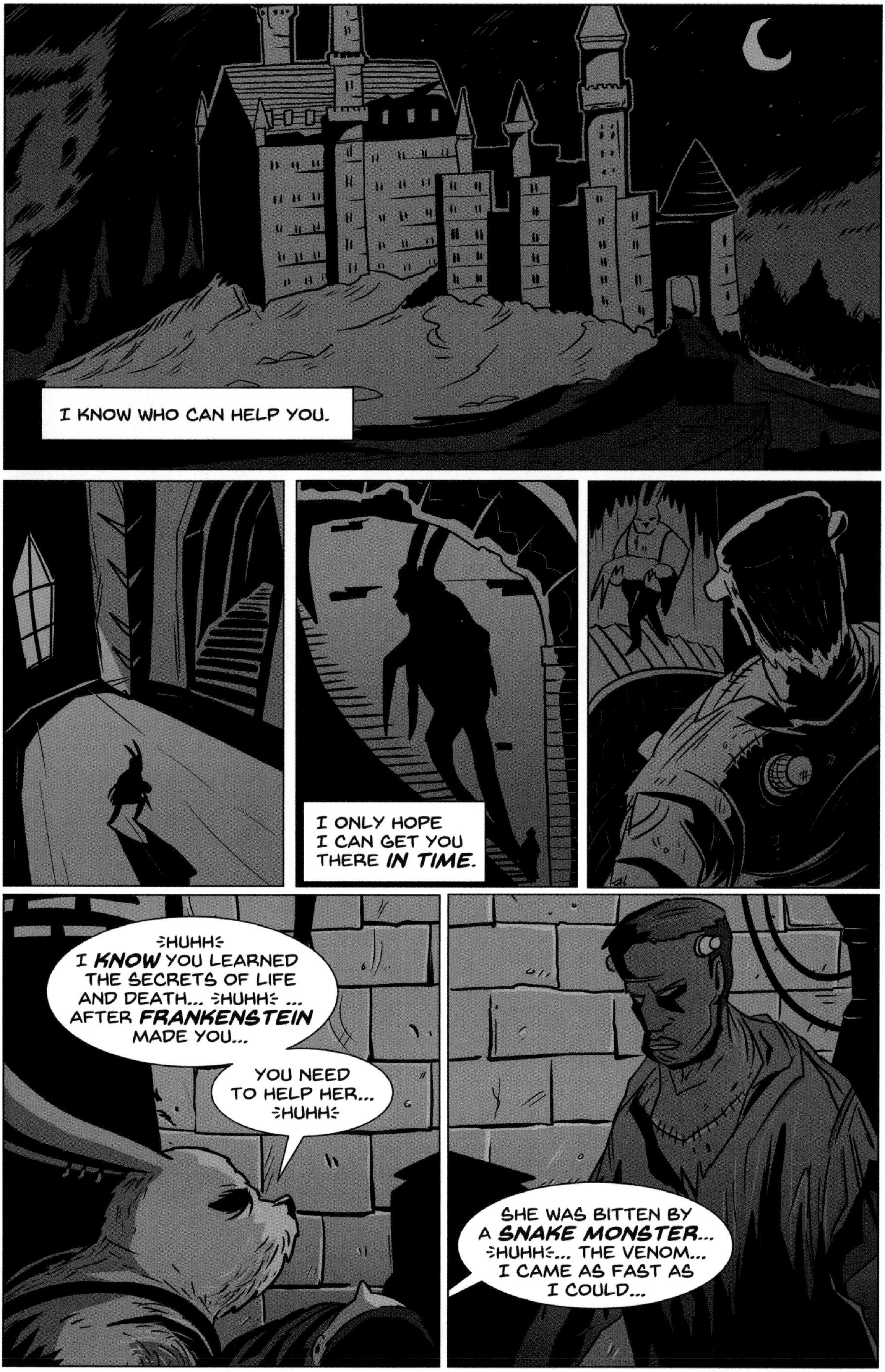
I KNOW WHO CAN HELP YOU.
I ONLY HOPE I CAN GET YOU THERE IN TIME.
HUHH I KNOW YOU LEARNED THE SECRETS OF LIFE AND DEATH... HUHH ... AFTER FRANKENSTEIN MADE YOU...
YOU NEED TO HELP HER... HUHH
SHE WAS BITTEN BY A SNAKE MONSTER... HUHH... THE VENOM... I CAME AS FAST AS I COULD...

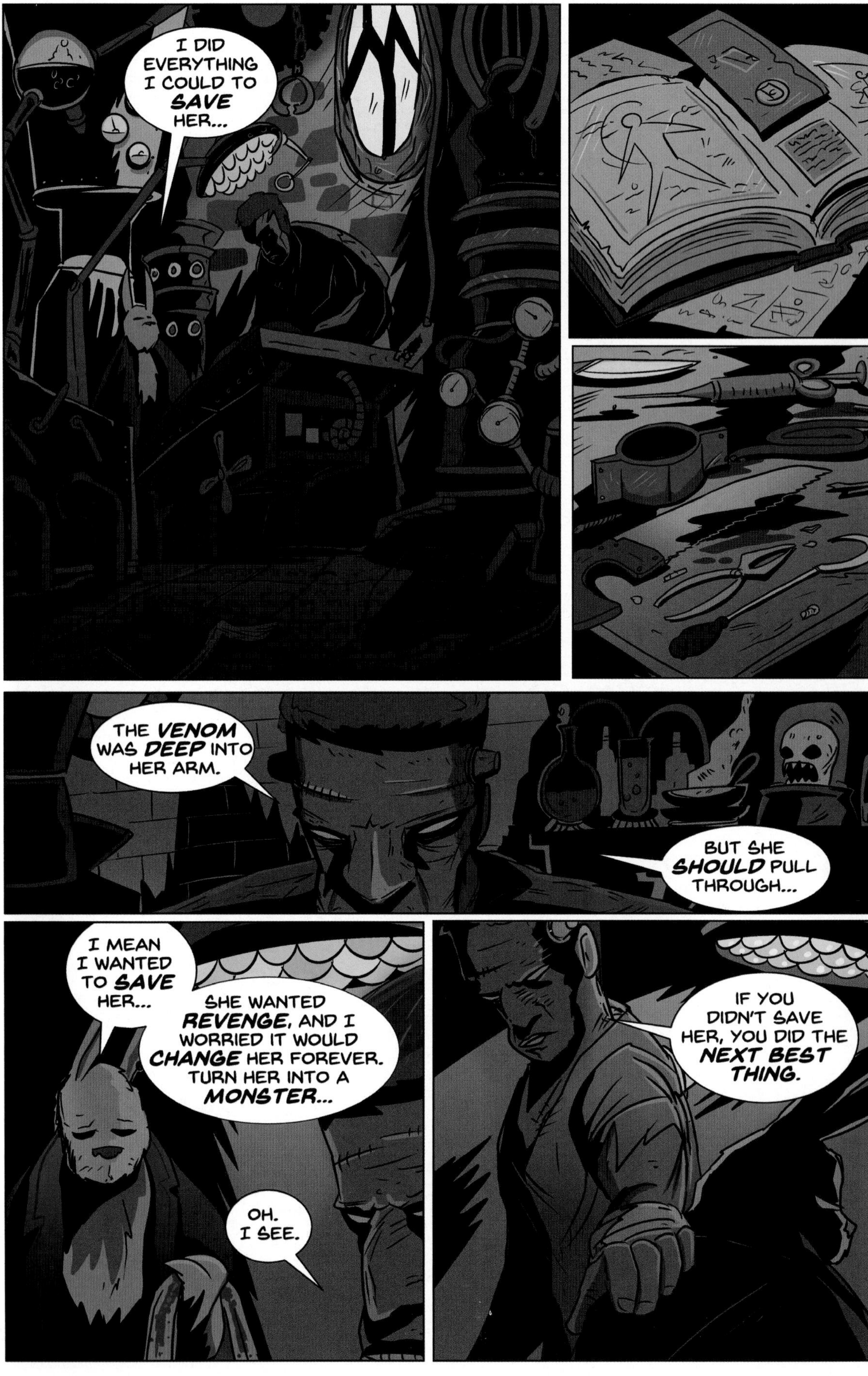
I DID EVERYTHING I COULD TO SAVE HER...
THE VENOM WAS DEEP INTO HER ARM.
BUT SHE SHOULD PULL THROUGH...
I MEAN I WANTED TO SAVE HER...
SHE WANTED REVENGE, AND I WORRIED IT WOULD CHANGE HER FOREVER. TURN HER INTO A MONSTER...
OH. I SEE.
IF YOU DIDN'T SAVE HER, YOU DID THE NEXT BEST THING.

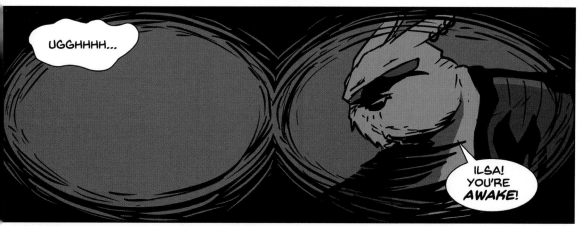

UGGHHHH...

ILSA! YOU'RE *AWAKE*!

IS KURT--?

JUSTICE WAS DONE. HE'LL NEVER *HURT* ANYONE EVER AGAIN...

SO I GOT MY *REVENGE* AFTER ALL?

AND I GOT AWAY WITH IT *UNHARMED*?

YOU'RE LUCKY TO BE *ALIVE*. THE VENOM WAS DEEP IN YOUR ARM...

HE COULDN'T *SAVE* IT...

!!!

SO HE DID THE *NEXT BEST THING*...

END.

Monstrous No. 2

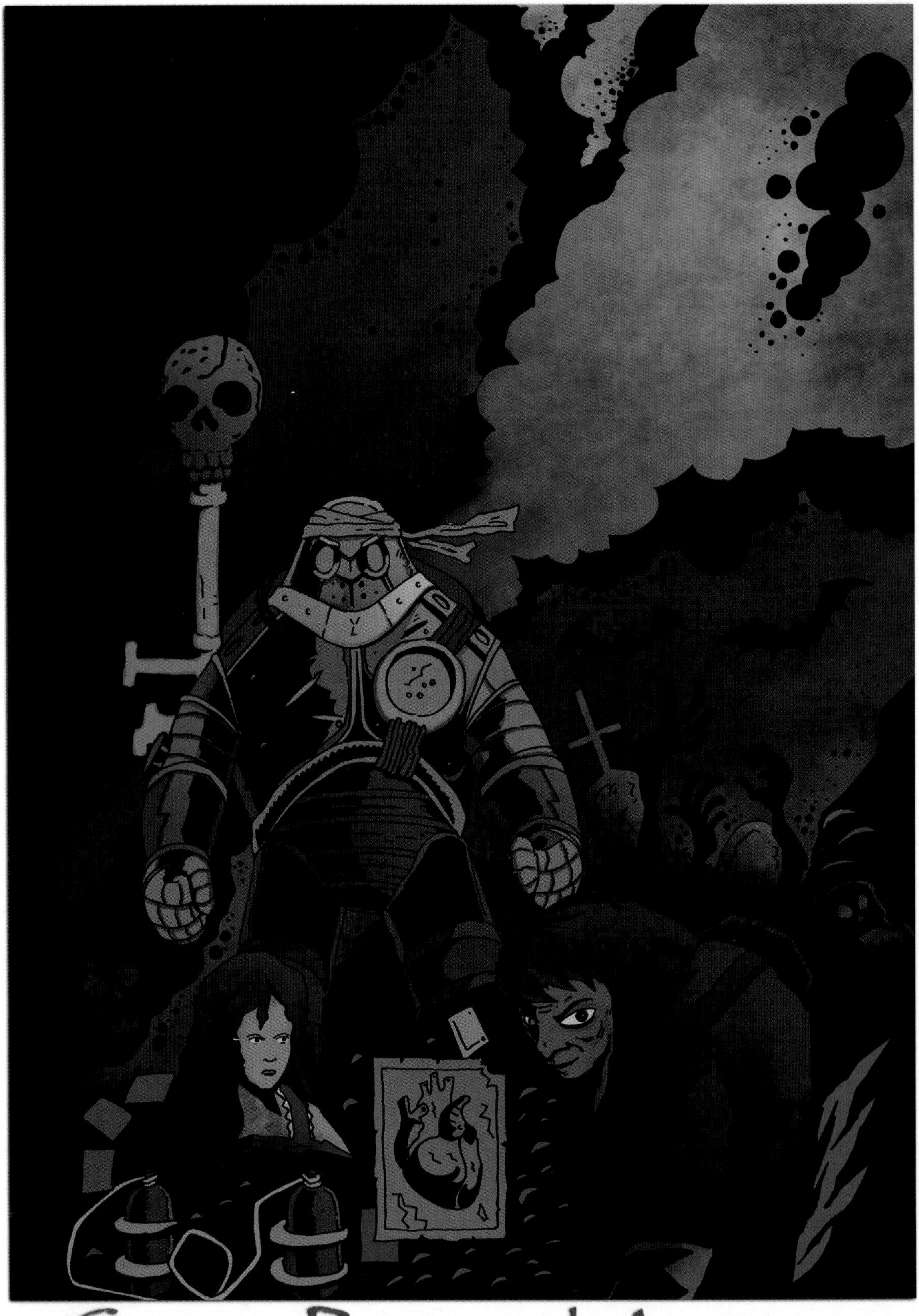

Steam-Powered Avenger

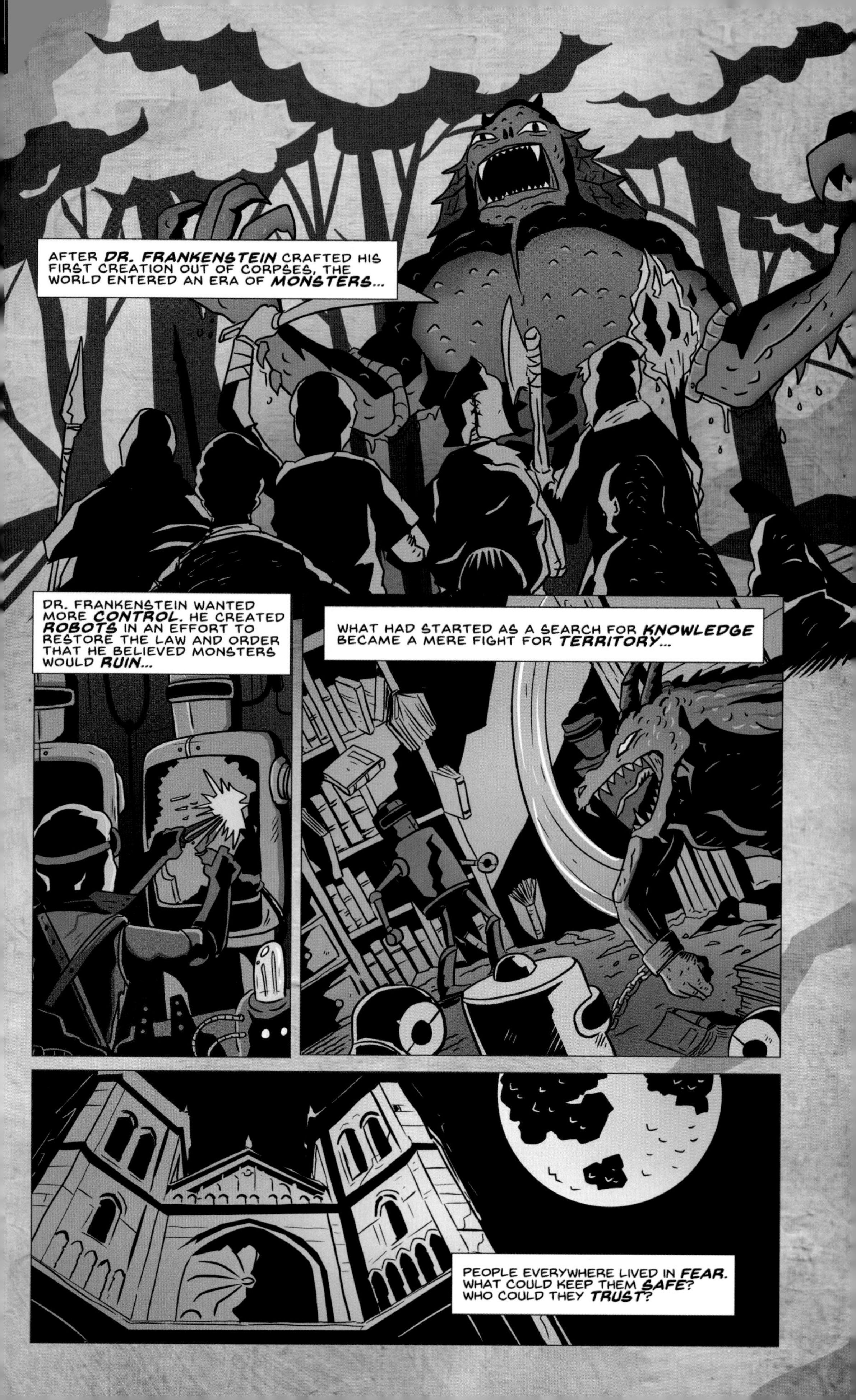

AFTER DR. FRANKENSTEIN CRAFTED HIS FIRST CREATION OUT OF CORPSES, THE WORLD ENTERED AN ERA OF MONSTERS...
DR. FRANKENSTEIN WANTED MORE CONTROL. HE CREATED ROBOTS IN AN EFFORT TO RESTORE THE LAW AND ORDER THAT HE BELIEVED MONSTERS WOULD RUIN...
WHAT HAD STARTED AS A SEARCH FOR KNOWLEDGE BECAME A MERE FIGHT FOR TERRITORY...
PEOPLE EVERYWHERE LIVED IN FEAR. WHAT COULD KEEP THEM SAFE? WHO COULD THEY TRUST?

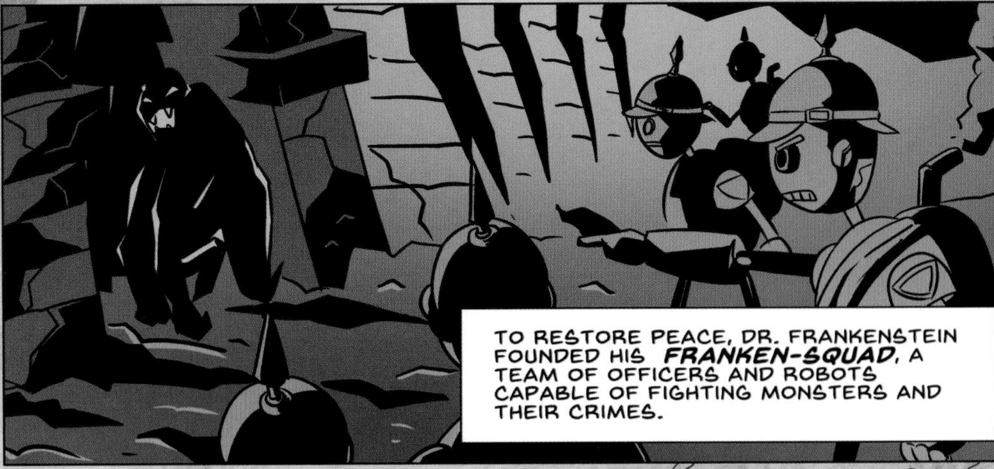
TO RESTORE PEACE, DR. FRANKENSTEIN FOUNDED HIS ***FRANKEN-SQUAD***, A TEAM OF OFFICERS AND ROBOTS CAPABLE OF FIGHTING MONSTERS AND THEIR CRIMES.

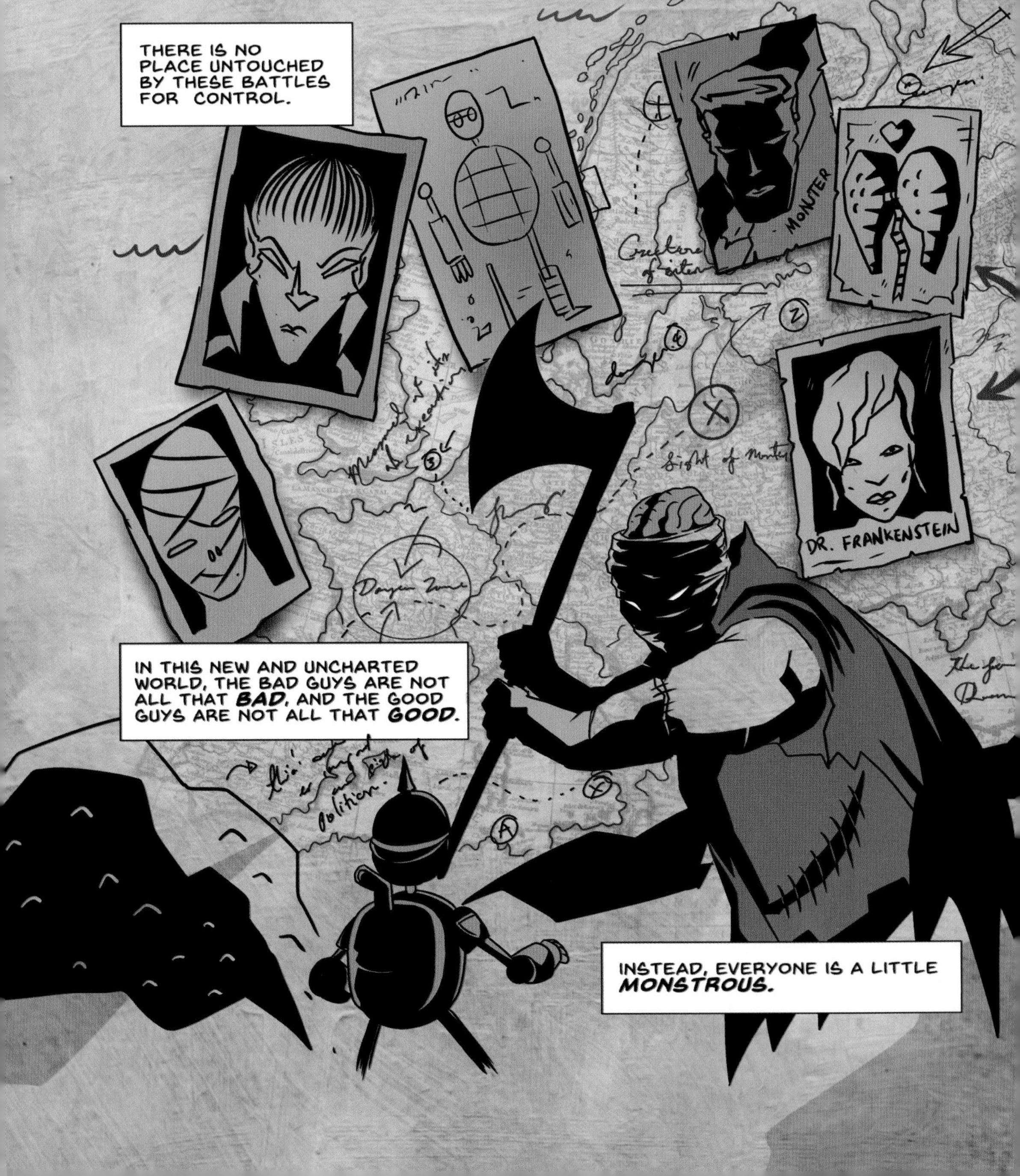
THERE IS NO PLACE UNTOUCHED BY THESE BATTLES FOR CONTROL.
MONSTER
DR. FRANKENSTEIN
IN THIS NEW AND UNCHARTED WORLD, THE BAD GUYS ARE NOT ALL THAT ***BAD***, AND THE GOOD GUYS ARE NOT ALL THAT ***GOOD***.
INSTEAD, EVERYONE IS A LITTLE ***MONSTROUS.***

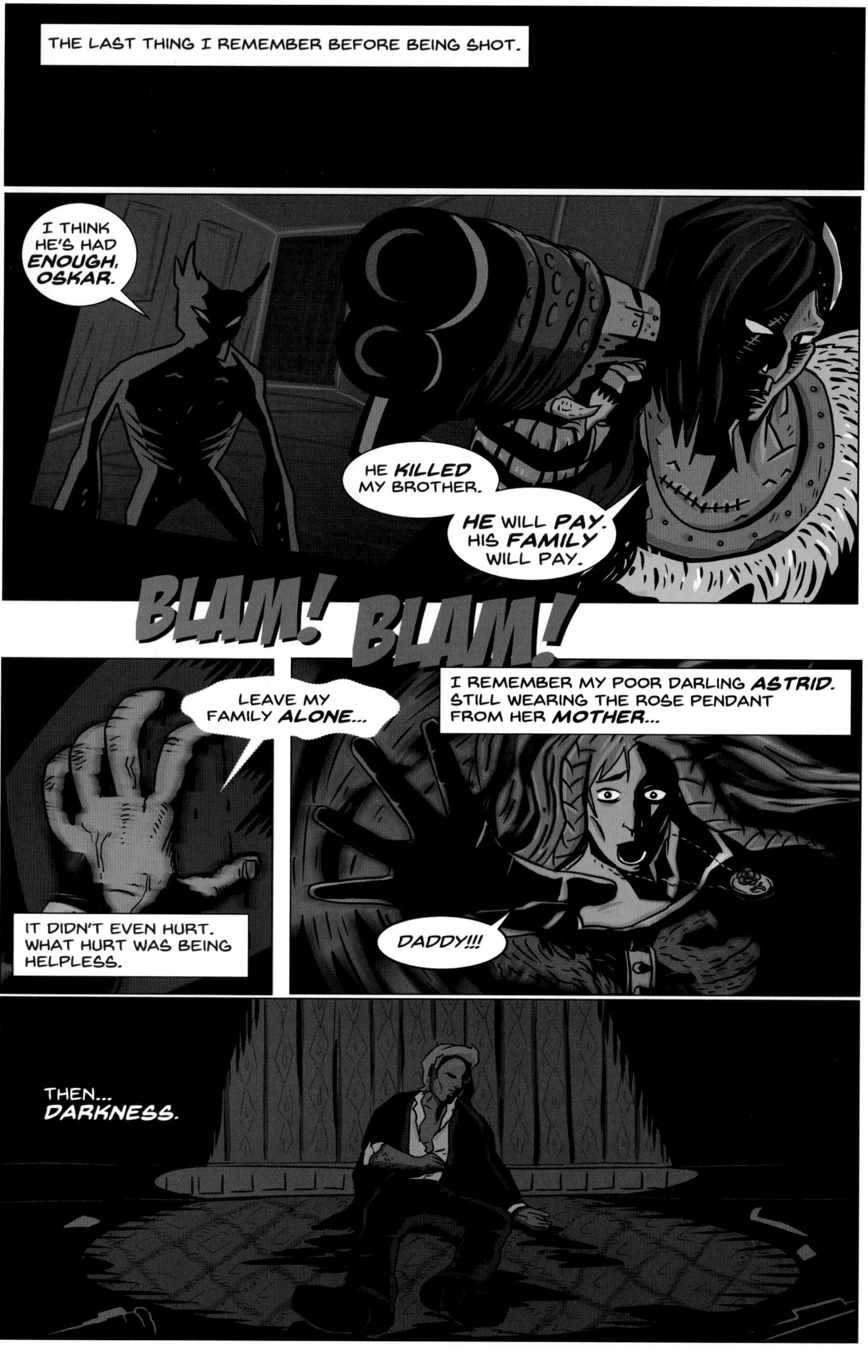
THE LAST THING I REMEMBER BEFORE BEING SHOT.
I THINK HE'S HAD ENOUGH, OSKAR.
HE KILLED MY BROTHER.
HE WILL PAY. HIS FAMILY WILL PAY.
BLAM! BLAM!
LEAVE MY FAMILY ALONE...
IT DIDN'T EVEN HURT. WHAT HURT WAS BEING HELPLESS.
I REMEMBER MY POOR DARLING ASTRID. STILL WEARING THE ROSE PENDANT FROM HER MOTHER...
DADDY!!!
THEN... DARKNESS.

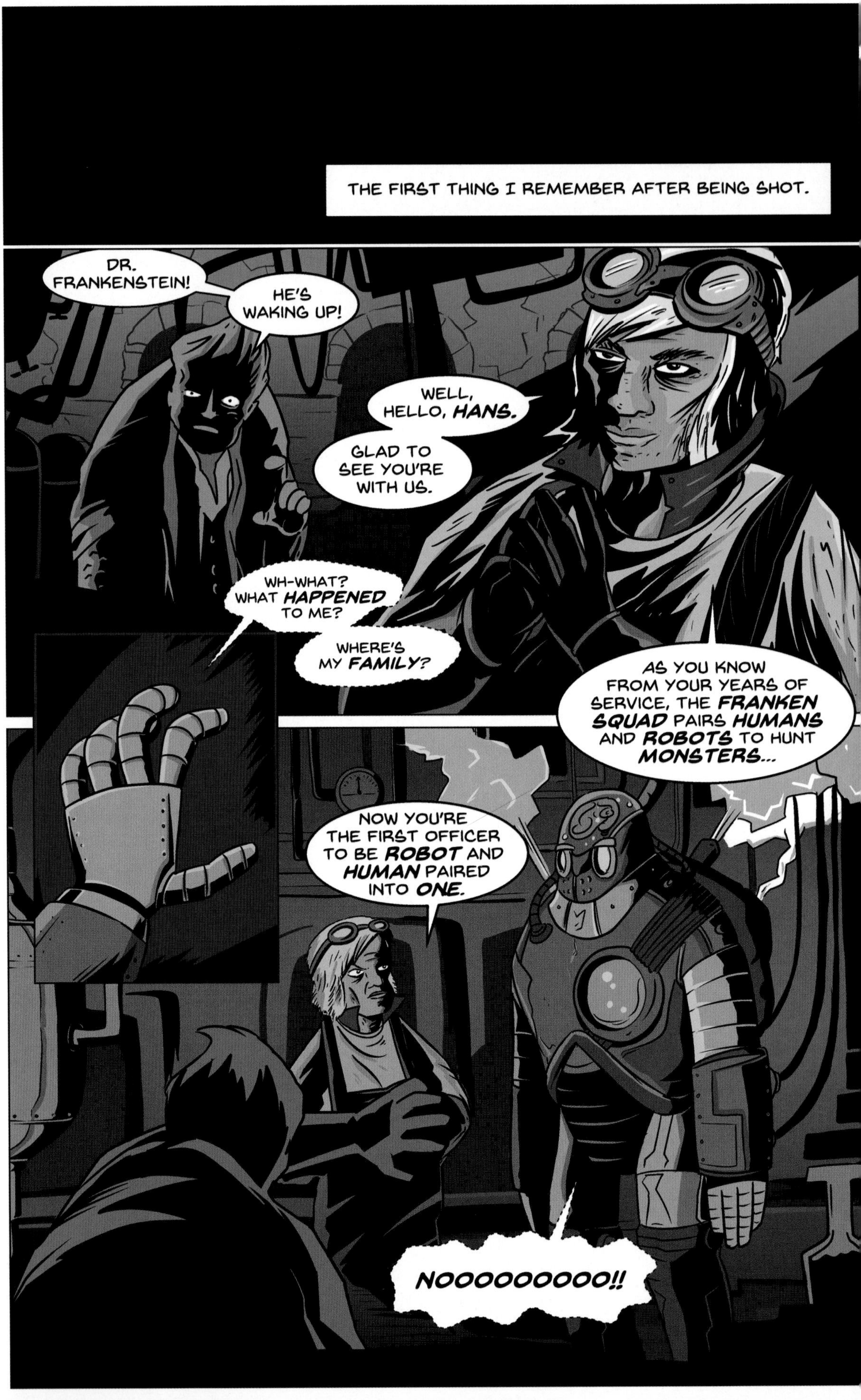
THE FIRST THING I REMEMBER AFTER BEING SHOT.
DR. FRANKENSTEIN!
HE'S WAKING UP!
WELL, HELLO, HANS.
GLAD TO SEE YOU'RE WITH US.
WH-WHAT? WHAT HAPPENED TO ME?
WHERE'S MY FAMILY?
AS YOU KNOW FROM YOUR YEARS OF SERVICE, THE FRANKEN SQUAD PAIRS HUMANS AND ROBOTS TO HUNT MONSTERS...
NOW YOU'RE THE FIRST OFFICER TO BE ROBOT AND HUMAN PAIRED INTO ONE.
NOOOOOOOOO!!

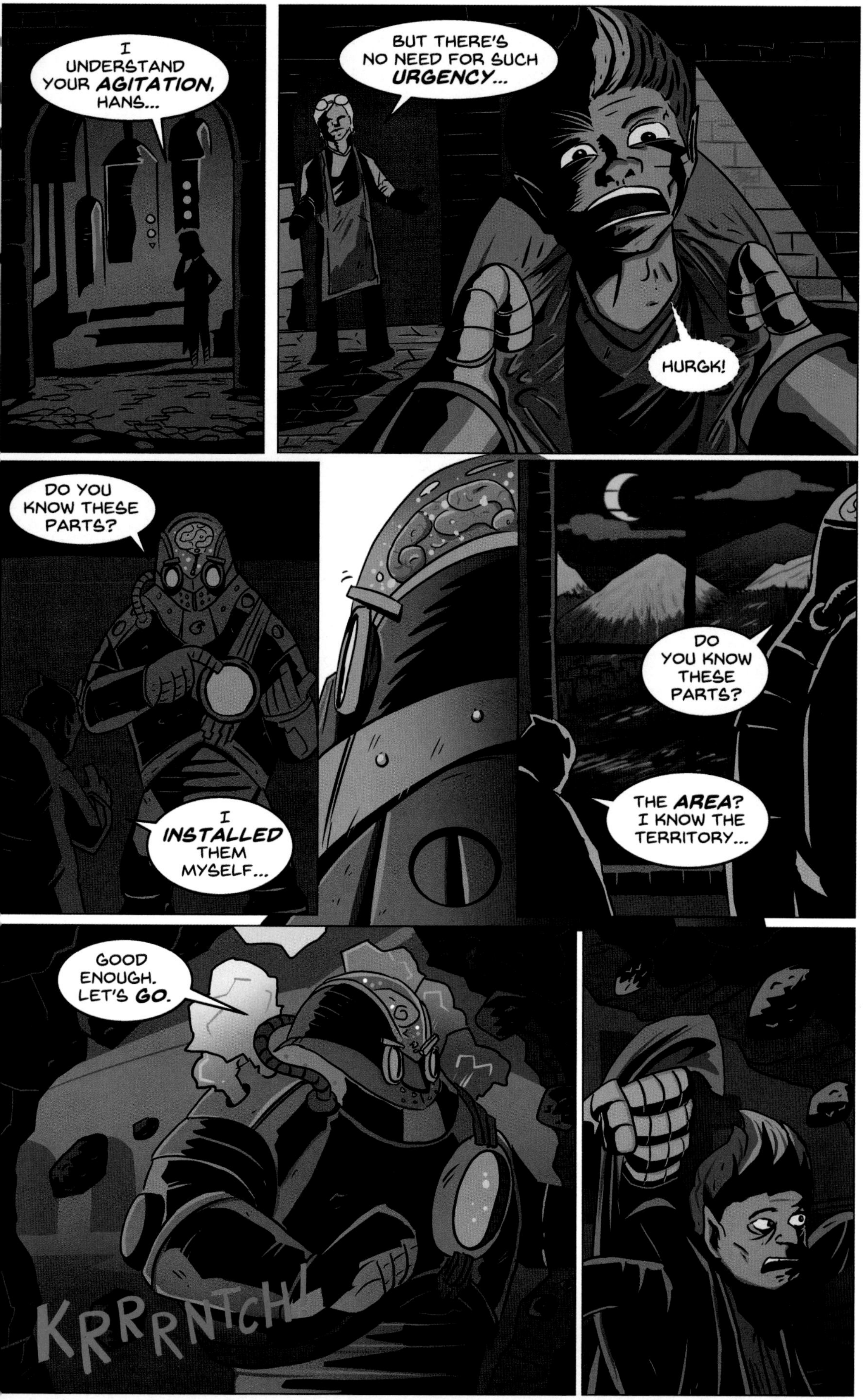
I UNDERSTAND YOUR AGITATION, HANS...
BUT THERE'S NO NEED FOR SUCH URGENCY...
HURGK!
DO YOU KNOW THESE PARTS?
I INSTALLED THEM MYSELF...
DO YOU KNOW THESE PARTS?
THE AREA? I KNOW THE TERRITORY...
GOOD ENOUGH. LET'S GO.
KRRRNTCH!

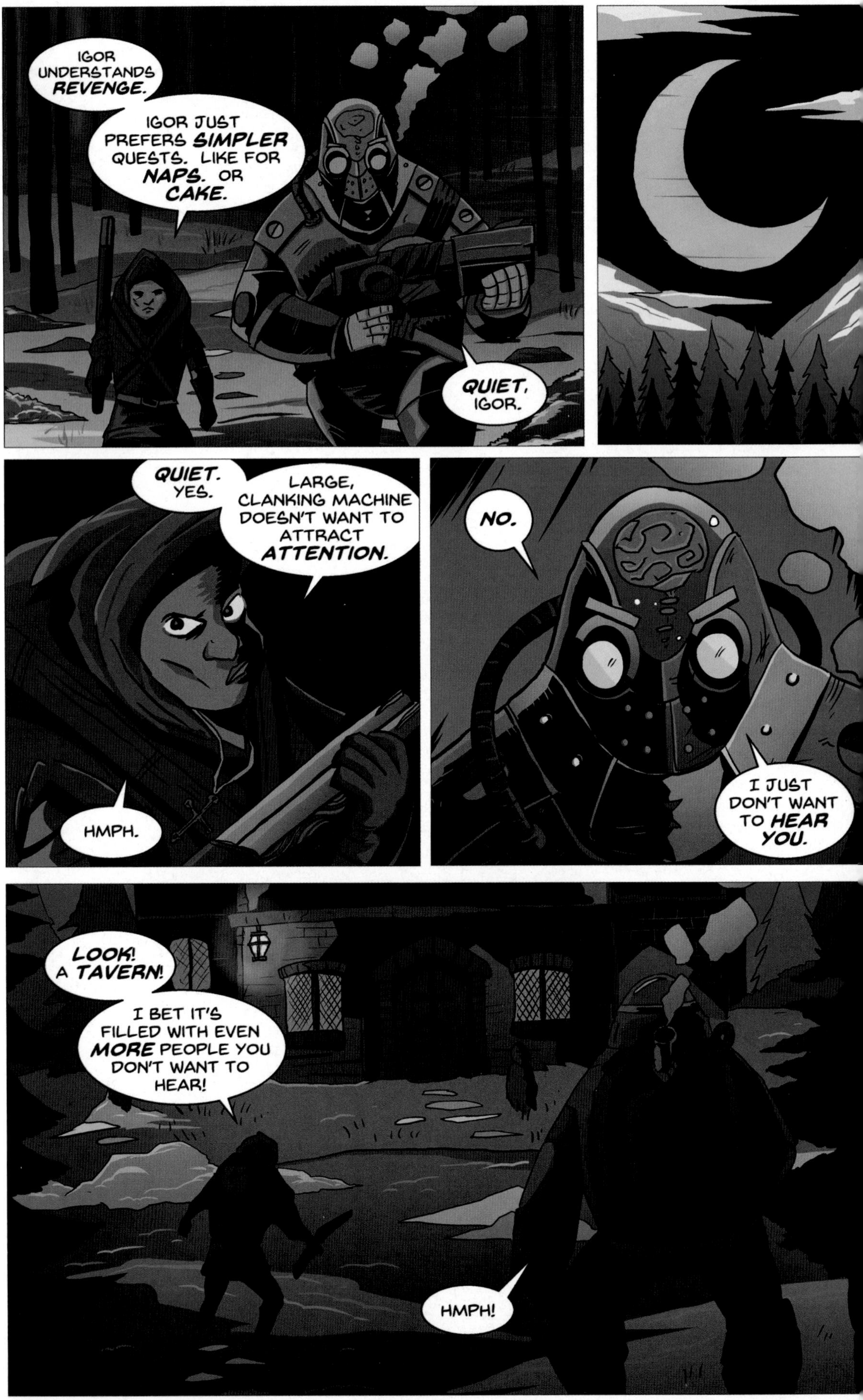
IGOR UNDERSTANDS REVENGE.
IGOR JUST PREFERS SIMPLER QUESTS. LIKE FOR NAPS. OR CAKE.
QUIET, IGOR.
QUIET. YES.
LARGE, CLANKING MACHINE DOESN'T WANT TO ATTRACT ATTENTION.
HMPH.
NO.
I JUST DON'T WANT TO HEAR YOU.
LOOK! A TAVERN!
I BET IT'S FILLED WITH EVEN MORE PEOPLE YOU DON'T WANT TO HEAR!
HMPH!

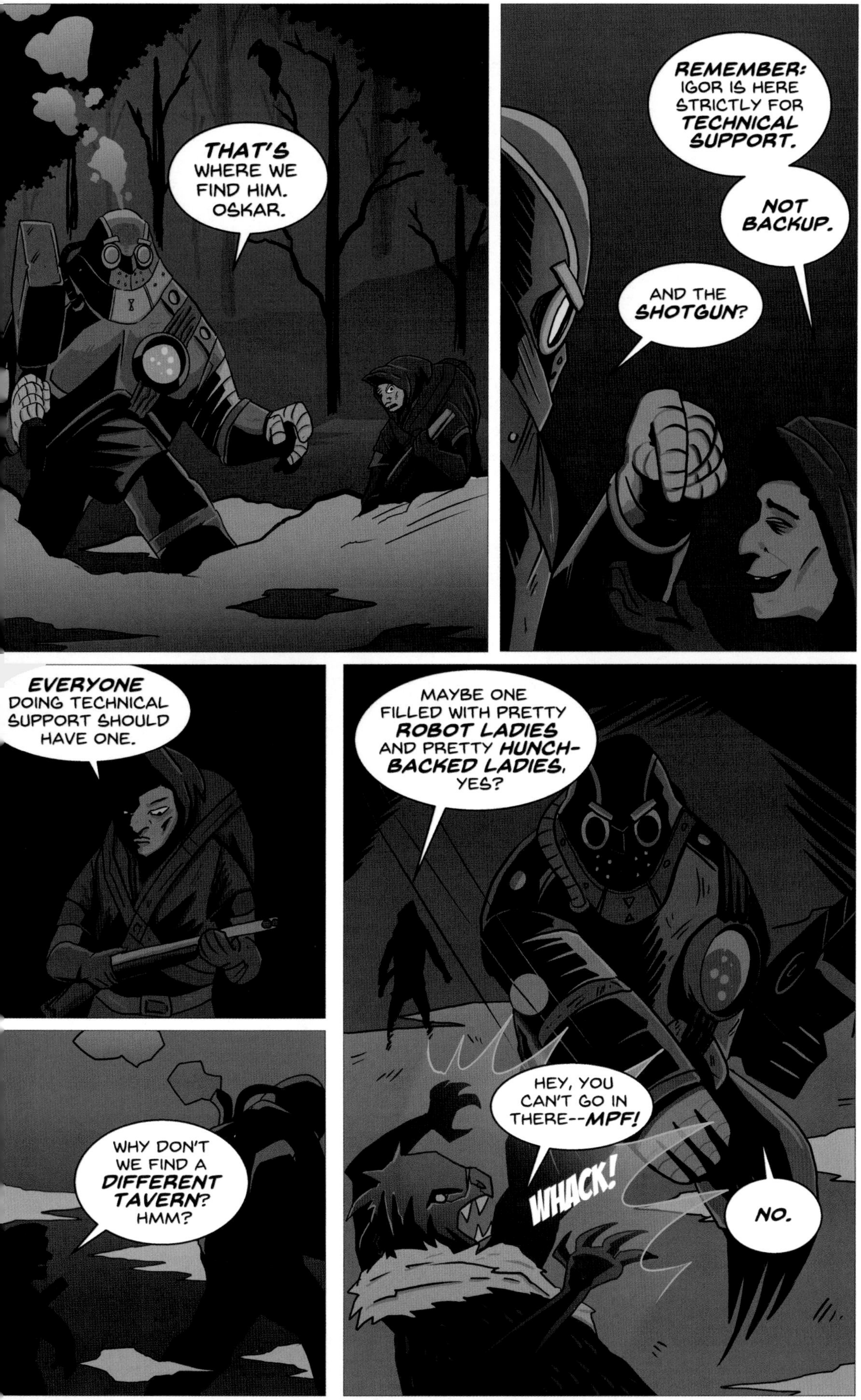
THAT'S WHERE WE FIND HIM. OSKAR.
REMEMBER: IGOR IS HERE STRICTLY FOR TECHNICAL SUPPORT.
NOT BACKUP.
AND THE SHOTGUN?
EVERYONE DOING TECHNICAL SUPPORT SHOULD HAVE ONE.
WHY DON'T WE FIND A DIFFERENT TAVERN? HMM?
MAYBE ONE FILLED WITH PRETTY ROBOT LADIES AND PRETTY HUNCH-BACKED LADIES, YES?
HEY, YOU CAN'T GO IN THERE--MPF!
WHACK!
NO.

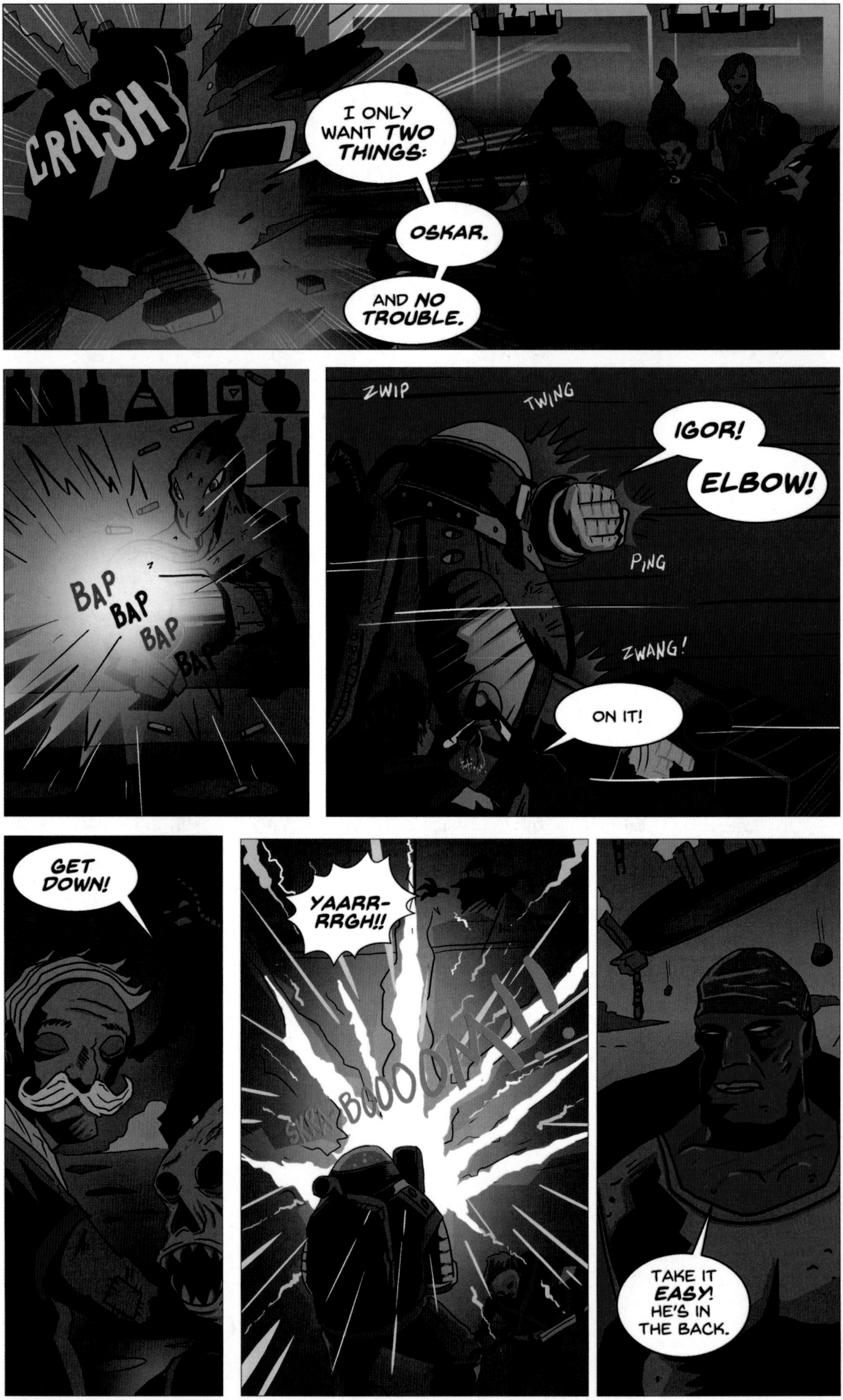
CRASH
I ONLY WANT TWO THINGS:
OSKAR.
AND NO TROUBLE.
BAP BAP BAP BAP
ZWIP
TWING
IGOR!
ELBOW!
PING
ZWANG!
ON IT!
GET DOWN!
YAARR-RRGH!!
SKRA-BOOOOM!!
TAKE IT EASY! HE'S IN THE BACK.

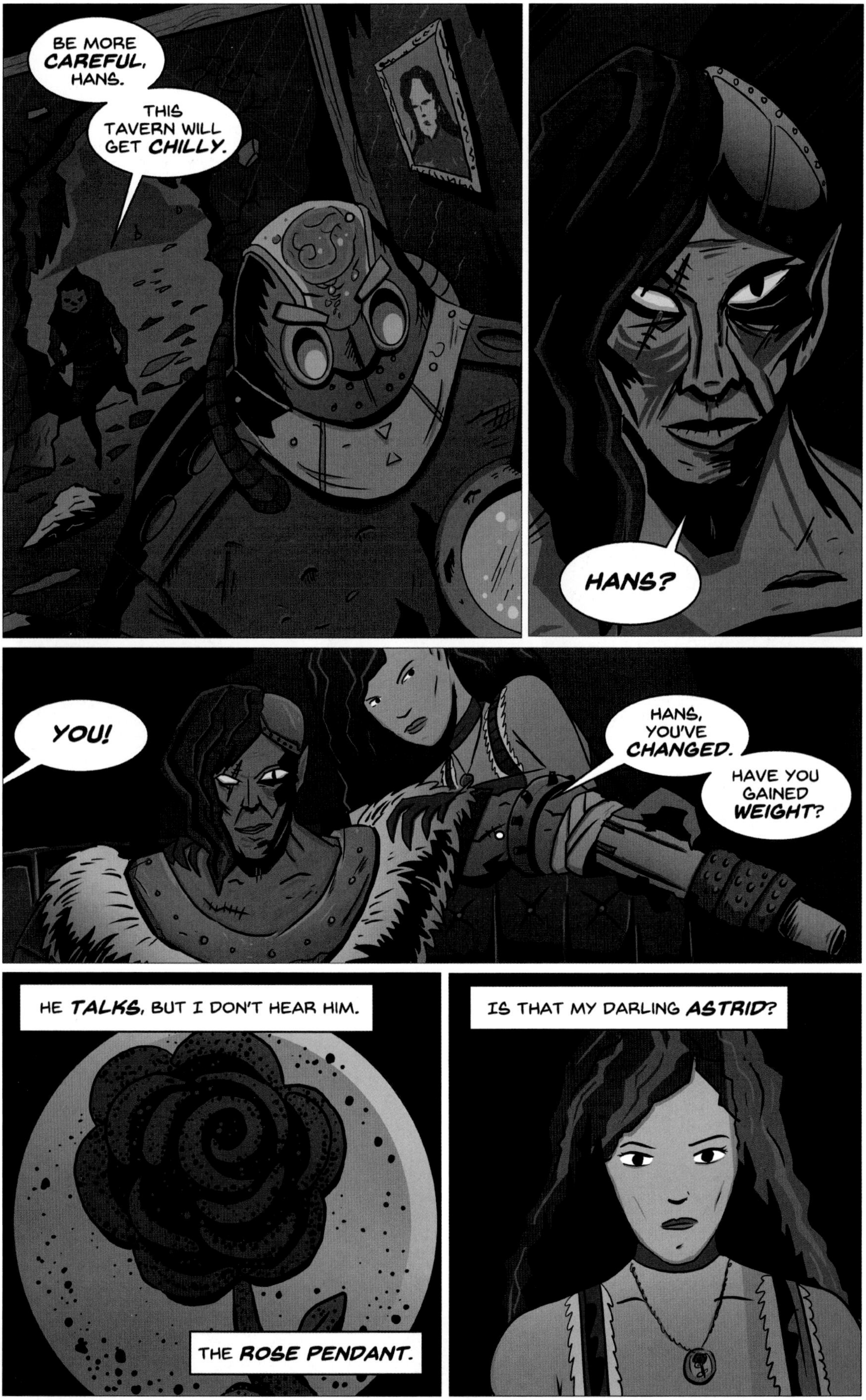
BE MORE CAREFUL, HANS.
THIS TAVERN WILL GET CHILLY.
HANS?
YOU!
HANS, YOU'VE CHANGED.
HAVE YOU GAINED WEIGHT?
HE TALKS, BUT I DON'T HEAR HIM.
THE ROSE PENDANT.
IS THAT MY DARLING ASTRID?

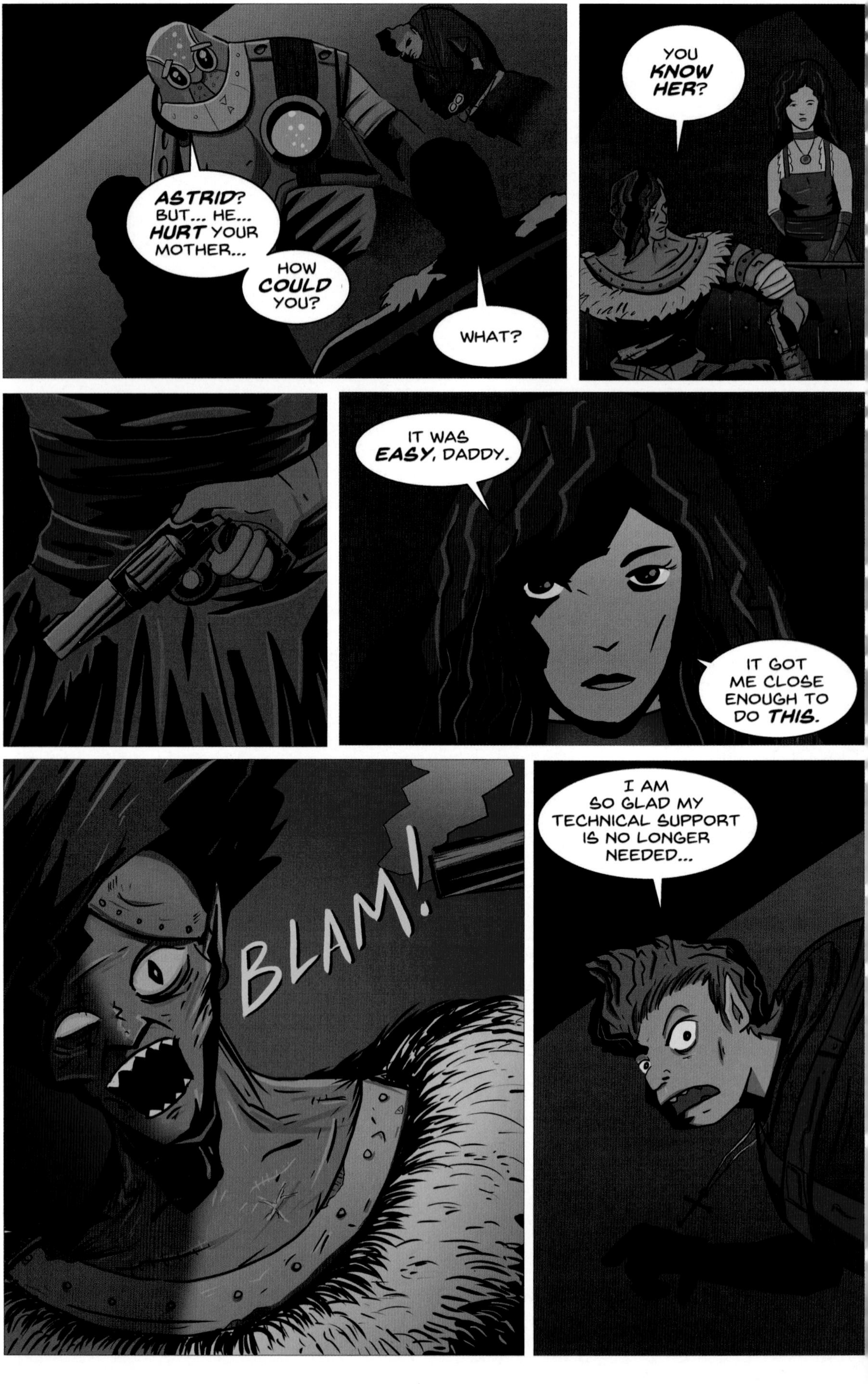
ASTRID? BUT... HE... HURT YOUR MOTHER...
HOW COULD YOU?
WHAT?
YOU KNOW HER?
IT WAS EASY, DADDY.
IT GOT ME CLOSE ENOUGH TO DO THIS.
BLAM!
I AM SO GLAD MY TECHNICAL SUPPORT IS NO LONGER NEEDED...

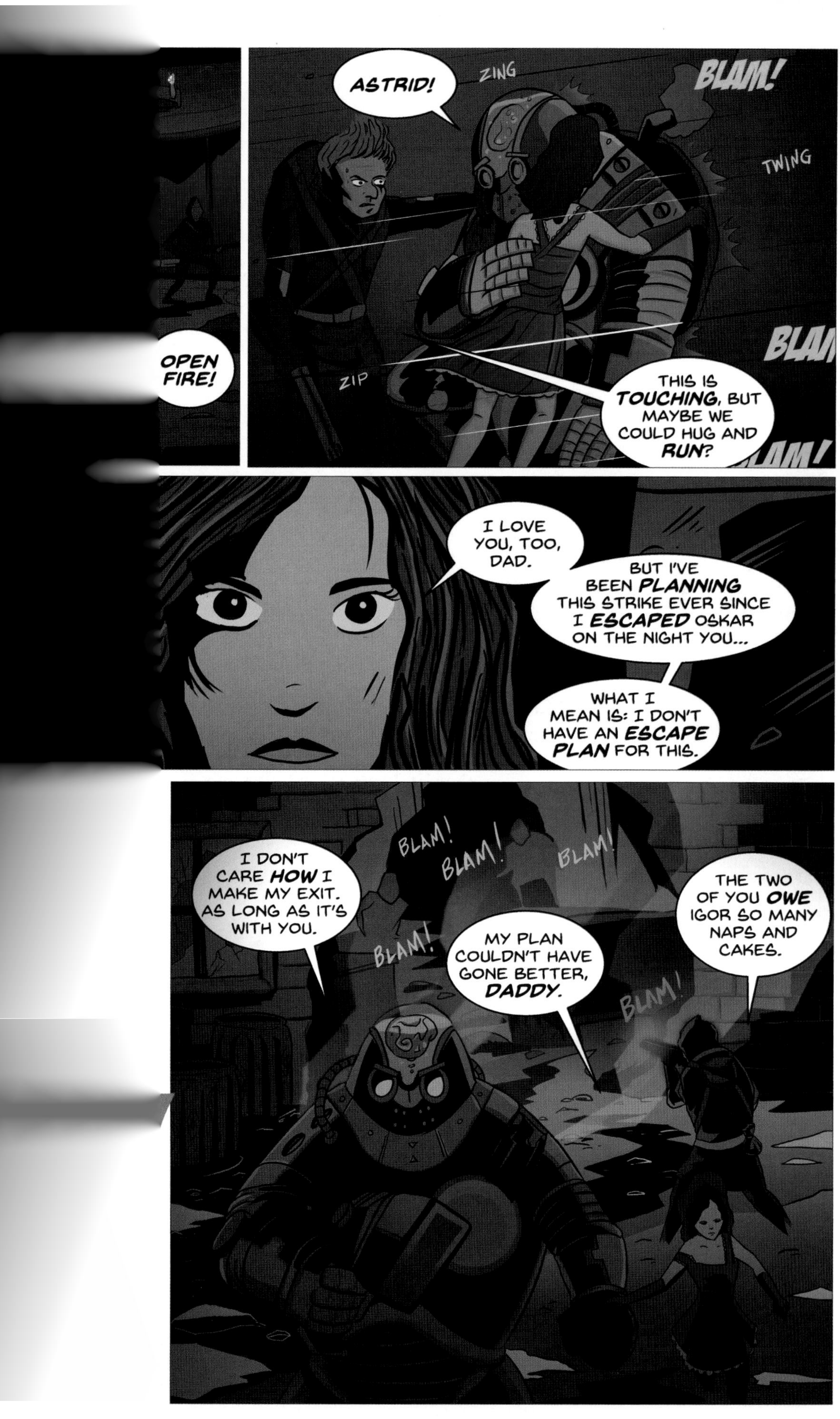
OPEN FIRE!
ASTRID!
ZING
BLAM!
TWING
BLAM
ZIP
THIS IS TOUCHING, BUT MAYBE WE COULD HUG AND RUN?
I LOVE YOU, TOO, DAD.
BUT I'VE BEEN PLANNING THIS STRIKE EVER SINCE I ESCAPED OSKAR ON THE NIGHT YOU...
WHAT I MEAN IS: I DON'T HAVE AN ESCAPE PLAN FOR THIS.
BLAM!
BLAM!
BLAM!
I DON'T CARE HOW I MAKE MY EXIT. AS LONG AS IT'S WITH YOU.
BLAM!
MY PLAN COULDN'T HAVE GONE BETTER, DADDY.
BLAM!
THE TWO OF YOU OWE IGOR SO MANY NAPS AND CAKES.

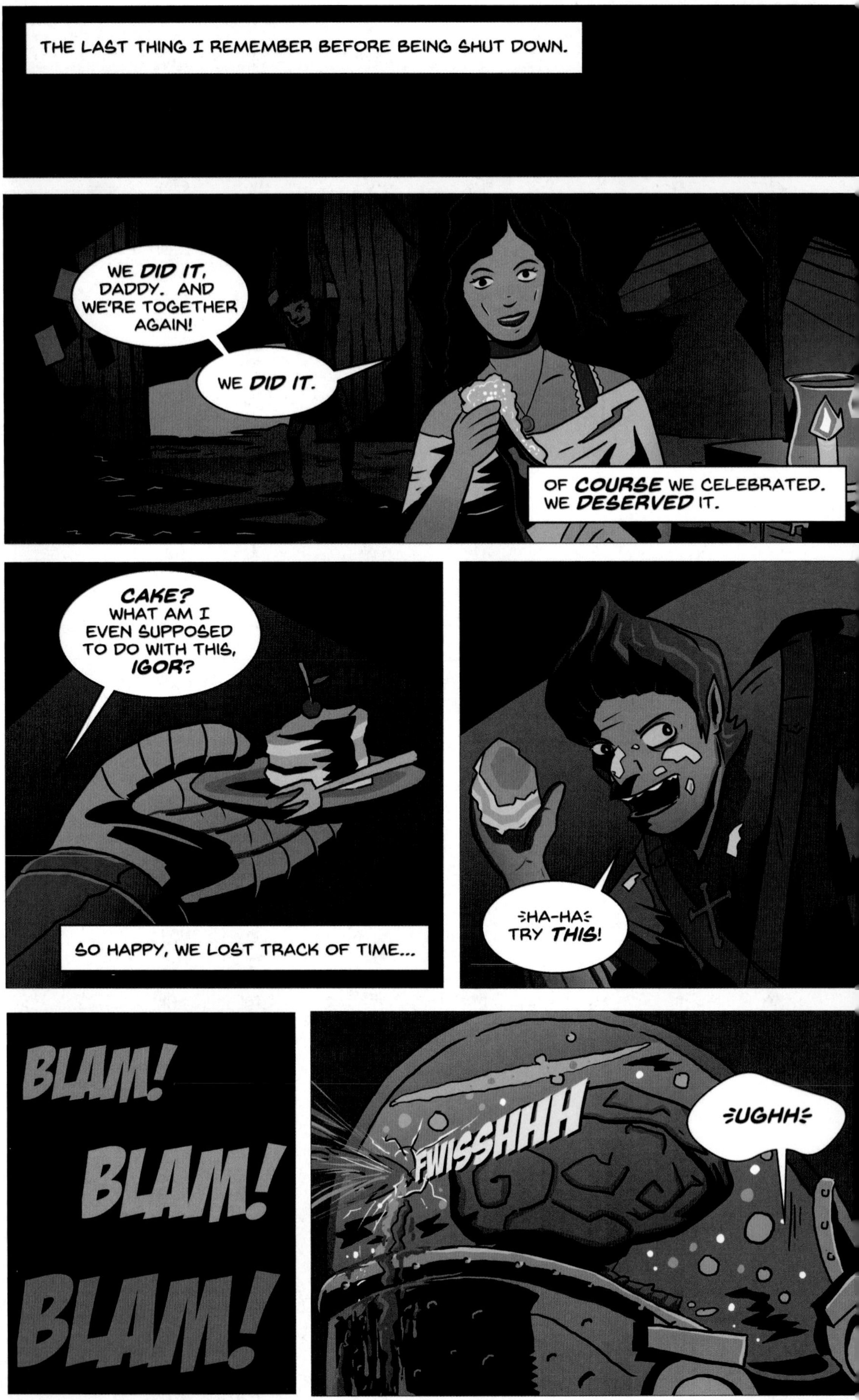
THE LAST THING I REMEMBER BEFORE BEING SHUT DOWN.
WE DID IT, DADDY. AND WE'RE TOGETHER AGAIN!
WE DID IT.
OF COURSE WE CELEBRATED. WE DESERVED IT.
CAKE? WHAT AM I EVEN SUPPOSED TO DO WITH THIS, IGOR?
SO HAPPY, WE LOST TRACK OF TIME...
HA-HA TRY THIS!
BLAM!
BLAM!
BLAM!
FWISSHHH
UGHH

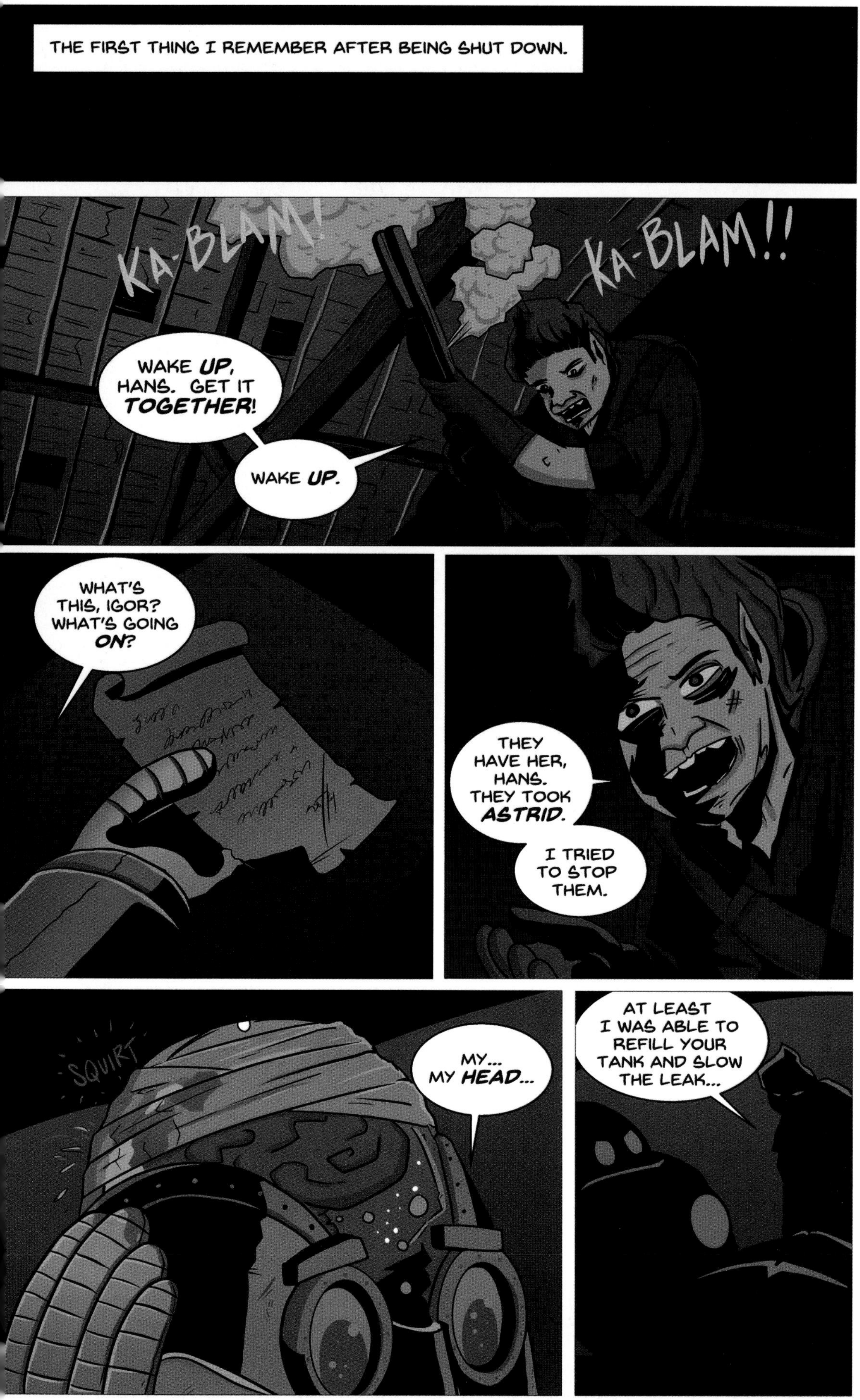
THE FIRST THING I REMEMBER AFTER BEING SHUT DOWN.
KA-BLAM!
KA-BLAM!!
WAKE UP, HANS. GET IT TOGETHER!
WAKE UP.
WHAT'S THIS, IGOR? WHAT'S GOING ON?
THEY HAVE HER, HANS. THEY TOOK ASTRID.
I TRIED TO STOP THEM.
SQUIRT
MY... MY HEAD...
AT LEAST I WAS ABLE TO REFILL YOUR TANK AND SLOW THE LEAK...

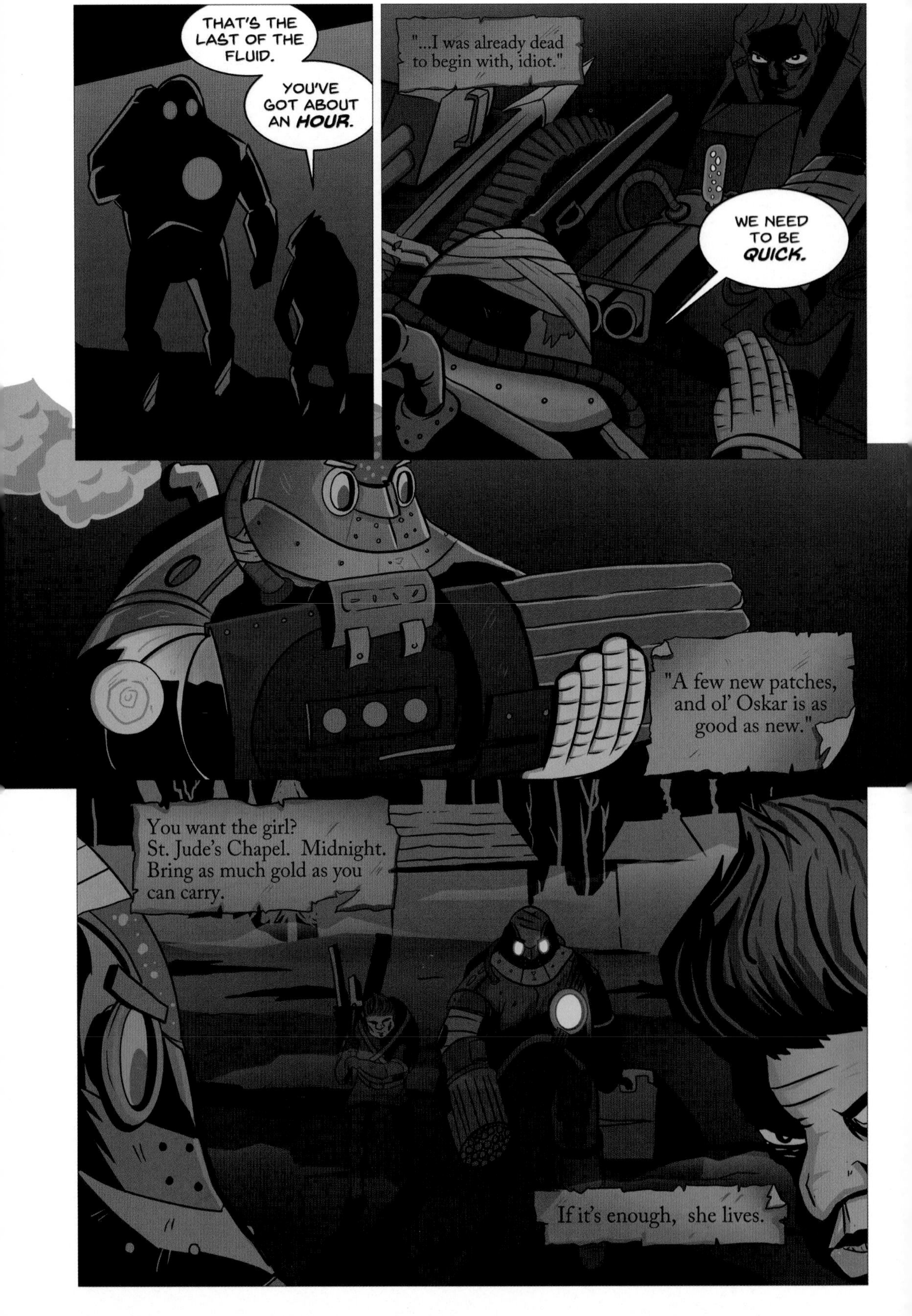
THAT'S THE LAST OF THE FLUID.
YOU'VE GOT ABOUT AN HOUR.
"...I was already dead to begin with, idiot."
WE NEED TO BE QUICK.
"A few new patches, and ol' Oskar is as good as new."
You want the girl? St. Jude's Chapel. Midnight. Bring as much gold as you can carry.
If it's enough, she lives.

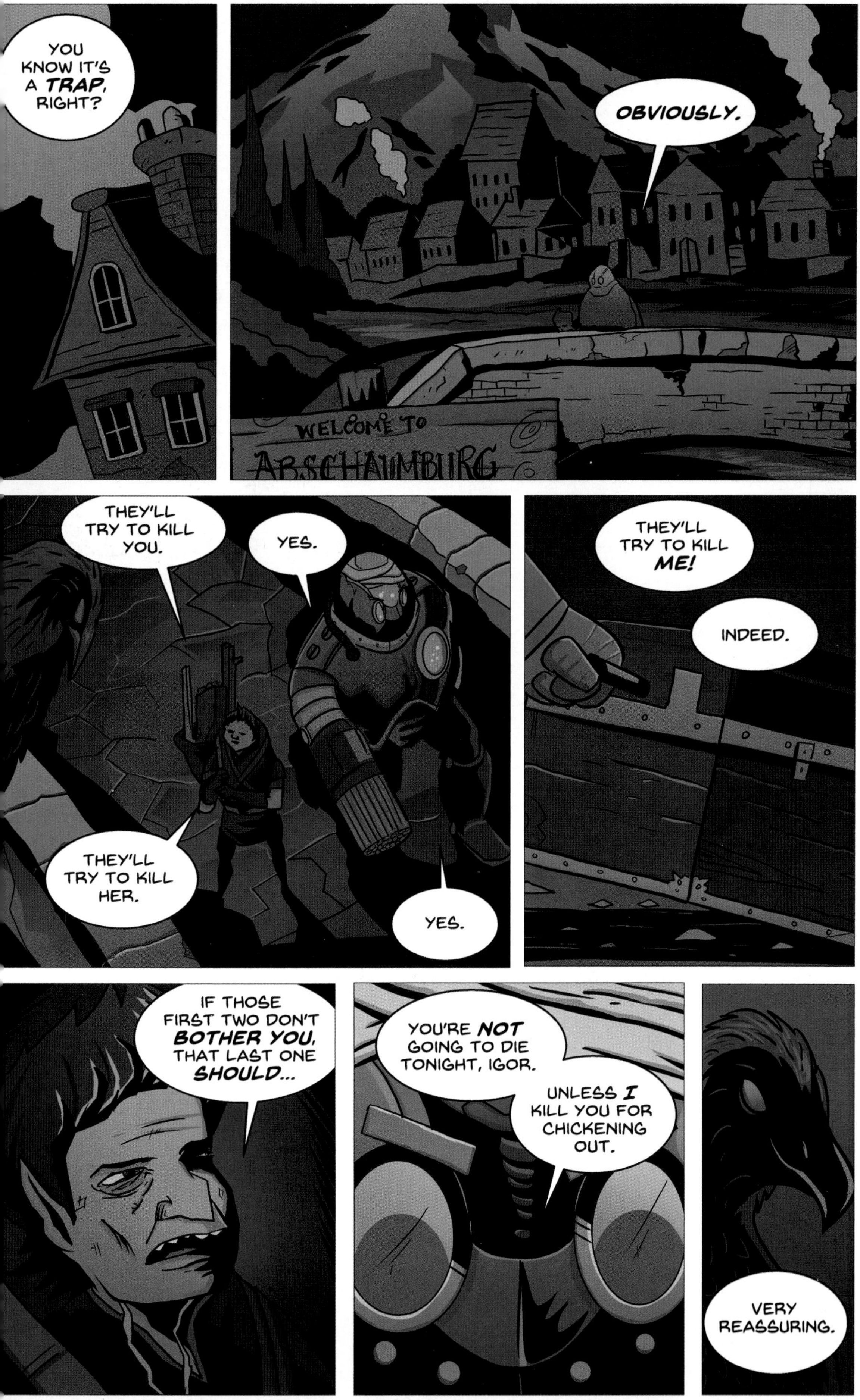

YOU KNOW IT'S A TRAP, RIGHT?
OBVIOUSLY.
WELCOME TO ABSCHAUMBURG
THEY'LL TRY TO KILL YOU.
YES.
THEY'LL TRY TO KILL HER.
YES.
THEY'LL TRY TO KILL ME!
INDEED.
IF THOSE FIRST TWO DON'T BOTHER YOU, THAT LAST ONE SHOULD...
YOU'RE NOT GOING TO DIE TONIGHT, IGOR.
UNLESS I KILL YOU FOR CHICKENING OUT.
VERY REASSURING.

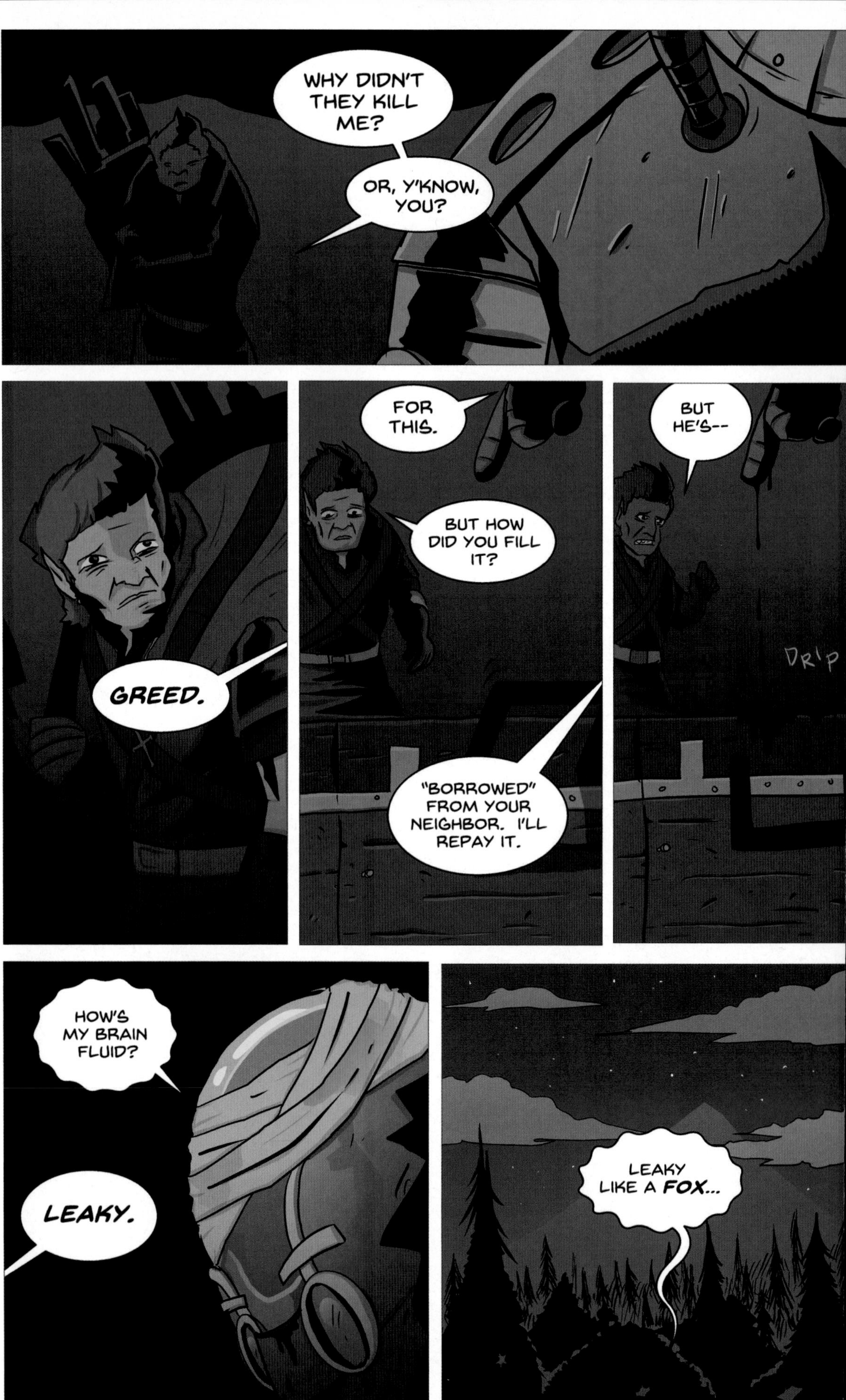
WHY DIDN'T THEY KILL ME?
OR, Y'KNOW, YOU?
GREED.
FOR THIS.
BUT HOW DID YOU FILL IT?
"BORROWED" FROM YOUR NEIGHBOR. I'LL REPAY IT.
BUT HE'S--
DRIP
HOW'S MY BRAIN FLUID?
LEAKY.
LEAKY LIKE A FOX...

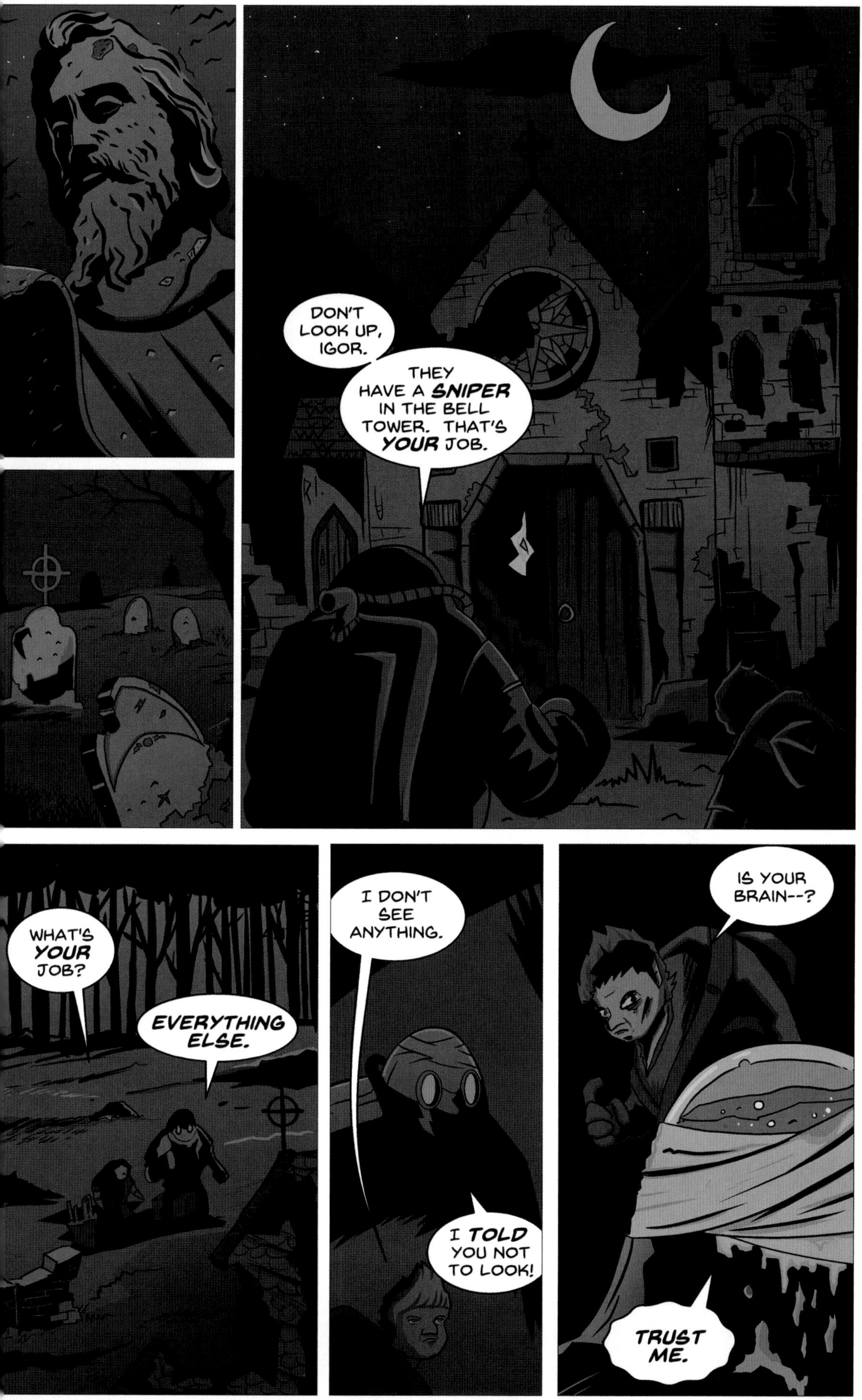
DON'T LOOK UP, IGOR.
THEY HAVE A SNIPER IN THE BELL TOWER. THAT'S YOUR JOB.
WHAT'S YOUR JOB?
EVERYTHING ELSE.
I DON'T SEE ANYTHING.
I TOLD YOU NOT TO LOOK!
IS YOUR BRAIN--?
TRUST ME.

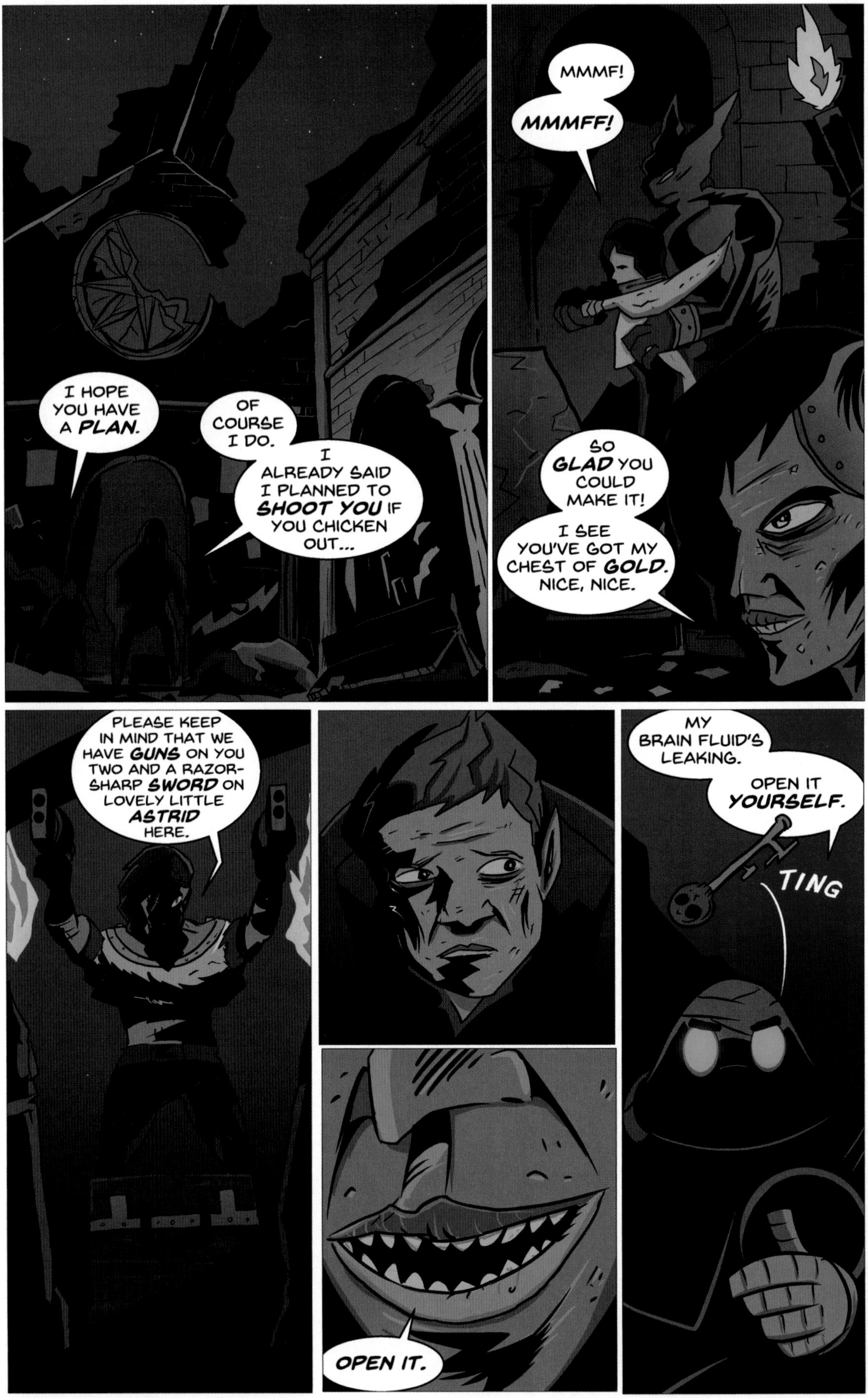
I HOPE YOU HAVE A PLAN.
OF COURSE I DO.
I ALREADY SAID I PLANNED TO SHOOT YOU IF YOU CHICKEN OUT...
MMMF!
MMMFF!
SO GLAD YOU COULD MAKE IT!
I SEE YOU'VE GOT MY CHEST OF GOLD. NICE, NICE.
PLEASE KEEP IN MIND THAT WE HAVE GUNS ON YOU TWO AND A RAZOR-SHARP SWORD ON LOVELY LITTLE ASTRID HERE.
OPEN IT.
MY BRAIN FLUID'S LEAKING.
OPEN IT YOURSELF.
TING

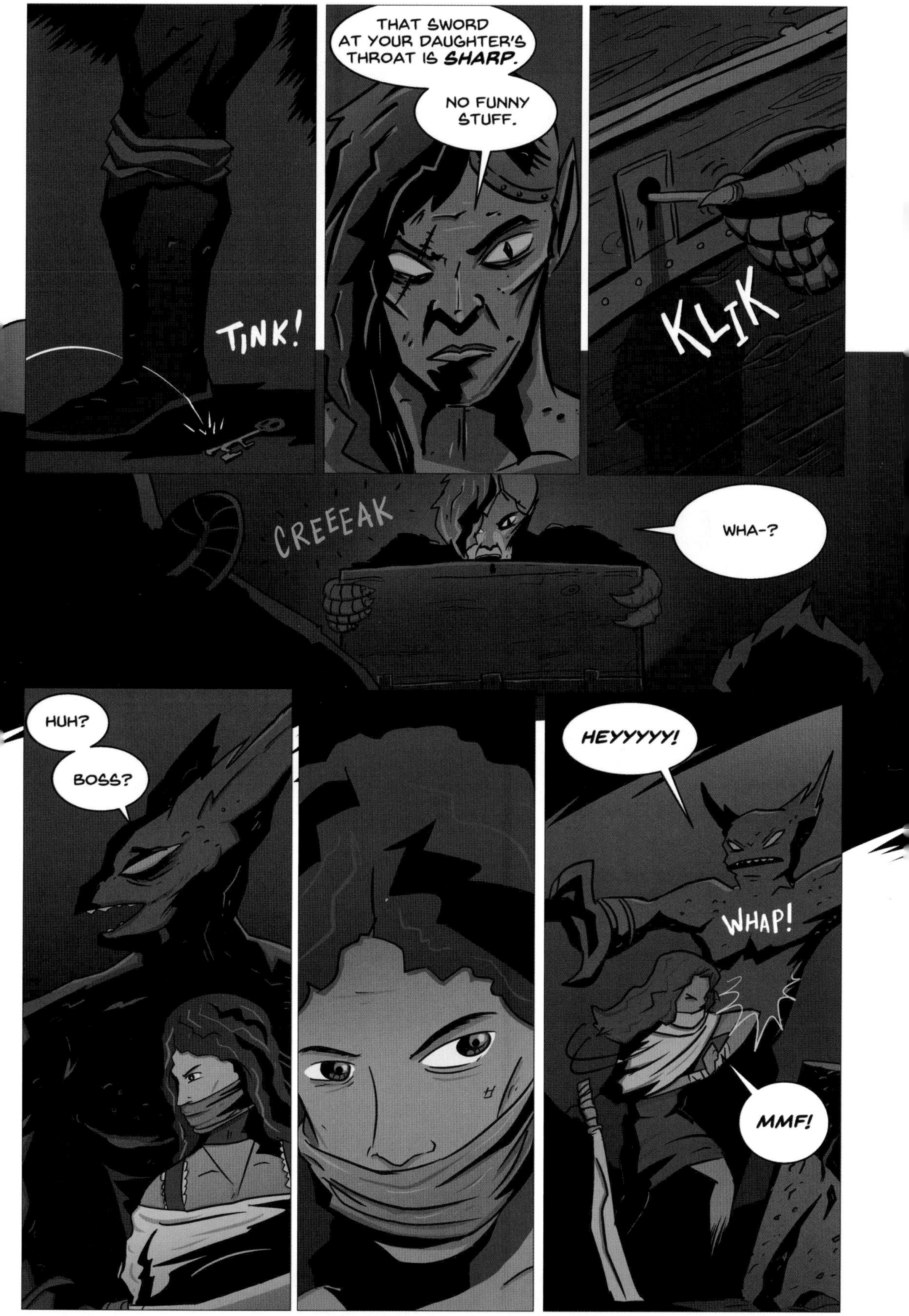
TINK!
THAT SWORD AT YOUR DAUGHTER'S THROAT IS **SHARP**.
NO FUNNY STUFF.
KLIK
CREEEAK
WHA-?
HUH?
BOSS?
HEYYYYY!
WHAP!
MMF!

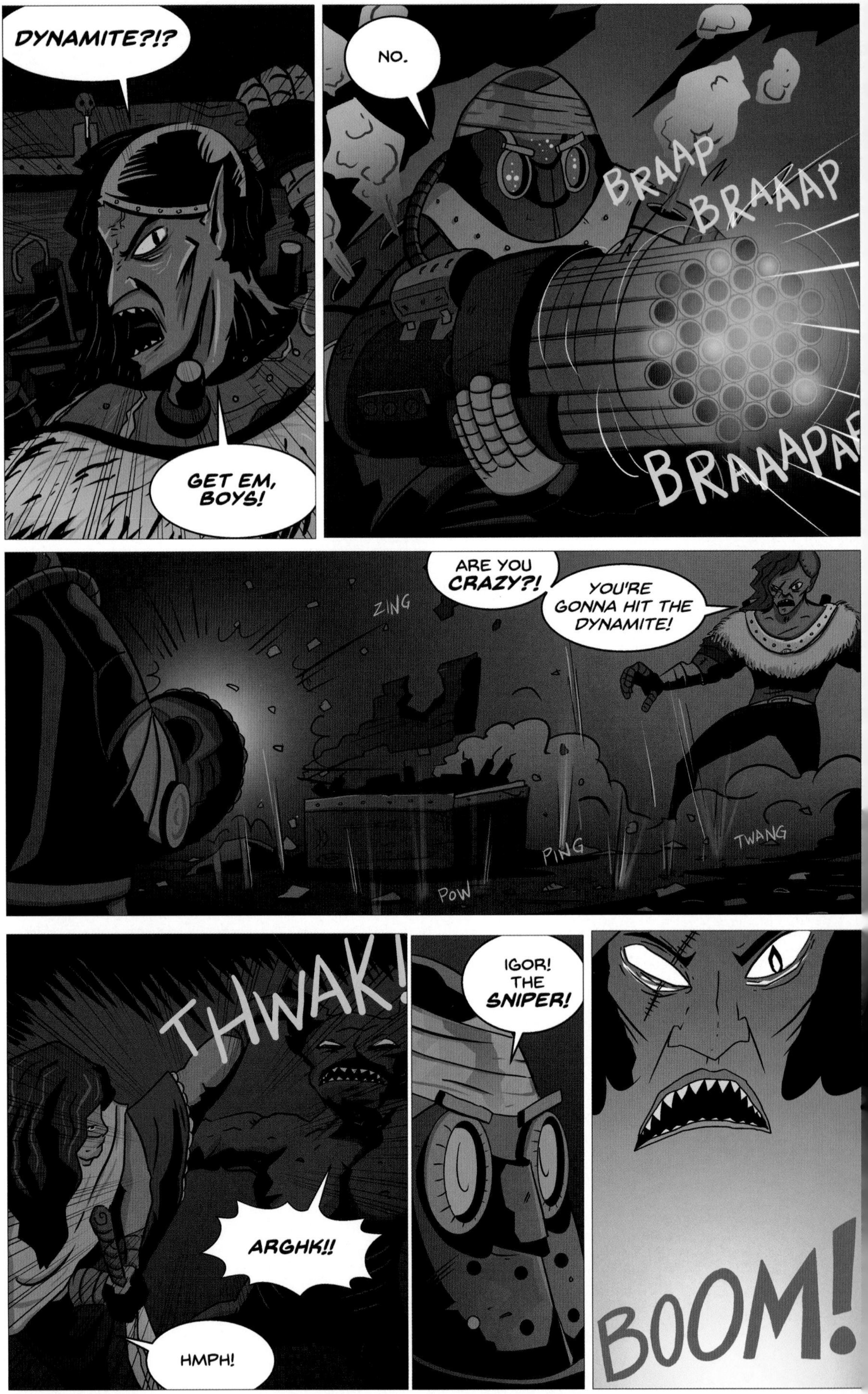
DYNAMITE?!?
GET EM, BOYS!
NO.
BRAAP
BRAAAP
BRAAAPAP
ARE YOU CRAZY?!
YOU'RE GONNA HIT THE DYNAMITE!
ZING
PING
TWANG
POW
THWAK!
ARGHK!!
HMPH!
IGOR! THE SNIPER!
BOOM!

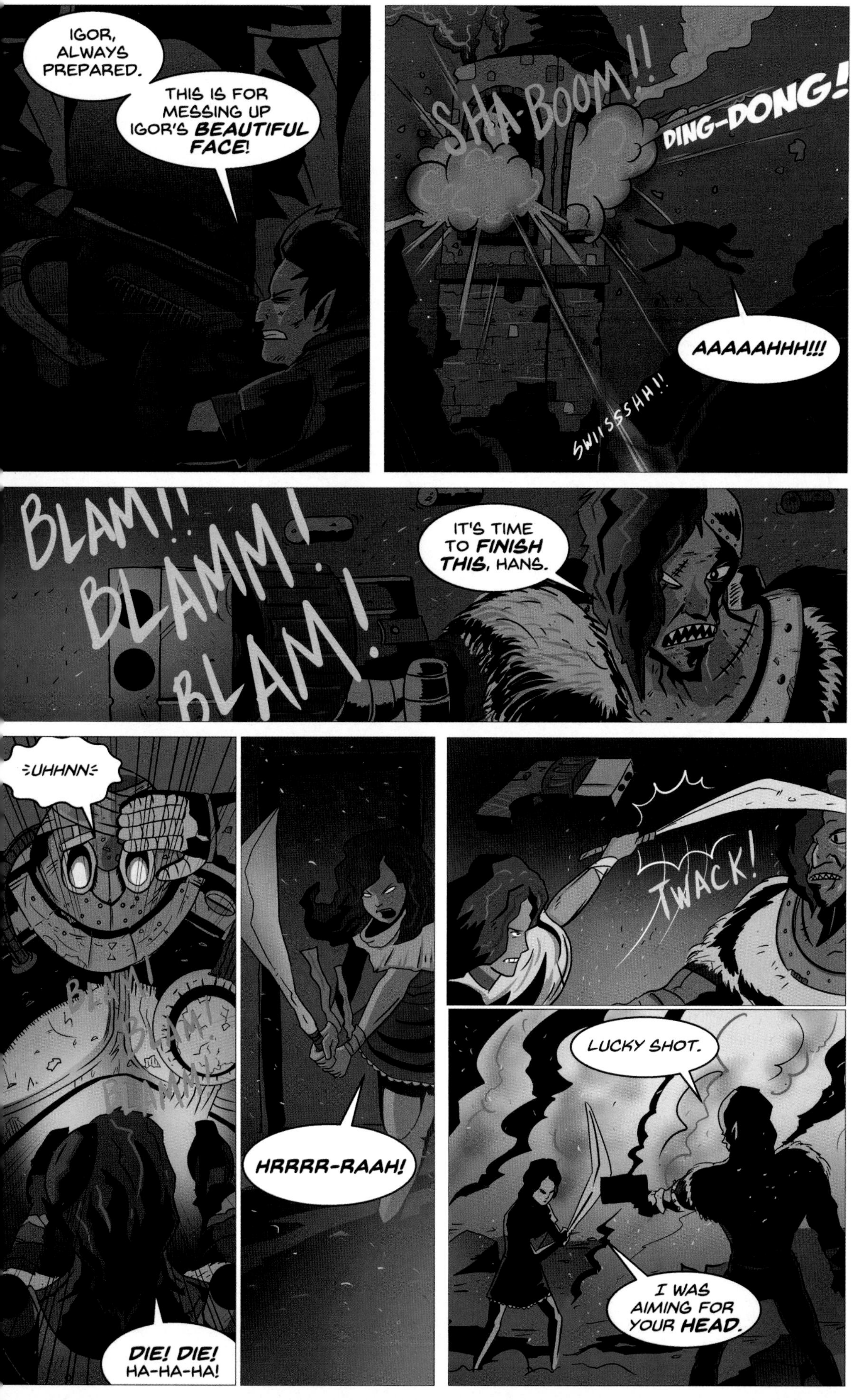
IGOR, ALWAYS PREPARED.
THIS IS FOR MESSING UP IGOR'S BEAUTIFUL FACE!
SHA-BOOM!!
DING-DONG!
AAAAAHHH!!!
SWIISSSHH!!
BLAM!! BLAMM! BLAM!
IT'S TIME TO FINISH THIS, HANS.
UHHNN
BLAM! BLAM! BLAMM!
DIE! DIE! HA-HA-HA!
HRRRR-RAAH!
TWACK!
LUCKY SHOT.
I WAS AIMING FOR YOUR HEAD.

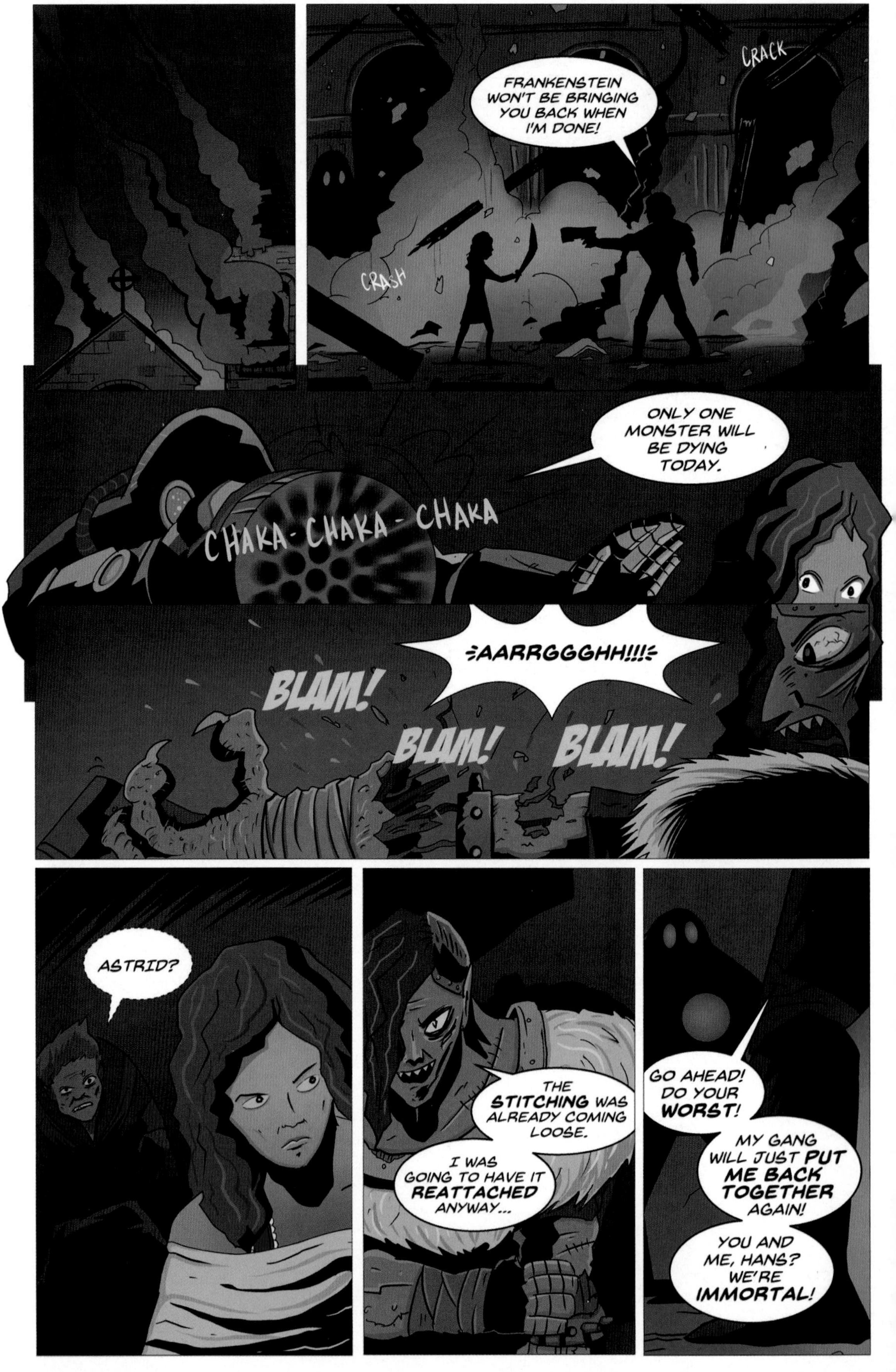

FRANKENSTEIN WON'T BE BRINGING YOU BACK WHEN I'M DONE!
CRACK
CRASH
ONLY ONE MONSTER WILL BE DYING TODAY.
CHAKA-CHAKA-CHAKA
AARRGGGHH!!!
BLAM!
BLAM!
BLAM!
ASTRID?
THE STITCHING WAS ALREADY COMING LOOSE.
I WAS GOING TO HAVE IT REATTACHED ANYWAY...
GO AHEAD! DO YOUR WORST!
MY GANG WILL JUST PUT ME BACK TOGETHER AGAIN!
YOU AND ME, HANS? WE'RE IMMORTAL!

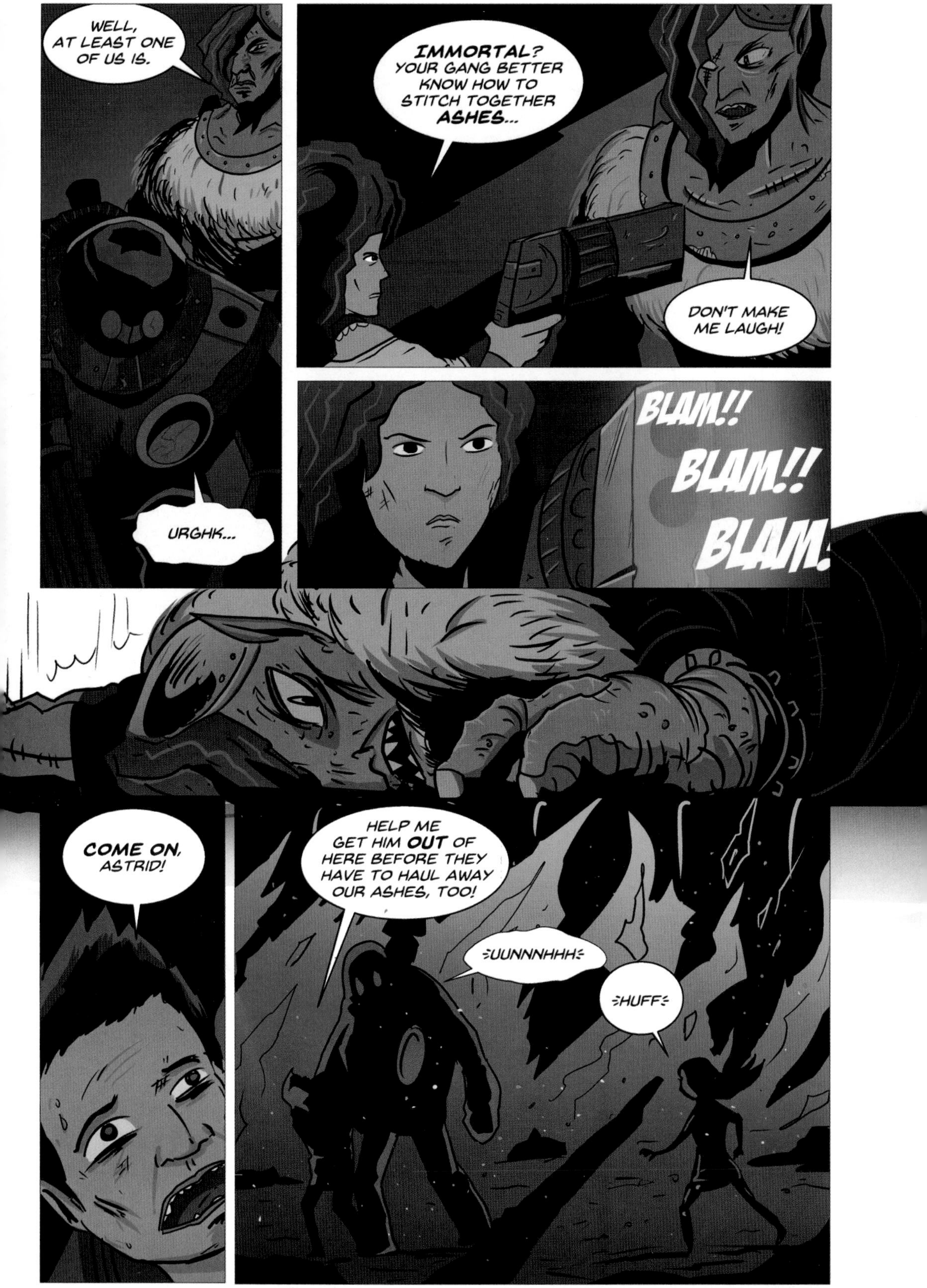
WELL, AT LEAST ONE OF US IS.
URGHK...
IMMORTAL? YOUR GANG BETTER KNOW HOW TO STITCH TOGETHER ASHES...
DON'T MAKE ME LAUGH!
BLAM!!
BLAM!!
BLAM!
COME ON, ASTRID!
HELP ME GET HIM OUT OF HERE BEFORE THEY HAVE TO HAUL AWAY OUR ASHES, TOO!
UUNNNHHH
HUFF

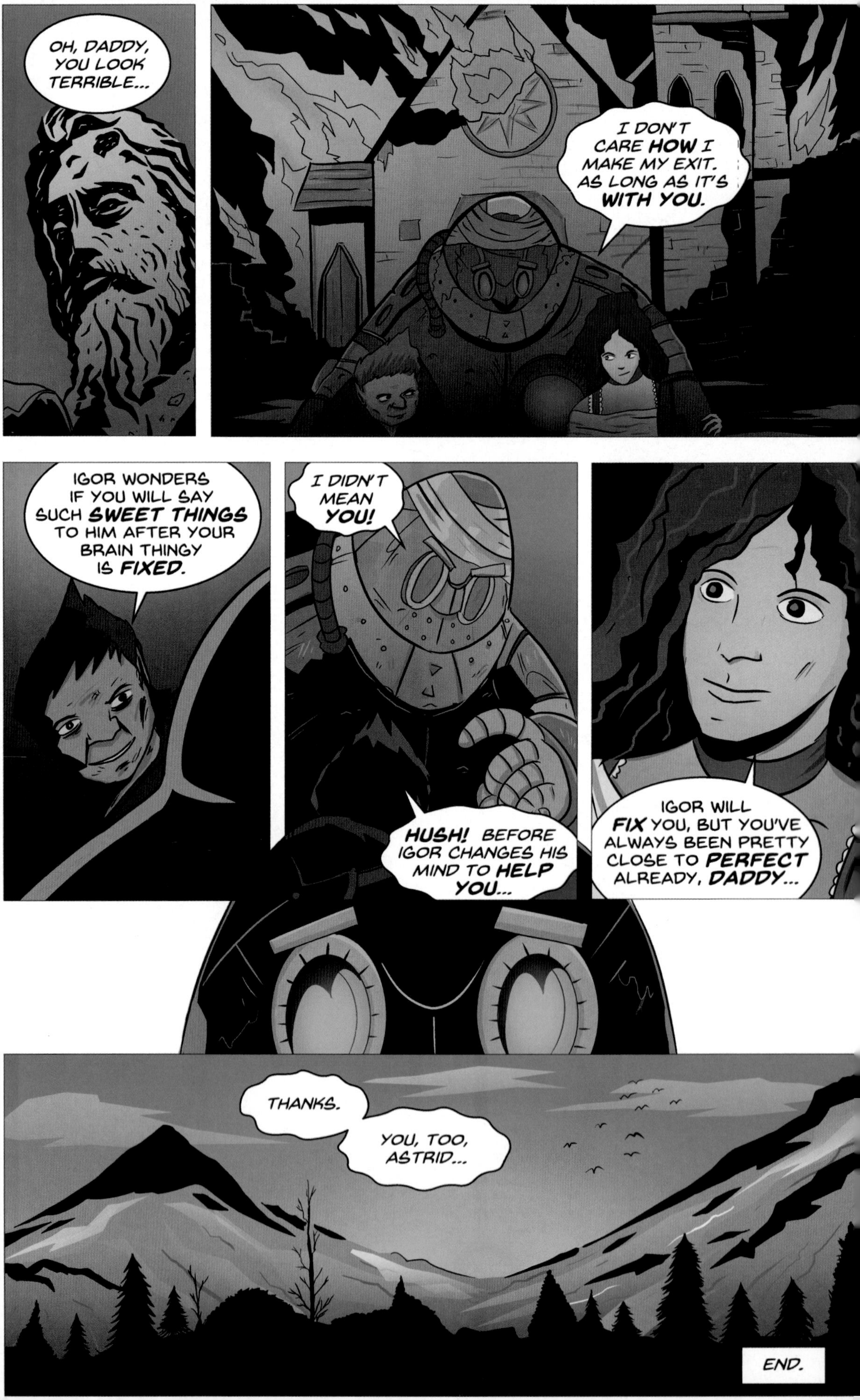
OH, DADDY, YOU LOOK TERRIBLE...
I DON'T CARE HOW I MAKE MY EXIT. AS LONG AS IT'S WITH YOU.
IGOR WONDERS IF YOU WILL SAY SUCH SWEET THINGS TO HIM AFTER YOUR BRAIN THINGY IS FIXED.
I DIDN'T MEAN YOU!
HUSH! BEFORE IGOR CHANGES HIS MIND TO HELP YOU...
IGOR WILL FIX YOU, BUT YOU'VE ALWAYS BEEN PRETTY CLOSE TO PERFECT ALREADY, DADDY...
THANKS.
YOU, TOO, ASTRID...
END.

Monstrous No. 3

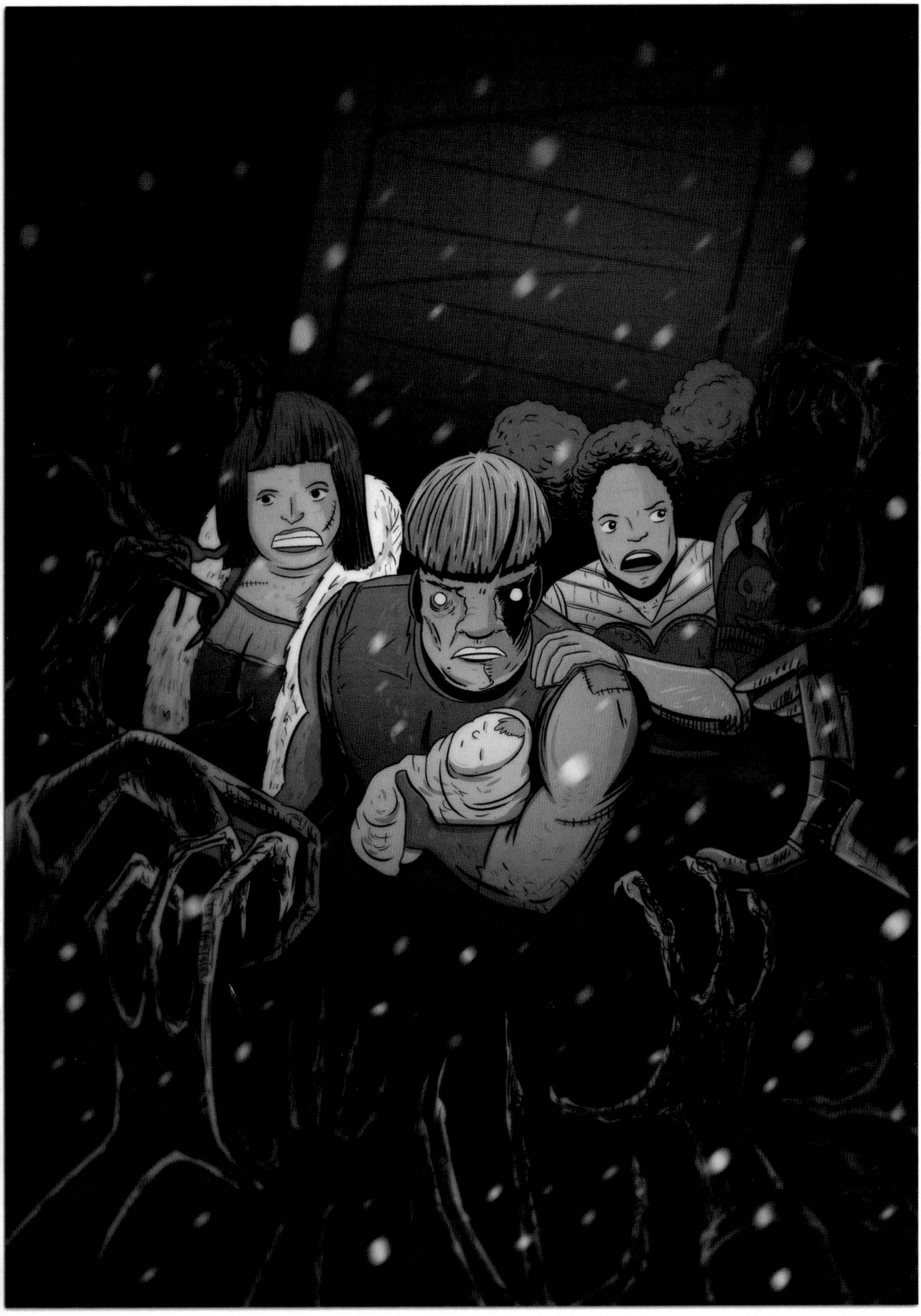

Three Monsters and a Baby

MANY YEARS AGO, **COUNT DRACULA RULED EVERYTHING** IN **SIGHT.**

ONLY THE GREAT PROFESSOR VAN HELSING WAS ABLE TO **STOP** THE **VAMPIRE.**

THE EVIL COUNT'S BODY FELL TO THE **ICY RIVER** BELOW...

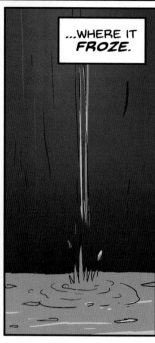

...WHERE IT **FROZE.**

HIS BODY, ENCASED IN ICE, WAS RECOVERED AND PUT UNDER GUARD IN THE TOWN OF **HAMPELMANN.** NEVER TO BE **THAWED...**

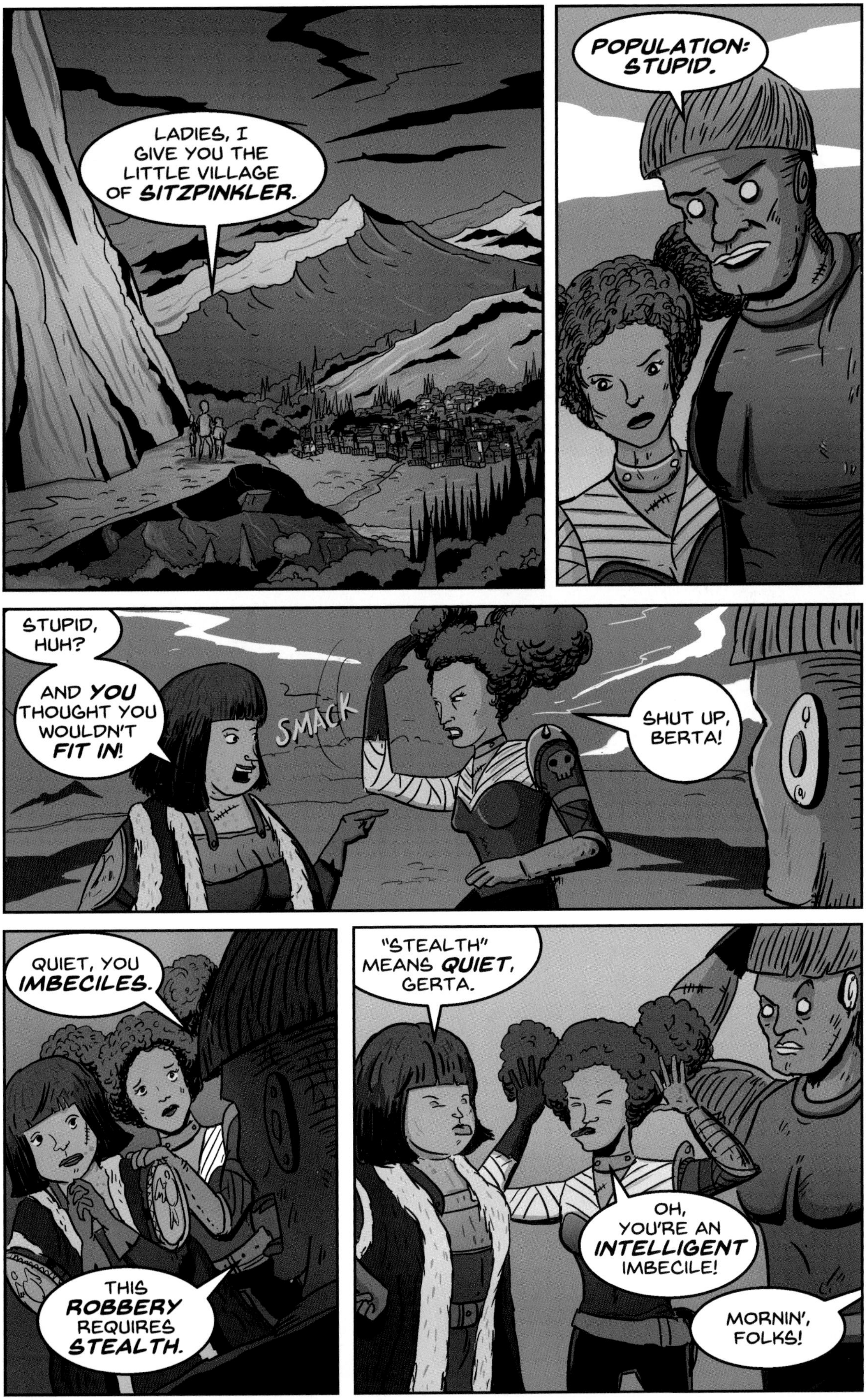
LADIES, I GIVE YOU THE LITTLE VILLAGE OF SITZPINKLER.
POPULATION: STUPID.
STUPID, HUH?
AND YOU THOUGHT YOU WOULDN'T FIT IN!
SMACK
SHUT UP, BERTA!
QUIET, YOU IMBECILES.
THIS ROBBERY REQUIRES STEALTH.
"STEALTH" MEANS QUIET, GERTA.
OH, YOU'RE AN INTELLIGENT IMBECILE!
MORNIN', FOLKS!

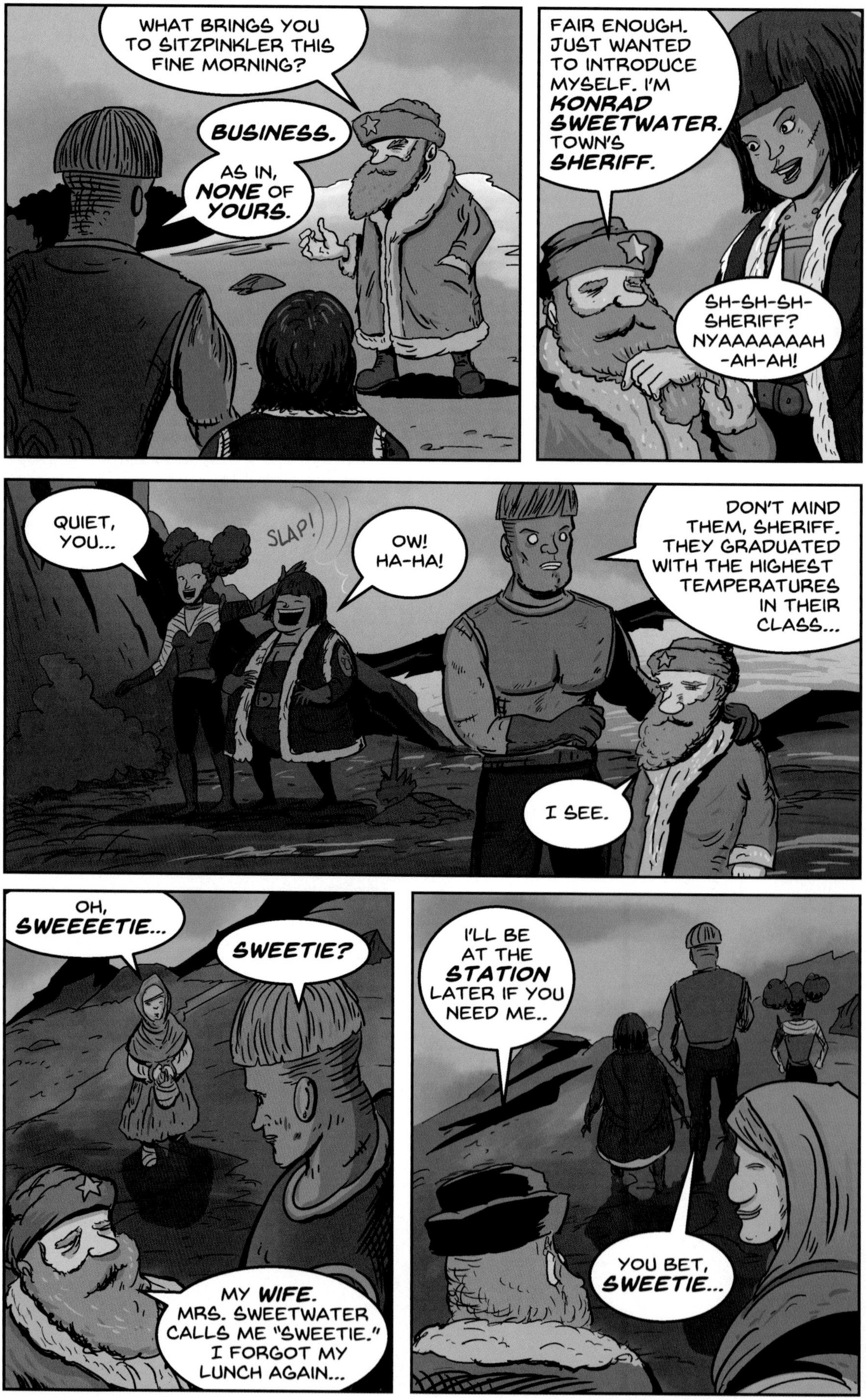
WHAT BRINGS YOU TO SITZPINKLER THIS FINE MORNING?
BUSINESS.
AS IN, NONE OF YOURS.
FAIR ENOUGH. JUST WANTED TO INTRODUCE MYSELF. I'M KONRAD SWEETWATER. TOWN'S SHERIFF.
SH-SH-SH-SHERIFF? NYAAAAAAAH-AH-AH!
QUIET, YOU...
SLAP!
OW! HA-HA!
DON'T MIND THEM, SHERIFF. THEY GRADUATED WITH THE HIGHEST TEMPERATURES IN THEIR CLASS...
I SEE.
OH, SWEEEETIE...
SWEETIE?
MY WIFE. MRS. SWEETWATER CALLS ME "SWEETIE." I FORGOT MY LUNCH AGAIN...
I'LL BE AT THE STATION LATER IF YOU NEED ME..
YOU BET, SWEETIE...

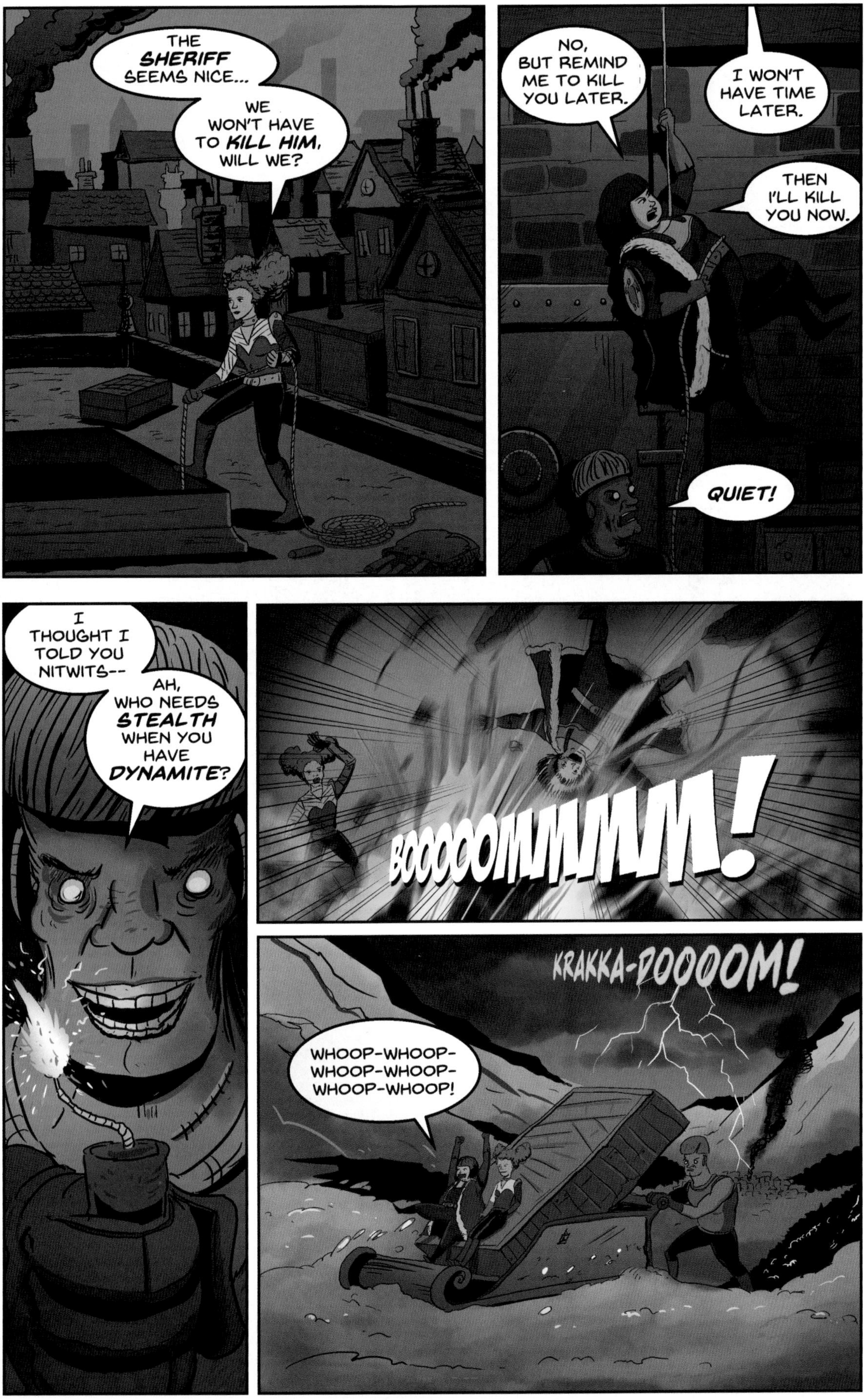
THE SHERIFF SEEMS NICE...
WE WON'T HAVE TO KILL HIM, WILL WE?
NO, BUT REMIND ME TO KILL YOU LATER.
I WON'T HAVE TIME LATER.
THEN I'LL KILL YOU NOW.
QUIET!
I THOUGHT I TOLD YOU NITWITS--
AH, WHO NEEDS STEALTH WHEN YOU HAVE DYNAMITE?
BOOOOOMMMMM!
KRAKKA-DOOOOM!
WHOOP-WHOOP-WHOOP-WHOOP-WHOOP-WHOOP!

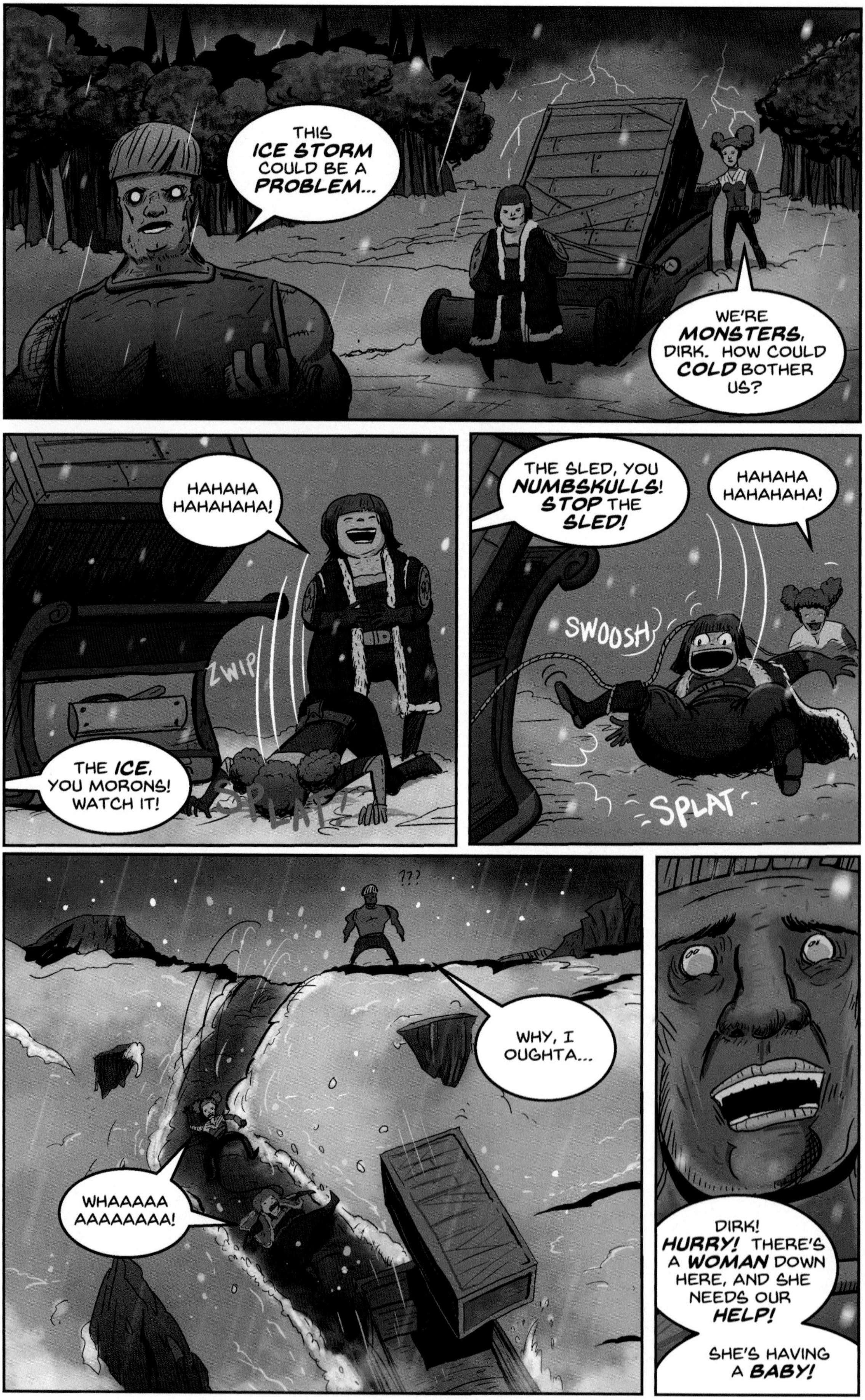
THIS ICE STORM COULD BE A PROBLEM...
WE'RE MONSTERS, DIRK. HOW COULD COLD BOTHER US?
HAHAHA HAHAHAHA!
ZWIP
THE ICE, YOU MORONS! WATCH IT!
SPLAT!
THE SLED, YOU NUMBSKULLS! STOP THE SLED!
HAHAHA HAHAHAHA!
SWOOSH
SPLAT
???
WHY, I OUGHTA...
WHAAAAA AAAAAAAA!
DIRK! HURRY! THERE'S A WOMAN DOWN HERE, AND SHE NEEDS OUR HELP!
SHE'S HAVING A BABY!

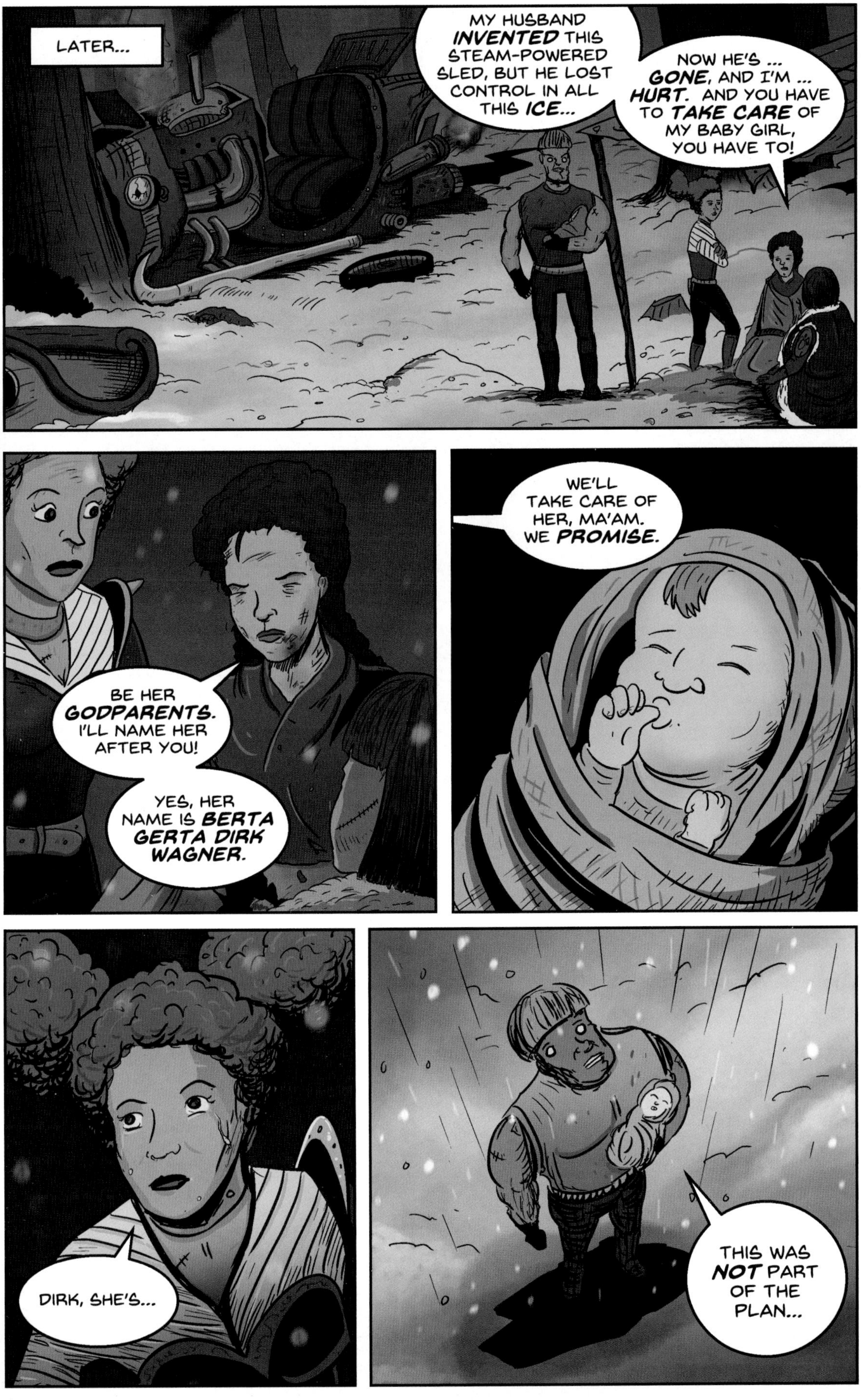
LATER...
MY HUSBAND INVENTED THIS STEAM-POWERED SLED, BUT HE LOST CONTROL IN ALL THIS ICE...
NOW HE'S ... GONE, AND I'M ... HURT. AND YOU HAVE TO TAKE CARE OF MY BABY GIRL, YOU HAVE TO!
BE HER GODPARENTS. I'LL NAME HER AFTER YOU!
YES, HER NAME IS BERTA GERTA DIRK WAGNER.
WE'LL TAKE CARE OF HER, MA'AM. WE PROMISE.
DIRK, SHE'S...
THIS WAS NOT PART OF THE PLAN...

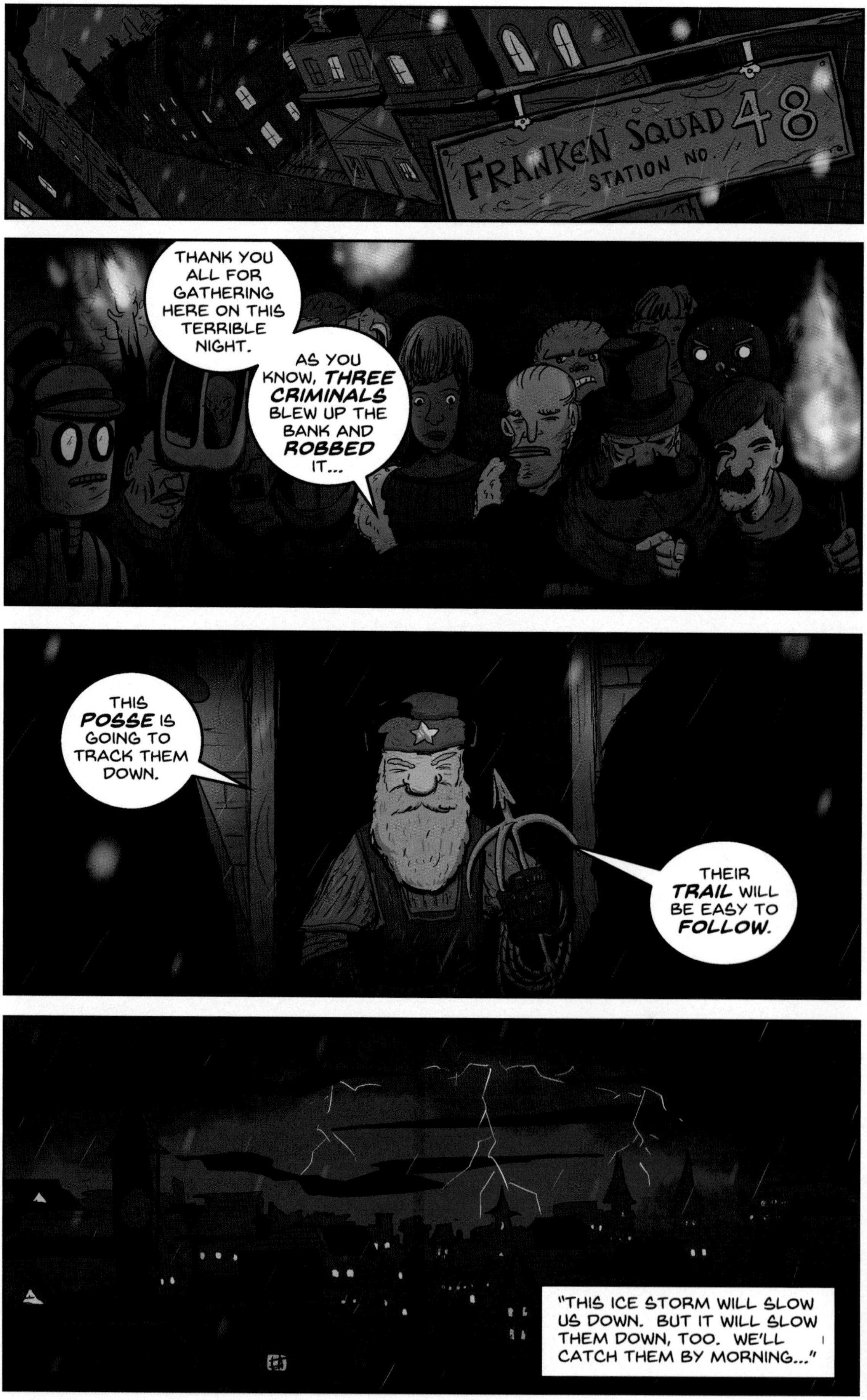
FRANKEN SQUAD STATION NO. 48
THANK YOU ALL FOR GATHERING HERE ON THIS TERRIBLE NIGHT.
AS YOU KNOW, THREE CRIMINALS BLEW UP THE BANK AND ROBBED IT...
THIS POSSE IS GOING TO TRACK THEM DOWN.
THEIR TRAIL WILL BE EASY TO FOLLOW.
"THIS ICE STORM WILL SLOW US DOWN. BUT IT WILL SLOW THEM DOWN, TOO. WE'LL CATCH THEM BY MORNING..."

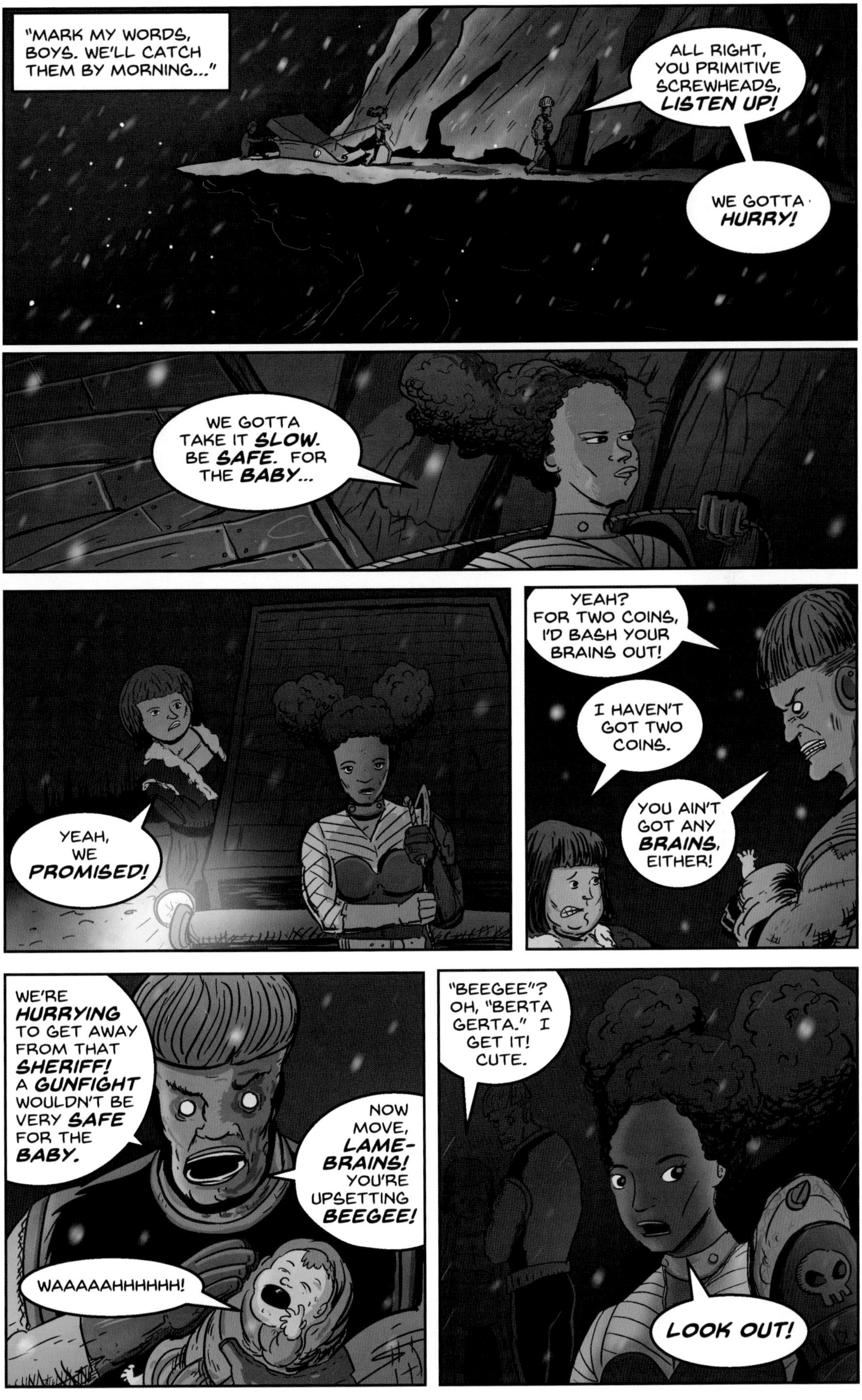
"MARK MY WORDS, BOYS. WE'LL CATCH THEM BY MORNING..."
ALL RIGHT, YOU PRIMITIVE SCREWHEADS, LISTEN UP!
WE GOTTA HURRY!
WE GOTTA TAKE IT SLOW. BE SAFE. FOR THE BABY...
YEAH, WE PROMISED!
YEAH? FOR TWO COINS, I'D BASH YOUR BRAINS OUT!
I HAVEN'T GOT TWO COINS.
YOU AIN'T GOT ANY BRAINS, EITHER!
WE'RE HURRYING TO GET AWAY FROM THAT SHERIFF! A GUNFIGHT WOULDN'T BE VERY SAFE FOR THE BABY.
NOW MOVE, LAME-BRAINS! YOU'RE UPSETTING BEEGEE!
WAAAAAHHHHHH!
"BEEGEE"? OH, "BERTA GERTA." I GET IT! CUTE.
LOOK OUT!

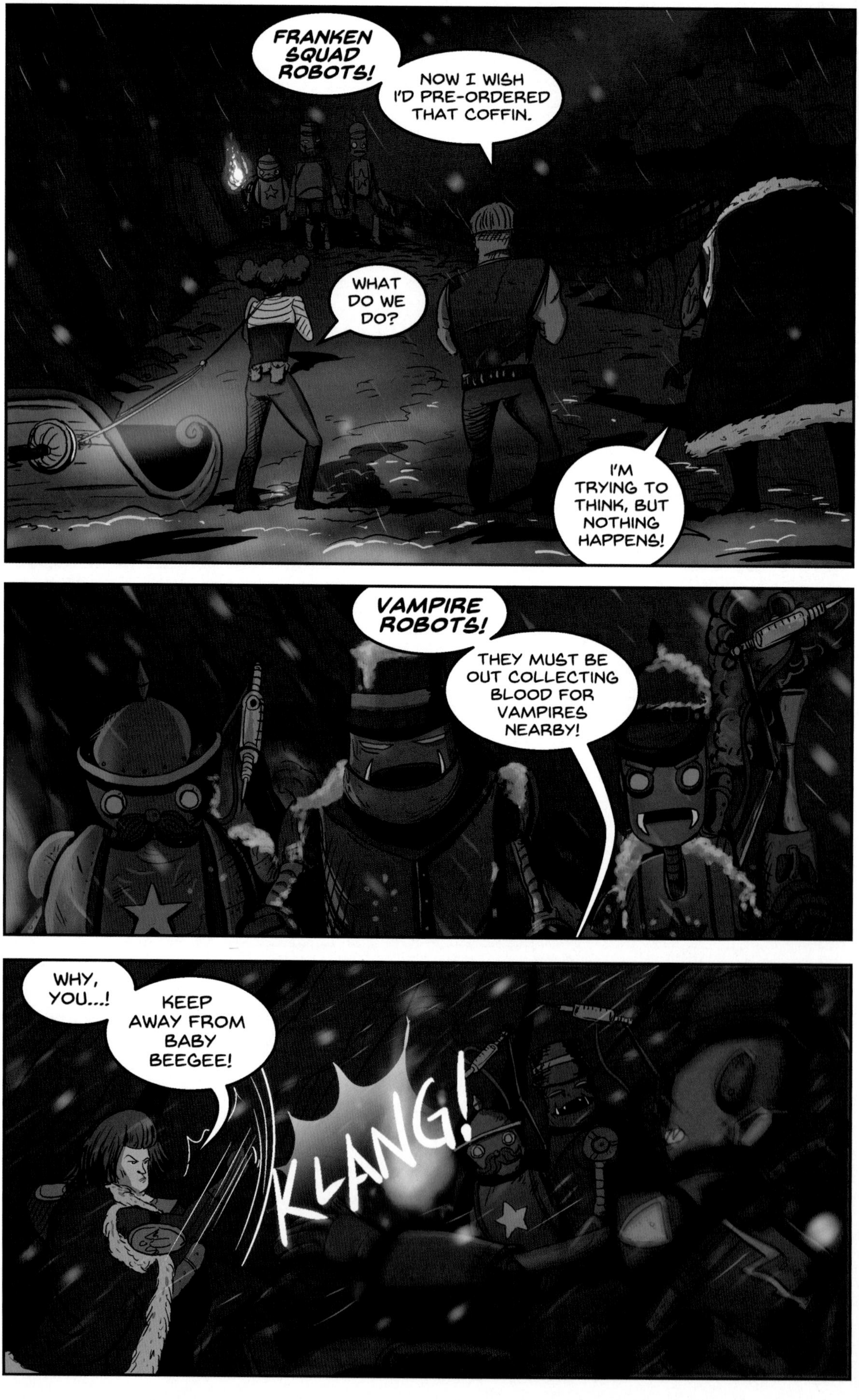
FRANKEN SQUAD ROBOTS!
NOW I WISH I'D PRE-ORDERED THAT COFFIN.
WHAT DO WE DO?
I'M TRYING TO THINK, BUT NOTHING HAPPENS!
VAMPIRE ROBOTS!
THEY MUST BE OUT COLLECTING BLOOD FOR VAMPIRES NEARBY!
WHY, YOU...!
KEEP AWAY FROM BABY BEEGEE!
KLANG!

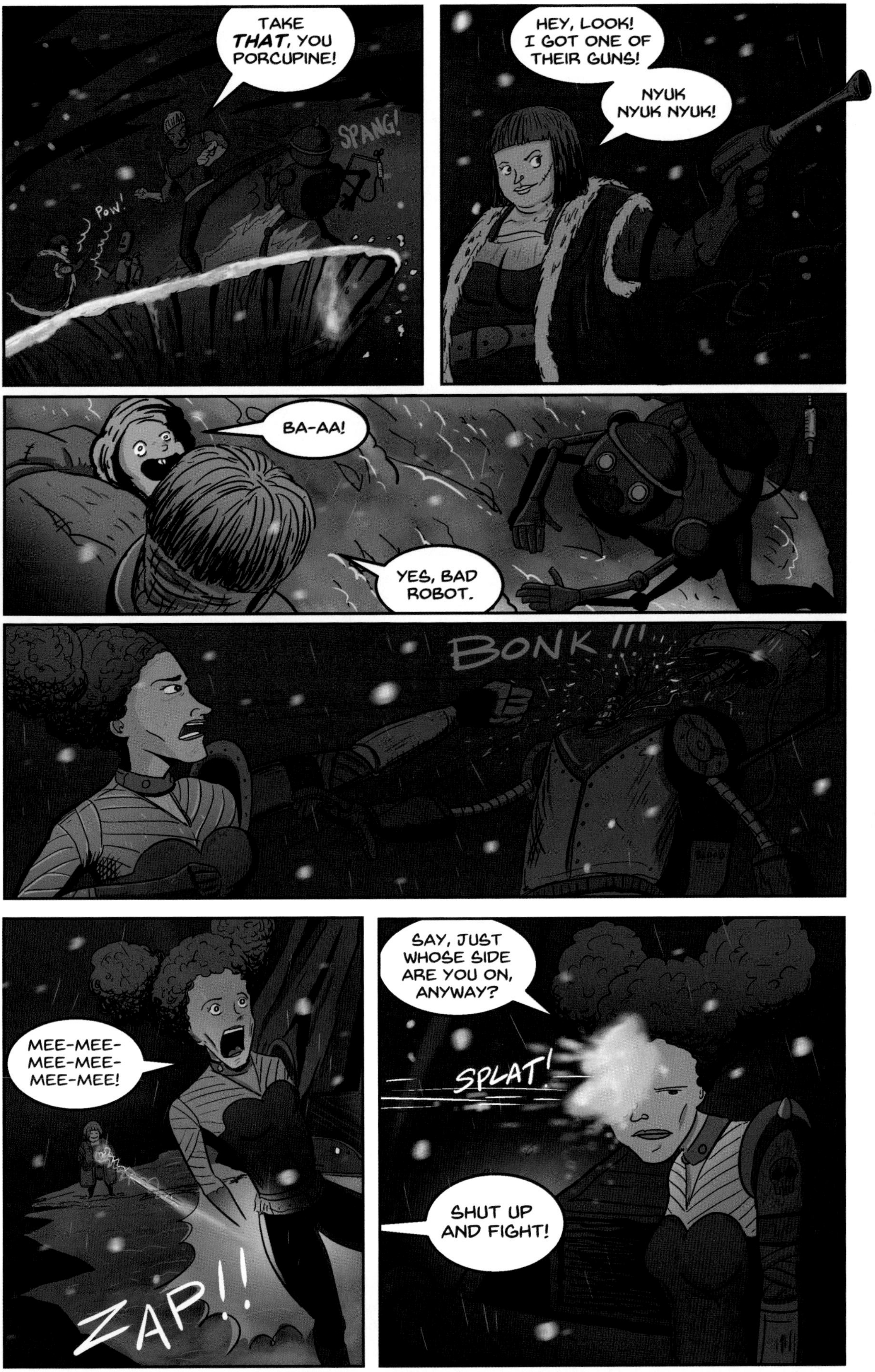
TAKE THAT, YOU PORCUPINE!
SPANG!
POW!
HEY, LOOK! I GOT ONE OF THEIR GUNS!
NYUK NYUK NYUK!
BA-AA!
YES, BAD ROBOT.
BONK!!!
MEE-MEE-MEE-MEE-MEE-MEE!
ZAP!!
SAY, JUST WHOSE SIDE ARE YOU ON, ANYWAY?
SPLAT!
SHUT UP AND FIGHT!

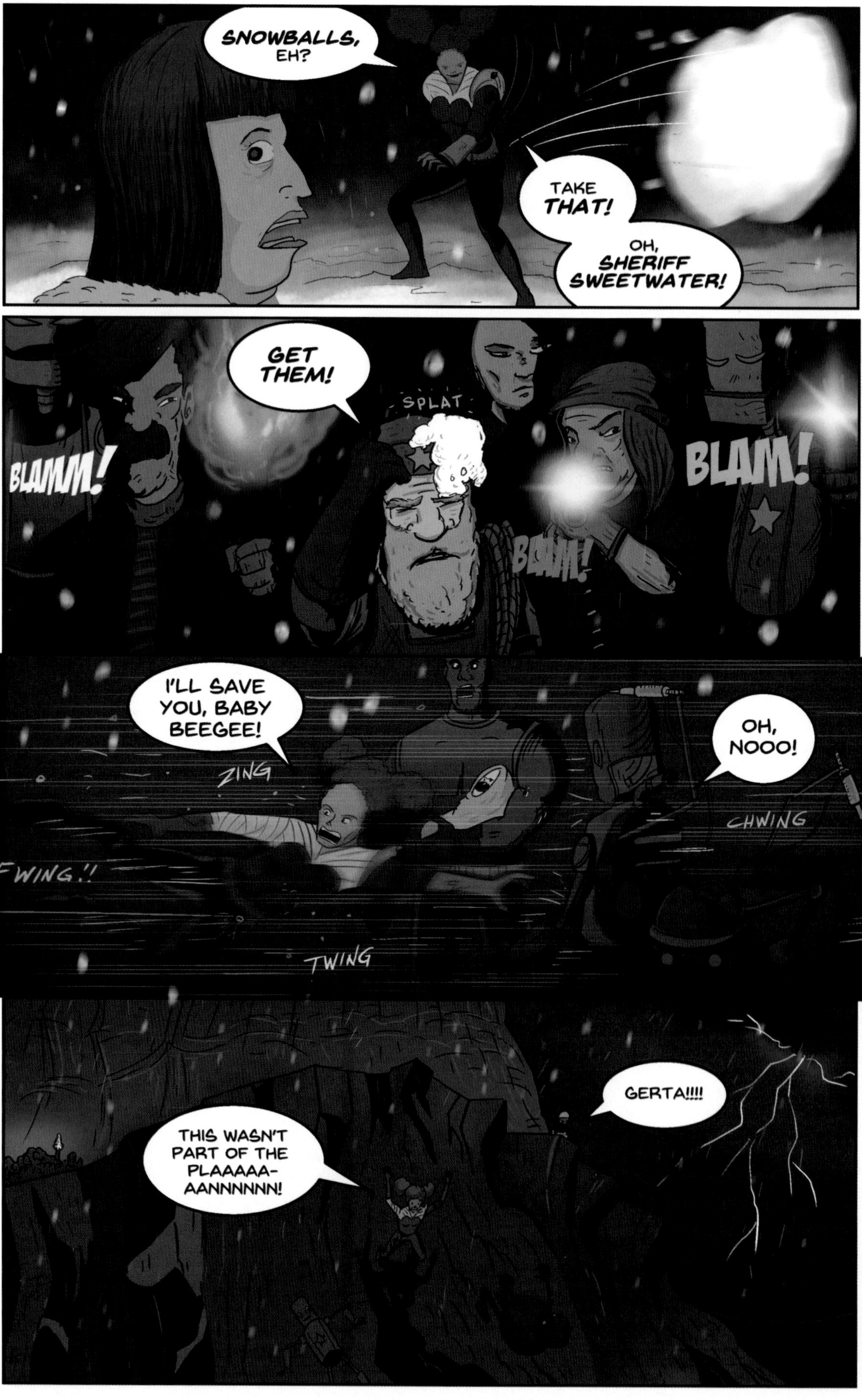
SNOWBALLS, EH?
TAKE THAT!
OH, SHERIFF SWEETWATER!
GET THEM!
SPLAT
BLAMM!
BLAM!
BLAM!
I'LL SAVE YOU, BABY BEEGEE!
OH, NOOO!
ZING
CHWING
FWING!!
TWING
GERTA!!!!
THIS WASN'T PART OF THE PLAAAAA-AANNNNNN!

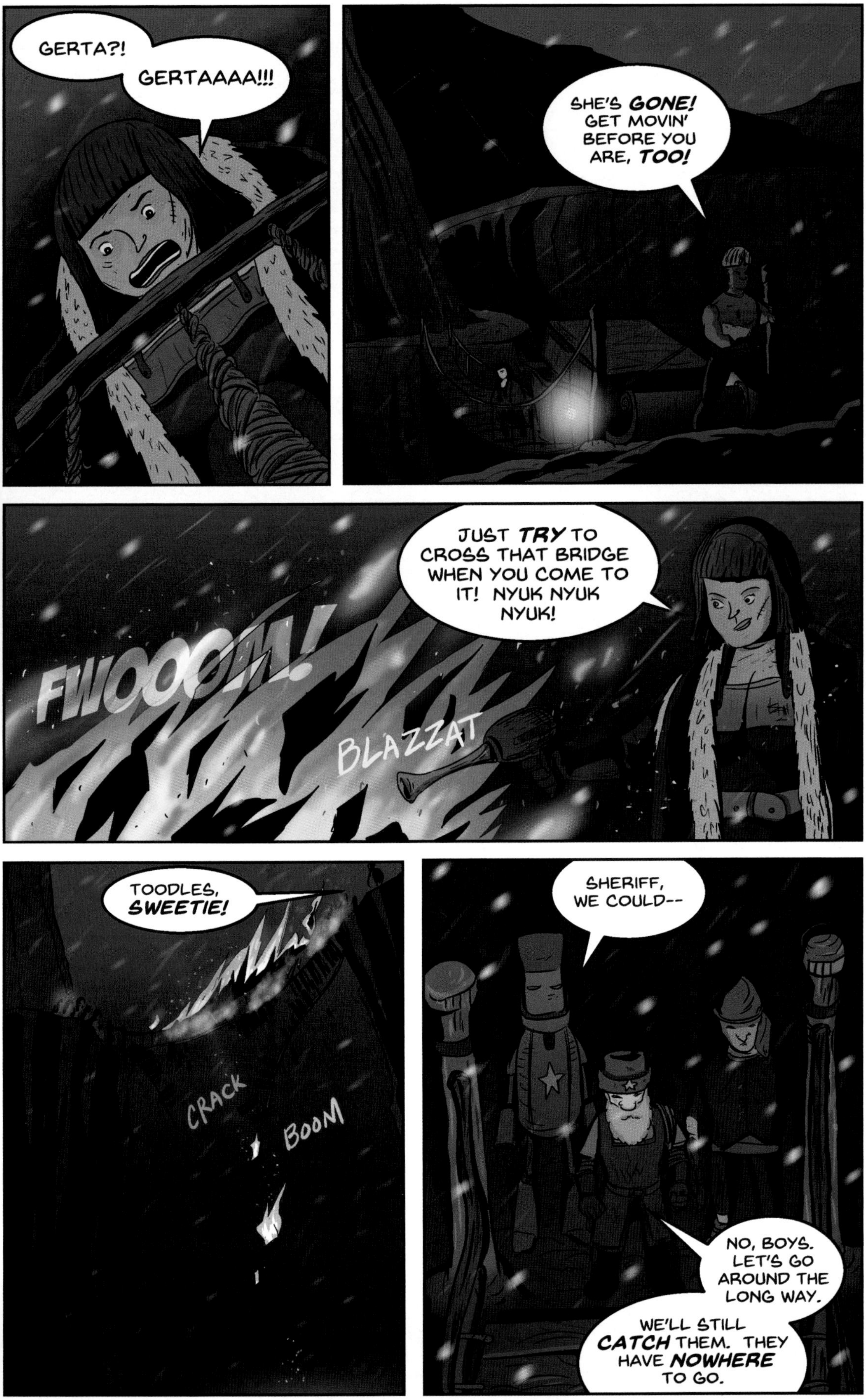
GERTA?!
GERTAAAA!!!
SHE'S GONE! GET MOVIN' BEFORE YOU ARE, TOO!
JUST TRY TO CROSS THAT BRIDGE WHEN YOU COME TO IT! NYUK NYUK NYUK!
FWOOOM!
BLAZZAT
TOODLES, SWEETIE!
CRACK
BOOM
SHERIFF, WE COULD--
NO, BOYS. LET'S GO AROUND THE LONG WAY.
WE'LL STILL CATCH THEM. THEY HAVE NOWHERE TO GO.

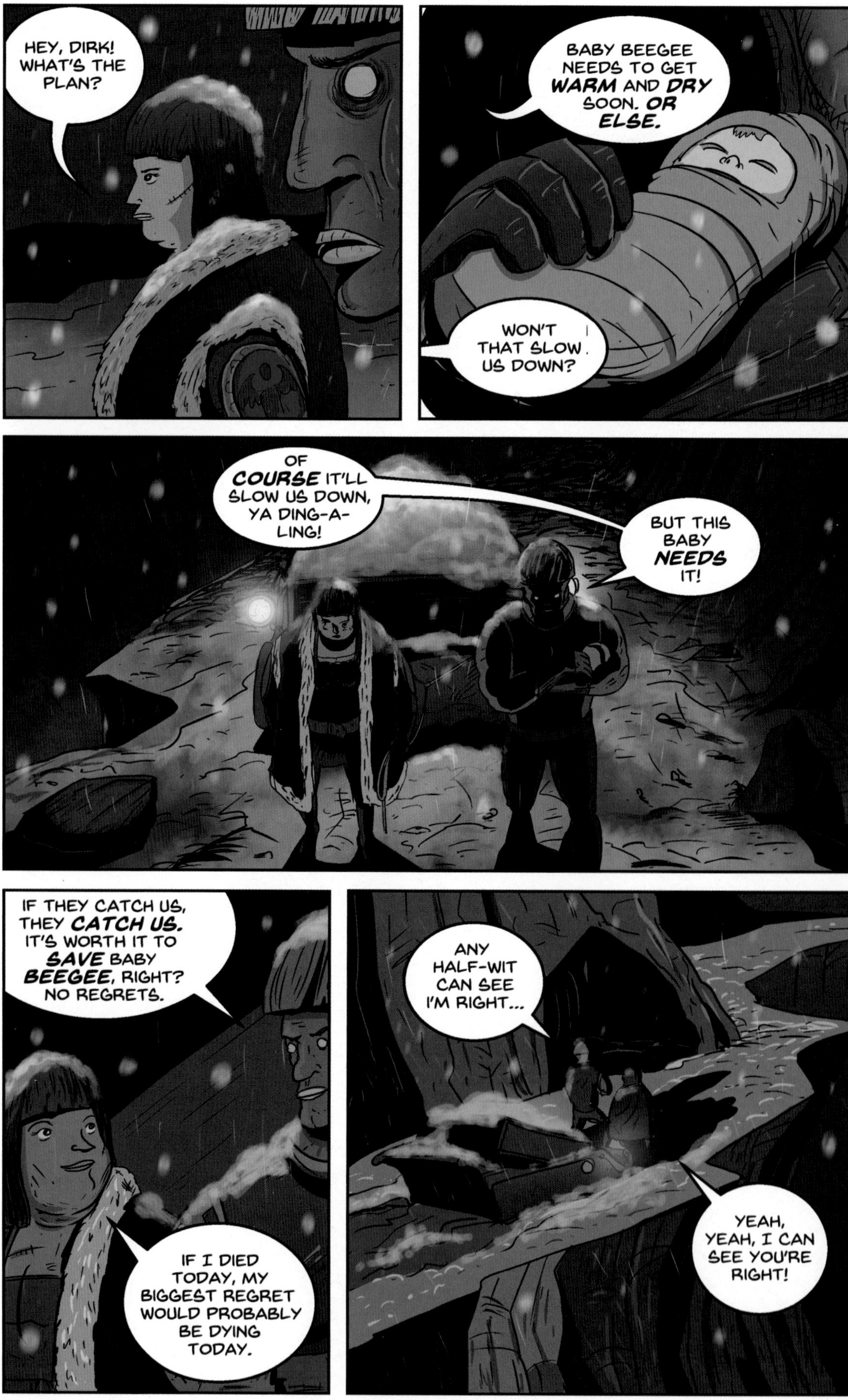
HEY, DIRK! WHAT'S THE PLAN?
BABY BEEGEE NEEDS TO GET **WARM** AND **DRY** SOON. **OR ELSE.**
WON'T THAT SLOW US DOWN?
OF **COURSE** IT'LL SLOW US DOWN, YA DING-A-LING!
BUT THIS BABY **NEEDS** IT!
IF THEY CATCH US, THEY **CATCH US.** IT'S WORTH IT TO **SAVE** BABY **BEEGEE**, RIGHT? NO REGRETS.
IF I DIED TODAY, MY BIGGEST REGRET WOULD PROBABLY BE DYING TODAY.
ANY HALF-WIT CAN SEE I'M RIGHT...
YEAH, YEAH, I CAN SEE YOU'RE RIGHT!

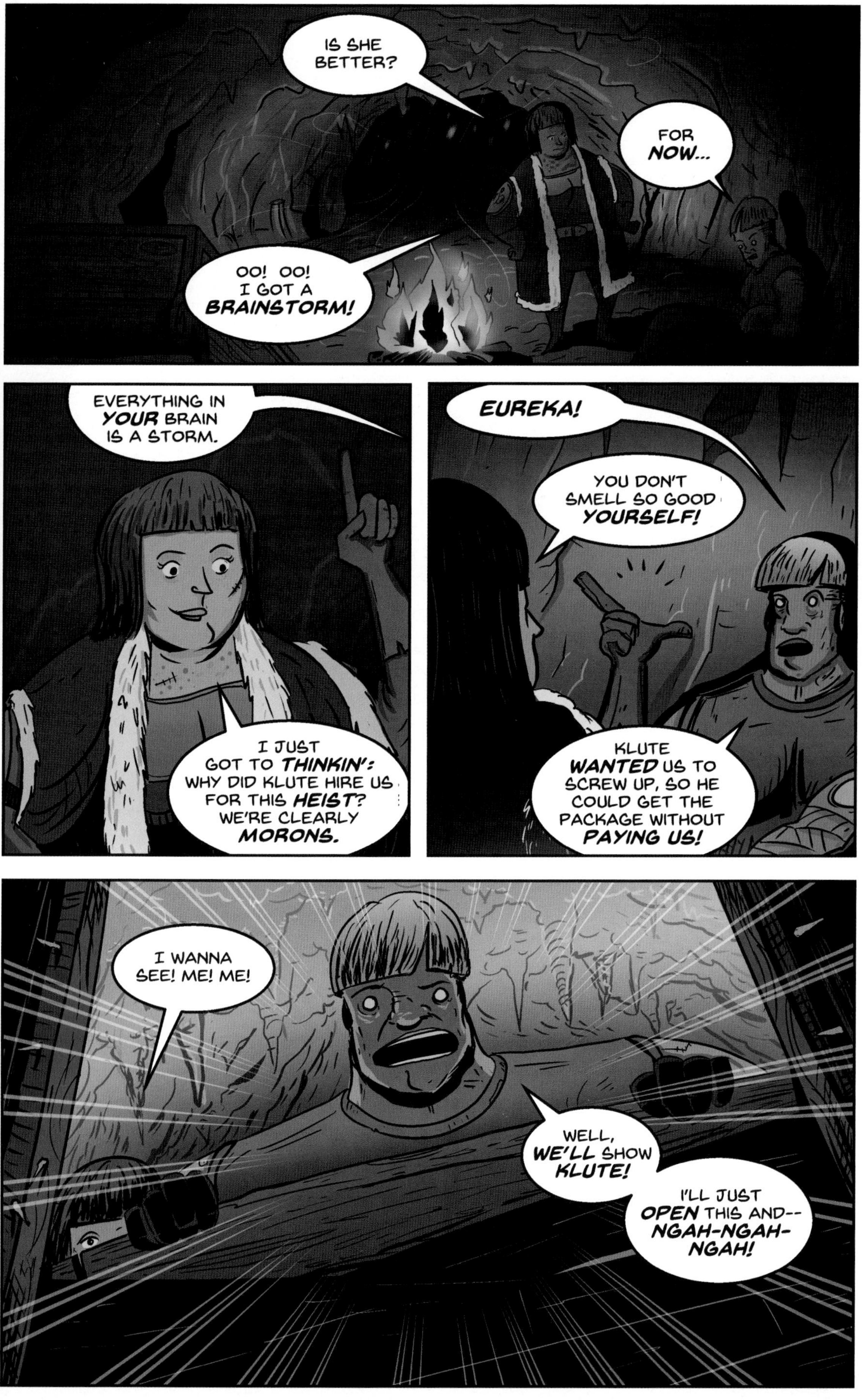
IS SHE BETTER?
FOR NOW...
OO! OO! I GOT A BRAINSTORM!
EVERYTHING IN YOUR BRAIN IS A STORM.
I JUST GOT TO THINKIN': WHY DID KLUTE HIRE US FOR THIS HEIST? WE'RE CLEARLY MORONS.
EUREKA!
YOU DON'T SMELL SO GOOD YOURSELF!
KLUTE WANTED US TO SCREW UP, SO HE COULD GET THE PACKAGE WITHOUT PAYING US!
I WANNA SEE! ME! ME!
WELL, WE'LL SHOW KLUTE!
I'LL JUST OPEN THIS AND-- NGAH-NGAH-NGAH!

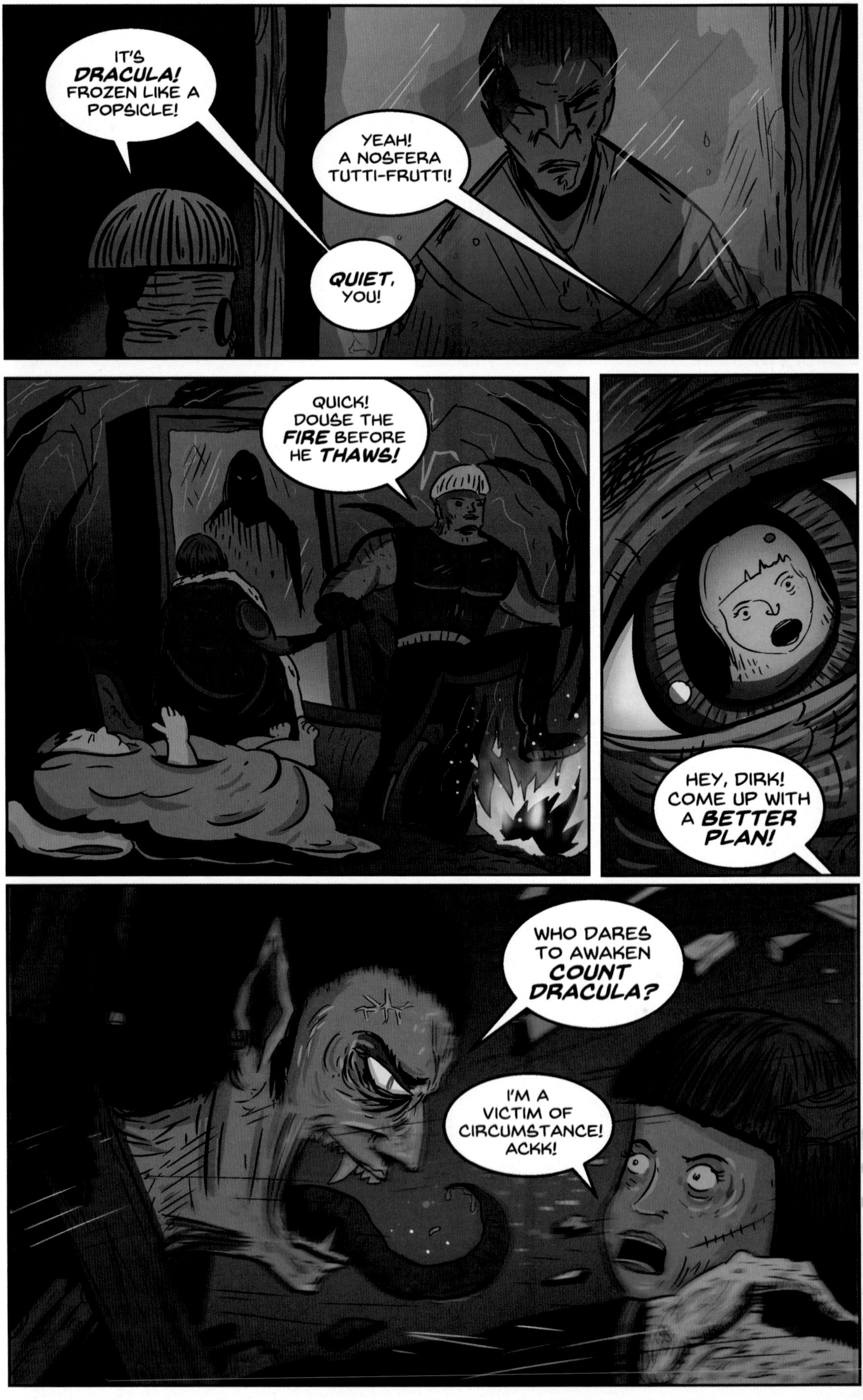
IT'S DRACULA! FROZEN LIKE A POPSICLE!
YEAH! A NOSFERA TUTTI-FRUTTI!
QUIET, YOU!
QUICK! DOUSE THE FIRE BEFORE HE THAWS!
HEY, DIRK! COME UP WITH A BETTER PLAN!
WHO DARES TO AWAKEN COUNT DRACULA?
I'M A VICTIM OF CIRCUMSTANCE! ACKK!

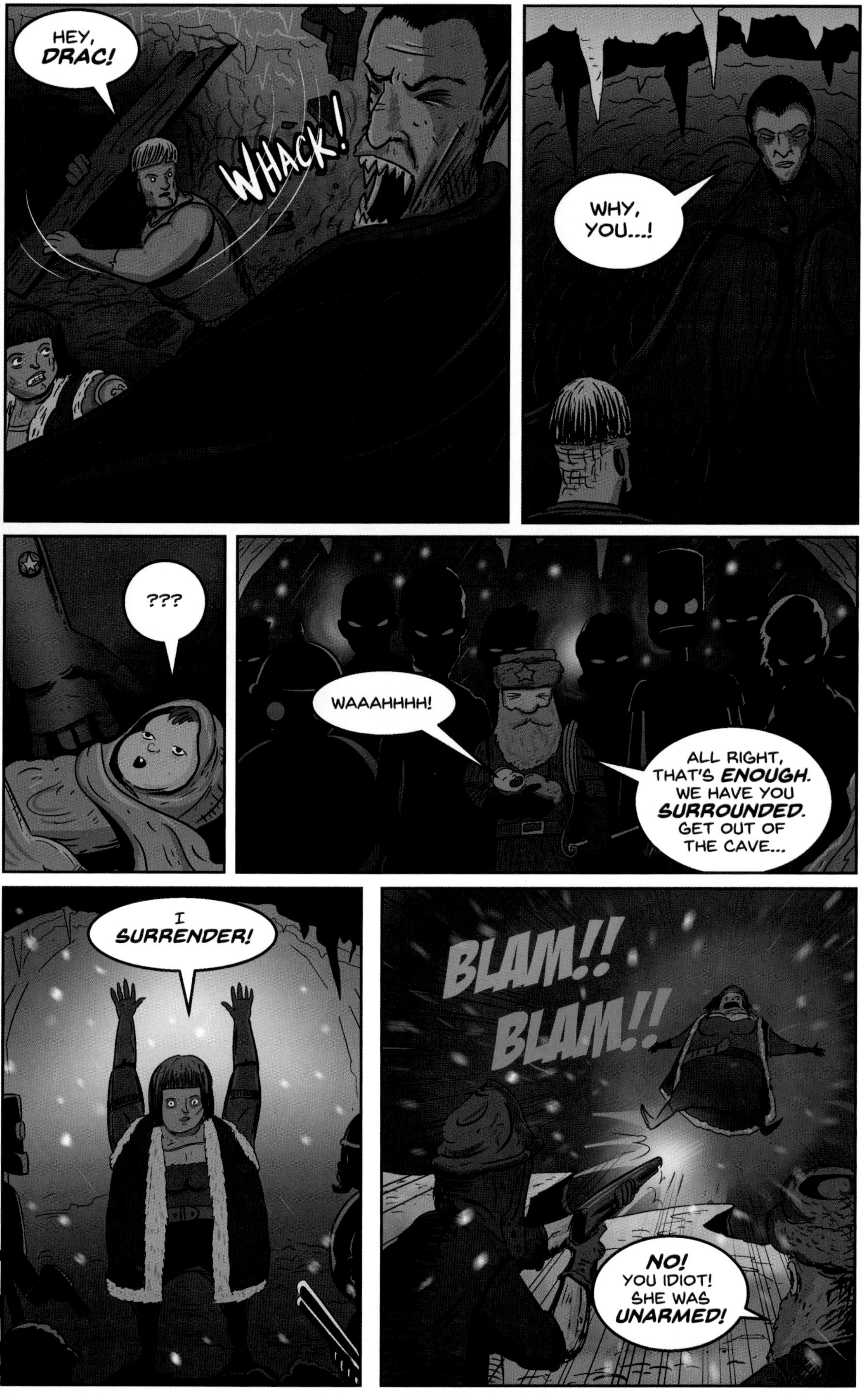
HEY, DRAC!
WHACK!
WHY, YOU...!
???
WAAAHHHH!
ALL RIGHT, THAT'S ENOUGH. WE HAVE YOU SURROUNDED. GET OUT OF THE CAVE...
I SURRENDER!
BLAM!! BLAM!!
NO! YOU IDIOT! SHE WAS UNARMED!

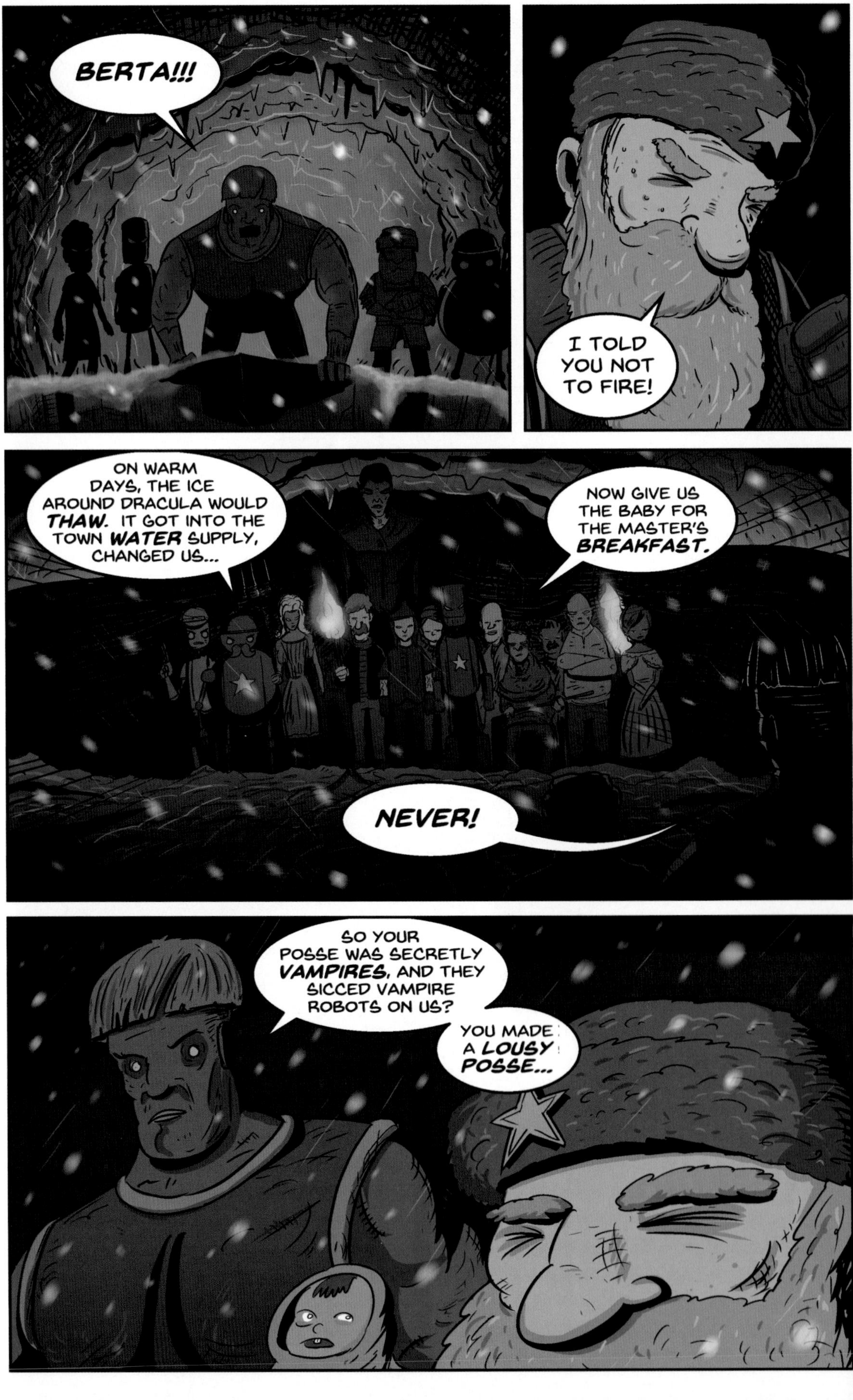
BERTA!!!
I TOLD YOU NOT TO FIRE!
ON WARM DAYS, THE ICE AROUND DRACULA WOULD THAW. IT GOT INTO THE TOWN WATER SUPPLY, CHANGED US...
NOW GIVE US THE BABY FOR THE MASTER'S BREAKFAST.
NEVER!
SO YOUR POSSE WAS SECRETLY VAMPIRES, AND THEY SICCED VAMPIRE ROBOTS ON US?
YOU MADE A LOUSY POSSE...

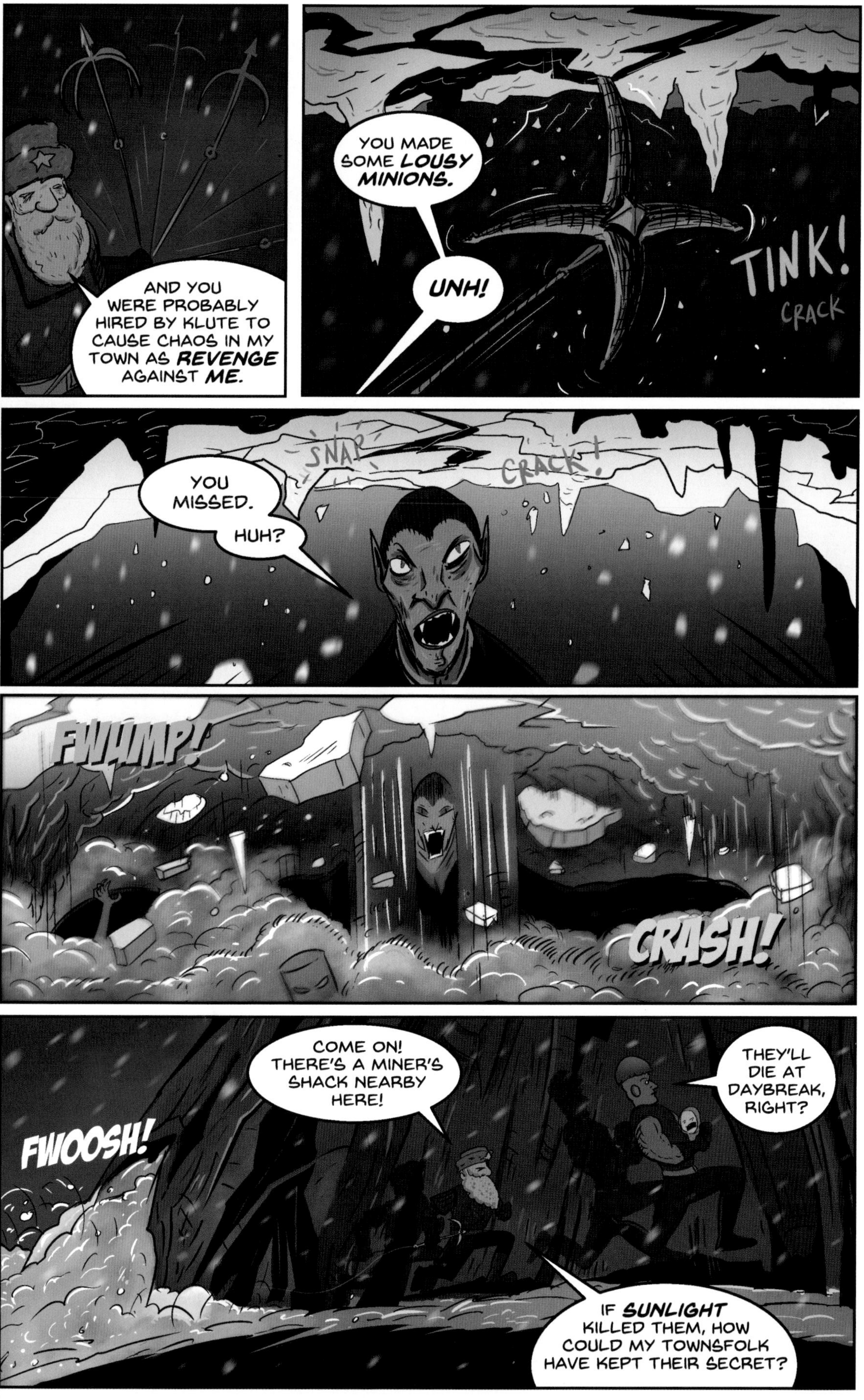
AND YOU WERE PROBABLY HIRED BY KLUTE TO CAUSE CHAOS IN MY TOWN AS REVENGE AGAINST ME.
YOU MADE SOME LOUSY MINIONS.
UNH!
TINK!
CRACK
SNAP
CRACK!
YOU MISSED.
HUH?
FWUMP!
CRASH!
FWOOSH!
COME ON! THERE'S A MINER'S SHACK NEARBY HERE!
THEY'LL DIE AT DAYBREAK, RIGHT?
IF SUNLIGHT KILLED THEM, HOW COULD MY TOWNSFOLK HAVE KEPT THEIR SECRET?

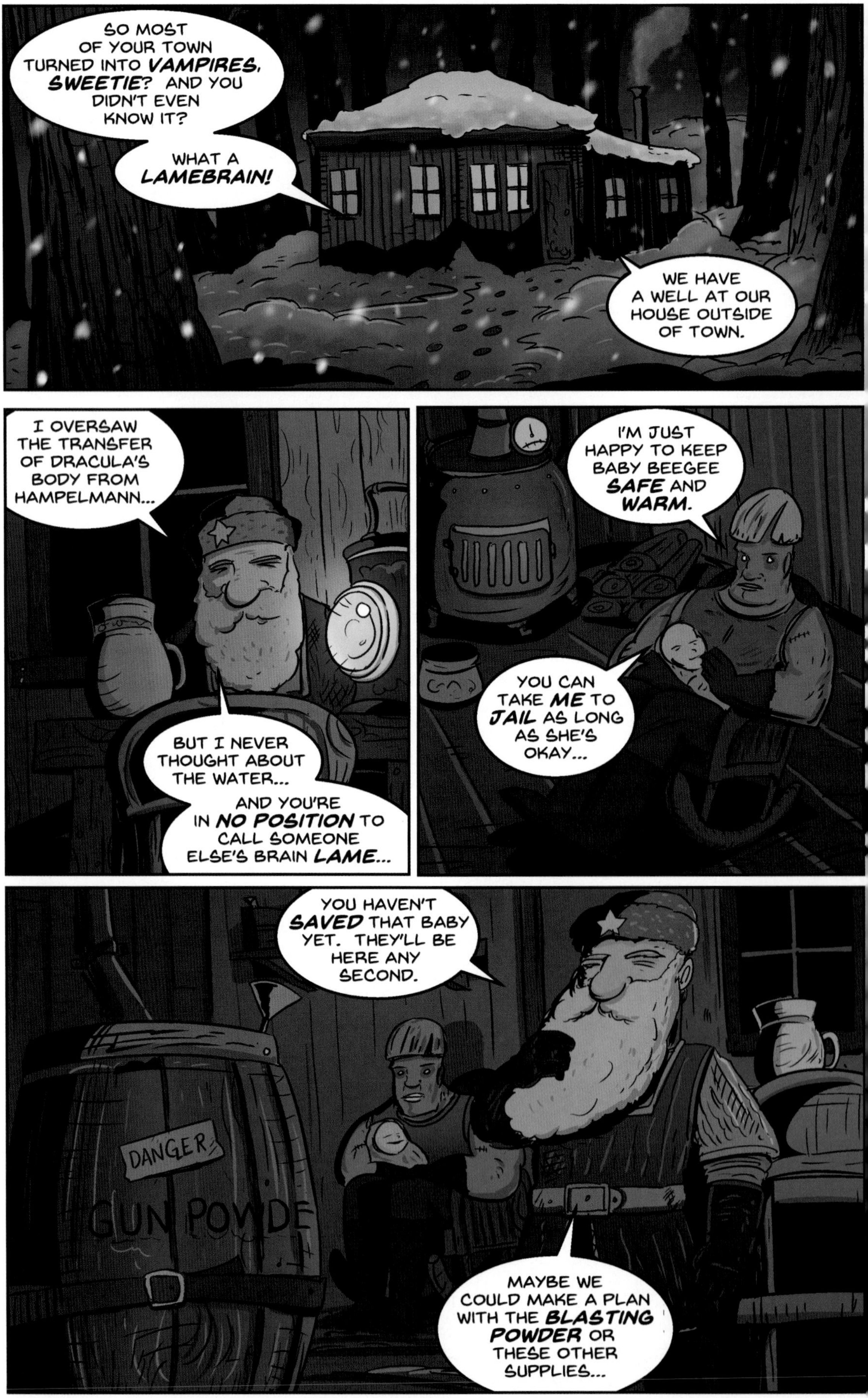
SO MOST OF YOUR TOWN TURNED INTO VAMPIRES, SWEETIE? AND YOU DIDN'T EVEN KNOW IT?
WHAT A LAMEBRAIN!
WE HAVE A WELL AT OUR HOUSE OUTSIDE OF TOWN.
I OVERSAW THE TRANSFER OF DRACULA'S BODY FROM HAMPELMANN...
BUT I NEVER THOUGHT ABOUT THE WATER...
AND YOU'RE IN NO POSITION TO CALL SOMEONE ELSE'S BRAIN LAME...
I'M JUST HAPPY TO KEEP BABY BEEGEE SAFE AND WARM.
YOU CAN TAKE ME TO JAIL AS LONG AS SHE'S OKAY...
YOU HAVEN'T SAVED THAT BABY YET. THEY'LL BE HERE ANY SECOND.
DANGER
GUN POWDE
MAYBE WE COULD MAKE A PLAN WITH THE BLASTING POWDER OR THESE OTHER SUPPLIES...

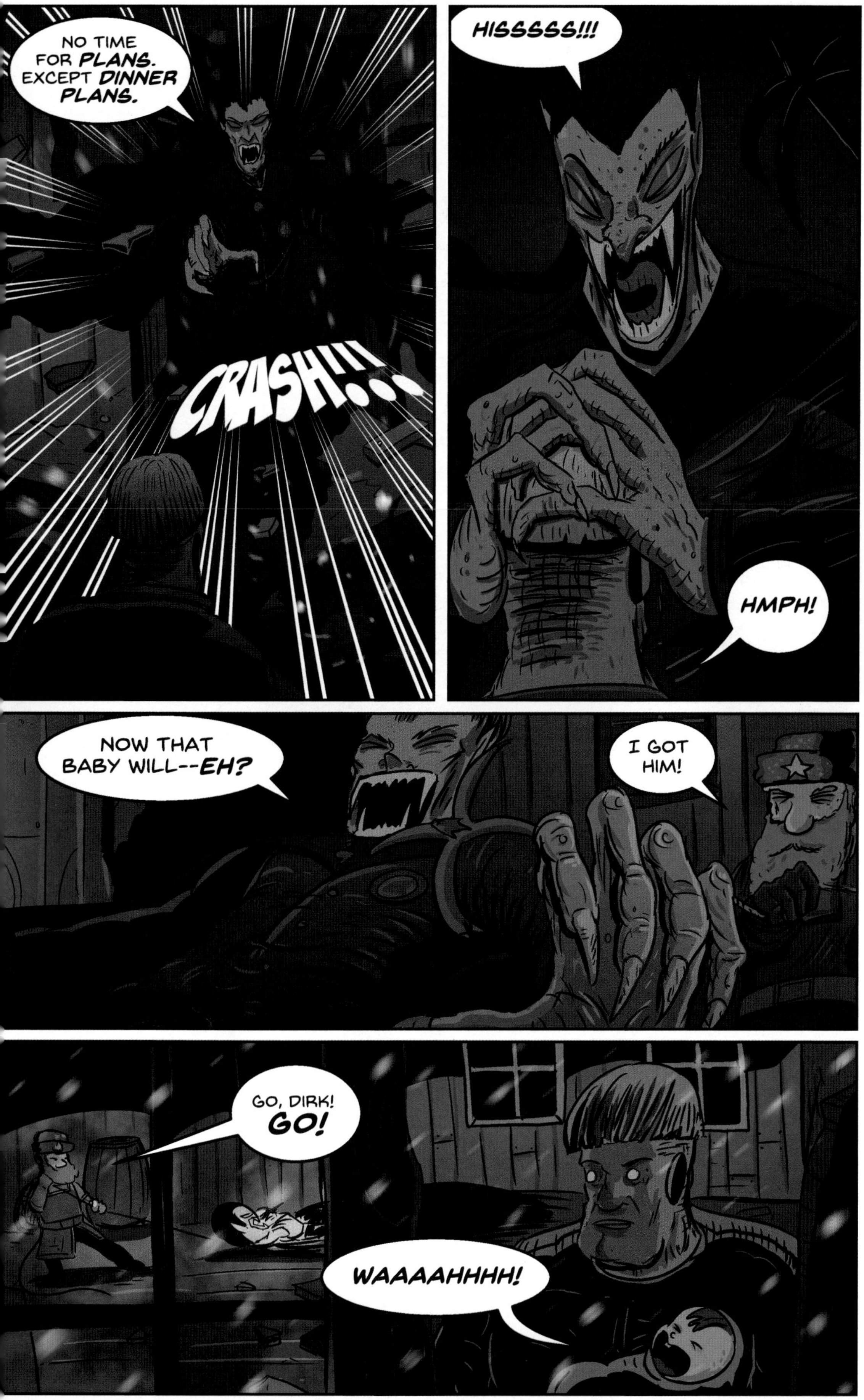
NO TIME FOR PLANS. EXCEPT DINNER PLANS.
CRASH!!!...
HISSSSSS!!!
HMPH!
NOW THAT BABY WILL--EH?
I GOT HIM!
GO, DIRK! GO!
WAAAAHHHH!

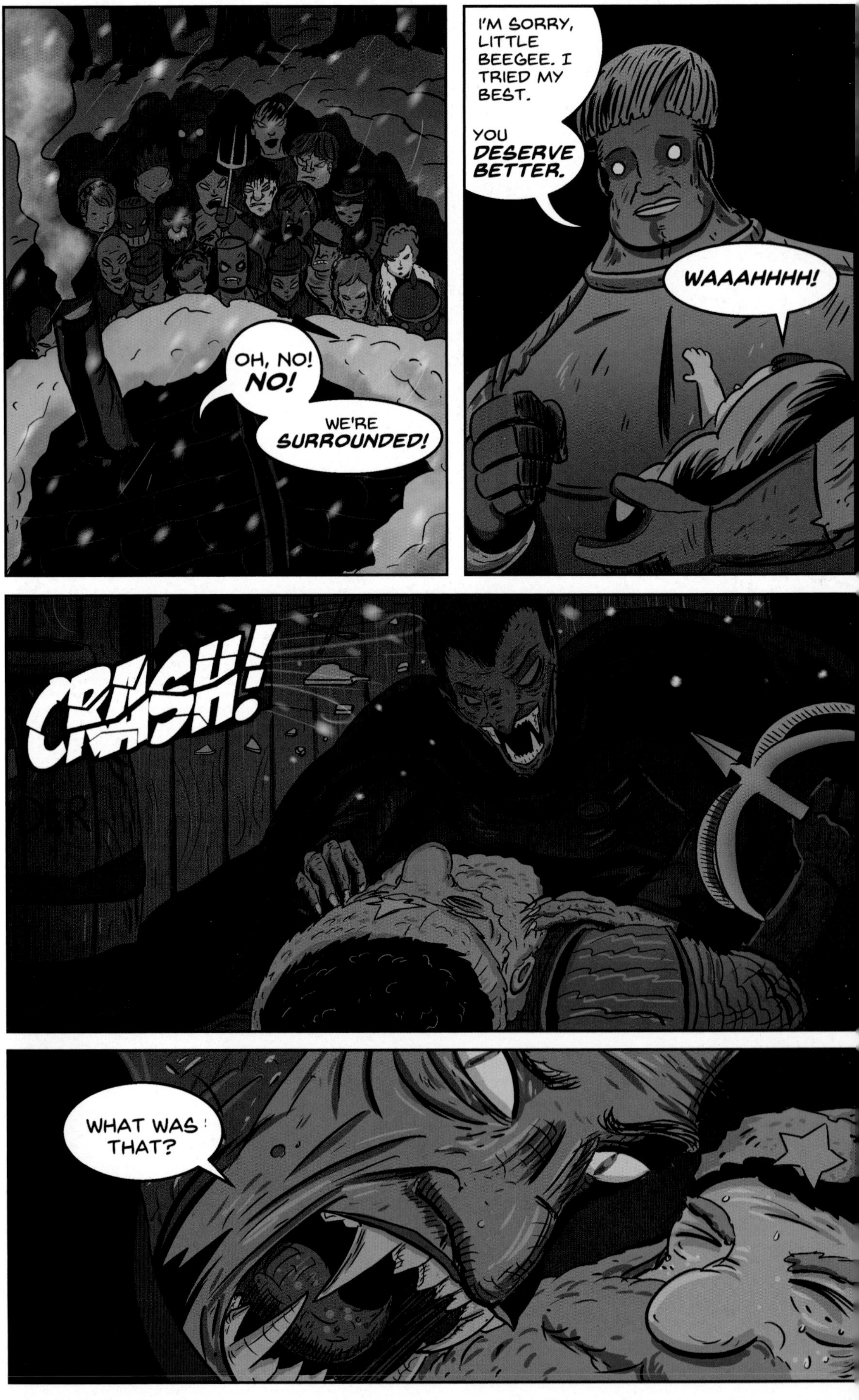
OH, NO! NO!
WE'RE SURROUNDED!
I'M SORRY, LITTLE BEEGEE. I TRIED MY BEST.
YOU DESERVE BETTER.
WAAAHHHH!
CRASH!
WHAT WAS THAT?

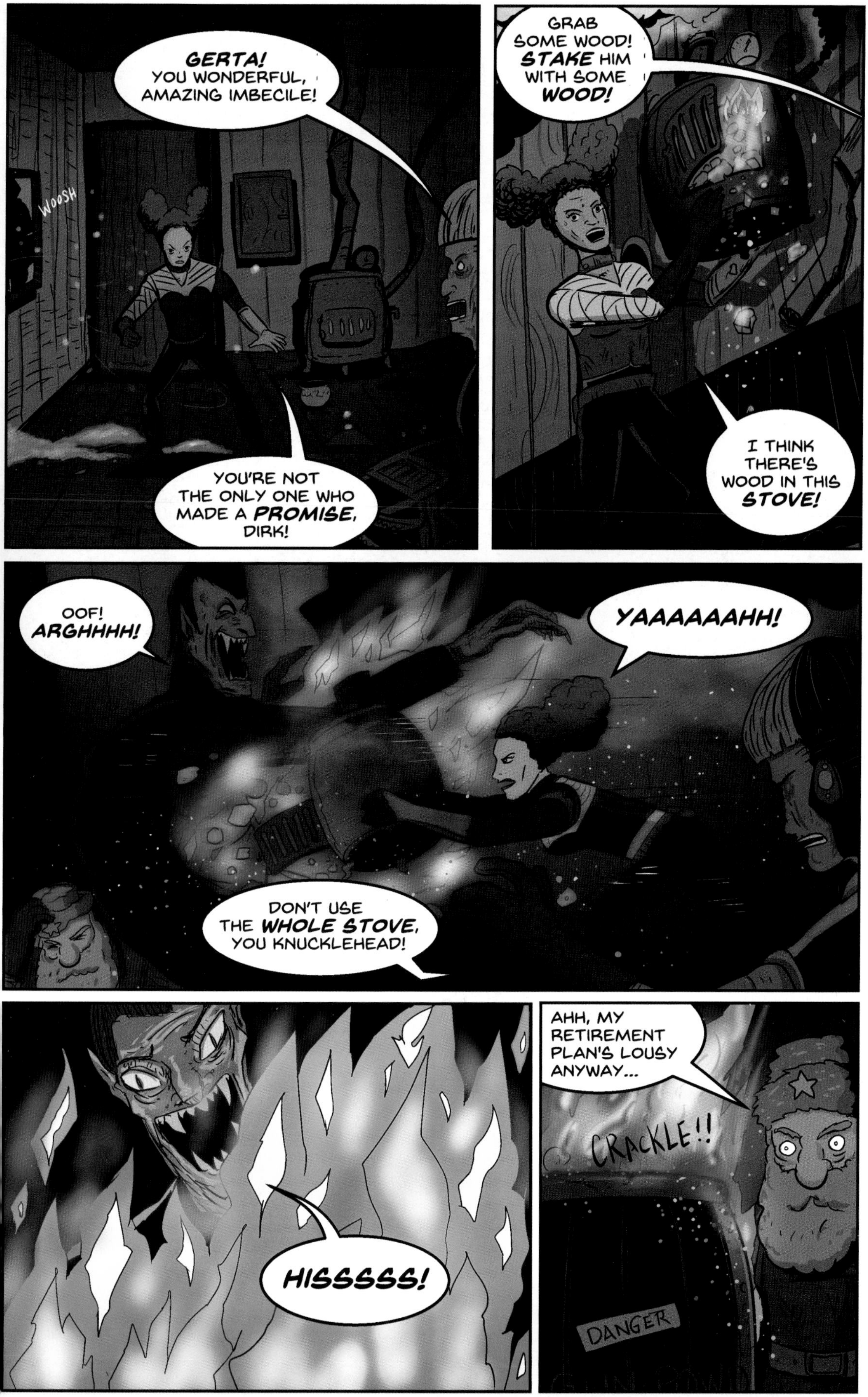
GERTA! YOU WONDERFUL, AMAZING IMBECILE!
WOOSH
YOU'RE NOT THE ONLY ONE WHO MADE A PROMISE, DIRK!
GRAB SOME WOOD! STAKE HIM WITH SOME WOOD!
I THINK THERE'S WOOD IN THIS STOVE!
OOF! ARGHHHH!
YAAAAAAHH!
DON'T USE THE WHOLE STOVE, YOU KNUCKLEHEAD!
HISSSSS!
AHH, MY RETIREMENT PLAN'S LOUSY ANYWAY...
CRACKLE!!
DANGER

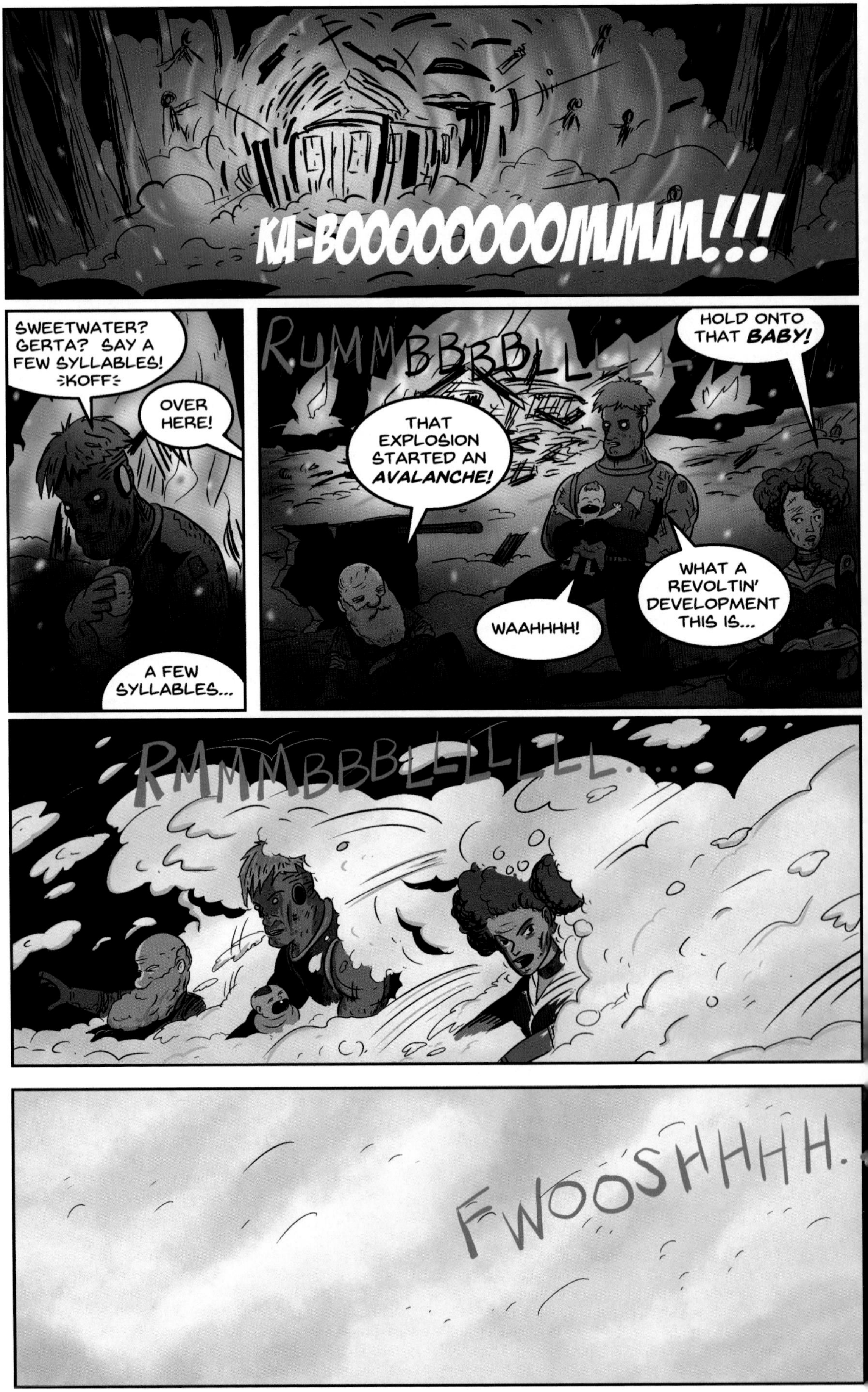
KA-BOOOOOOOOMMM!!!
SWEETWATER? GERTA? SAY A FEW SYLLABLES! *KOFF*
OVER HERE!
A FEW SYLLABLES...
RUMMBBBLLLLL
HOLD ONTO THAT BABY!
THAT EXPLOSION STARTED AN AVALANCHE!
WAAHHHH!
WHAT A REVOLTIN' DEVELOPMENT THIS IS...
RMMMBBBLLLLLLL...
FWOOSHHHH..

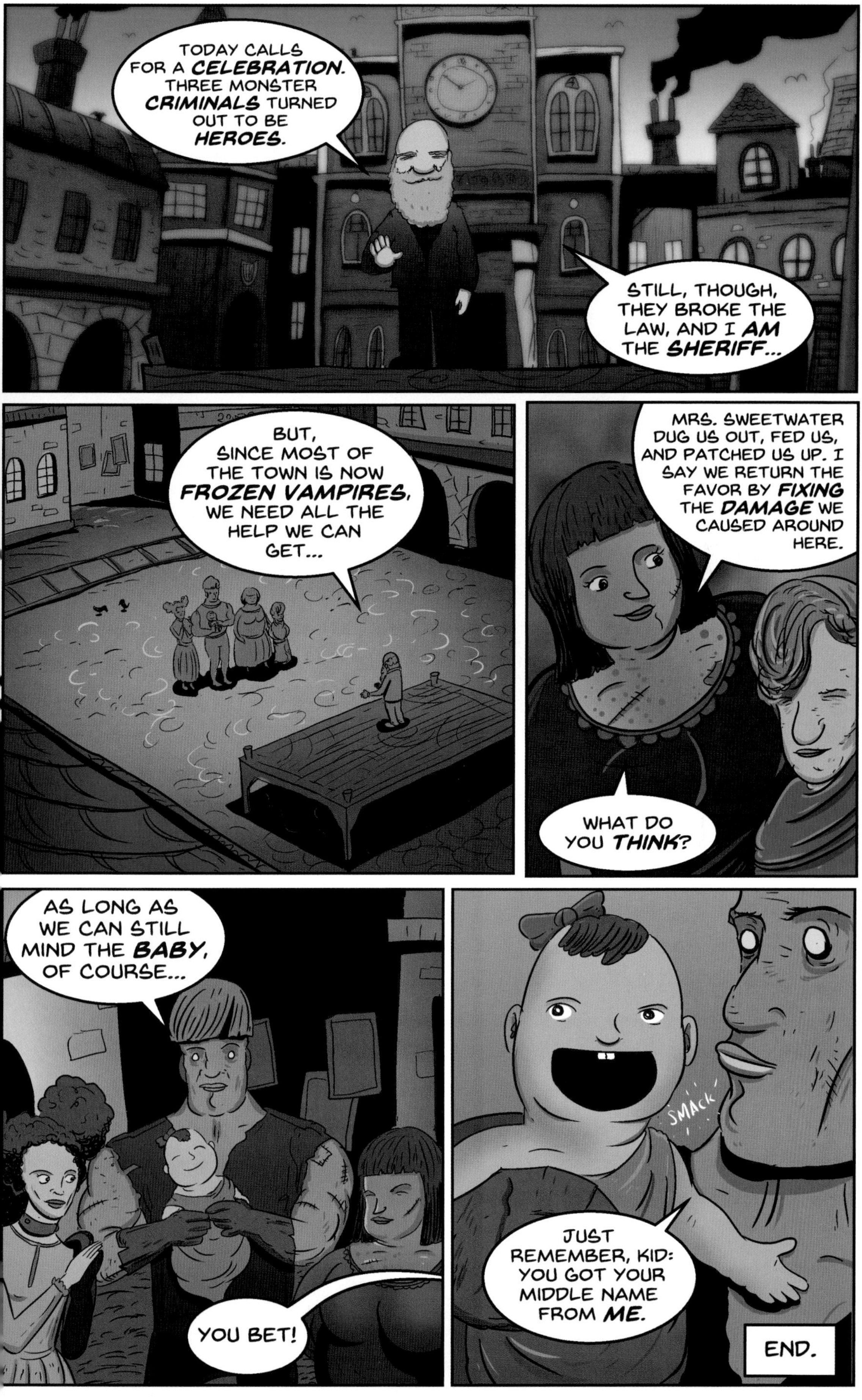
TODAY CALLS FOR A CELEBRATION. THREE MONSTER CRIMINALS TURNED OUT TO BE HEROES.
STILL, THOUGH, THEY BROKE THE LAW, AND I AM THE SHERIFF...
BUT, SINCE MOST OF THE TOWN IS NOW FROZEN VAMPIRES, WE NEED ALL THE HELP WE CAN GET...
MRS. SWEETWATER DUG US OUT, FED US, AND PATCHED US UP. I SAY WE RETURN THE FAVOR BY FIXING THE DAMAGE WE CAUSED AROUND HERE.
WHAT DO YOU THINK?
AS LONG AS WE CAN STILL MIND THE BABY, OF COURSE...
YOU BET!
SMACK
JUST REMEMBER, KID: YOU GOT YOUR MIDDLE NAME FROM ME.
END.

Monstrous No. 4

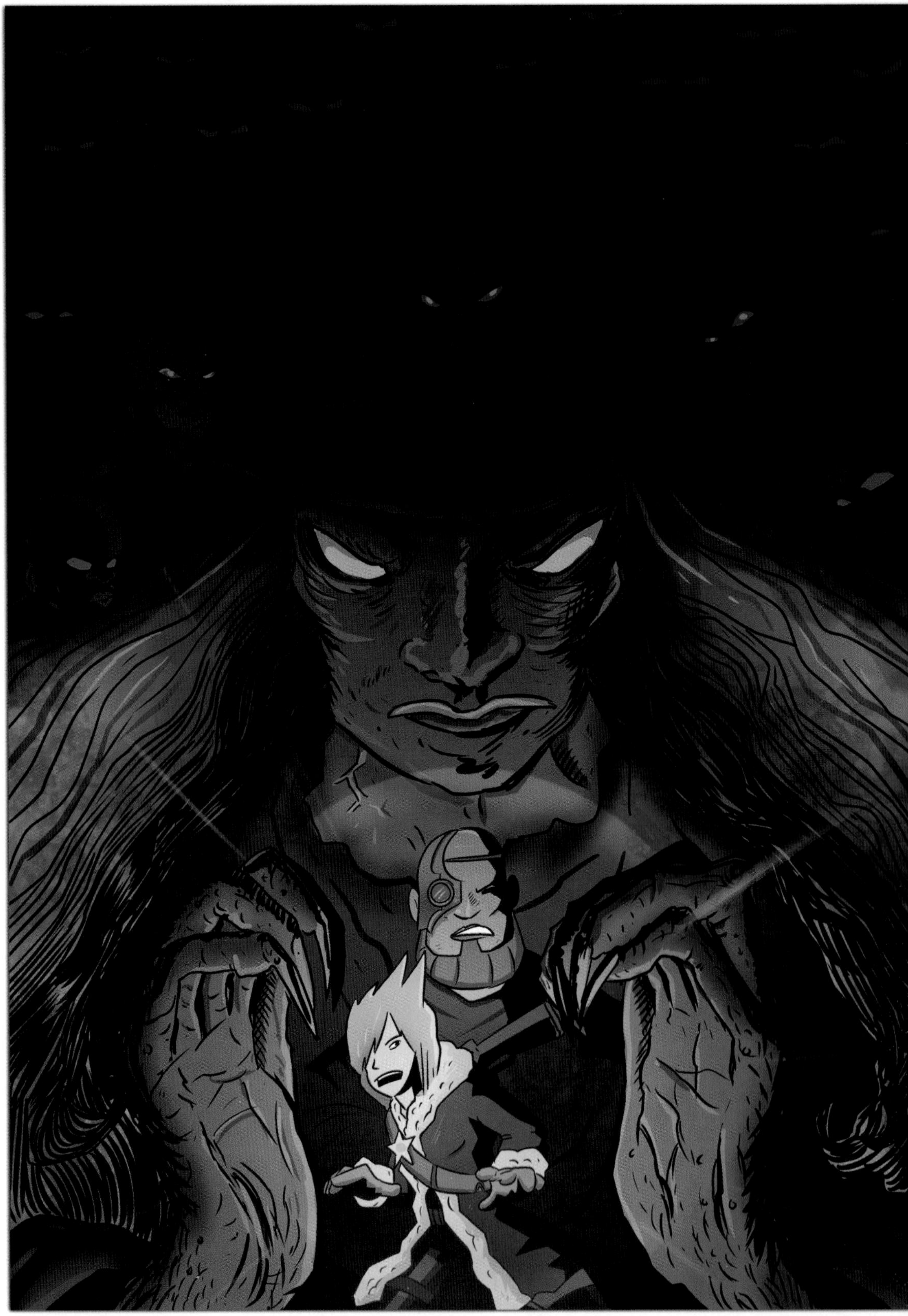

Keepin' Em Out of Jail

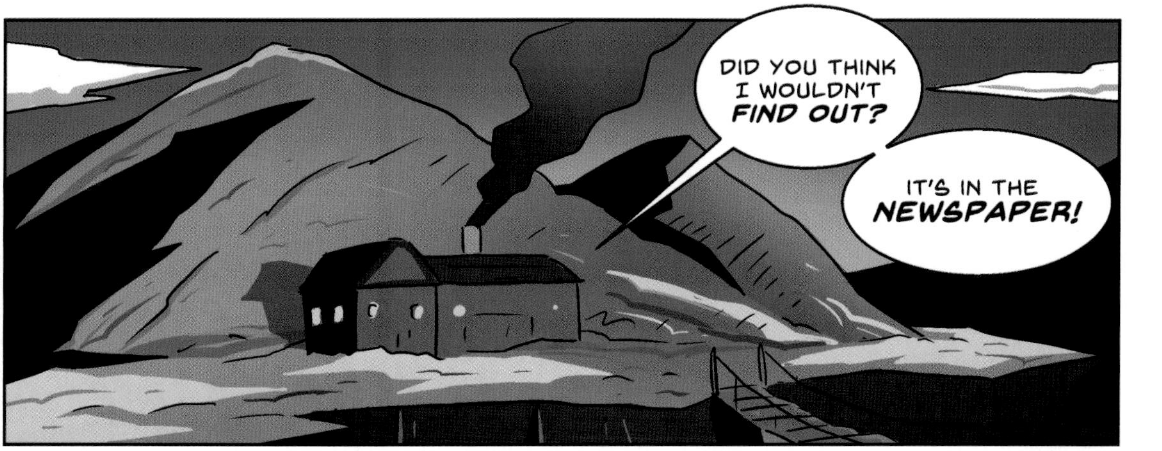
DID YOU THINK I WOULDN'T FIND OUT?
IT'S IN THE NEWSPAPER!

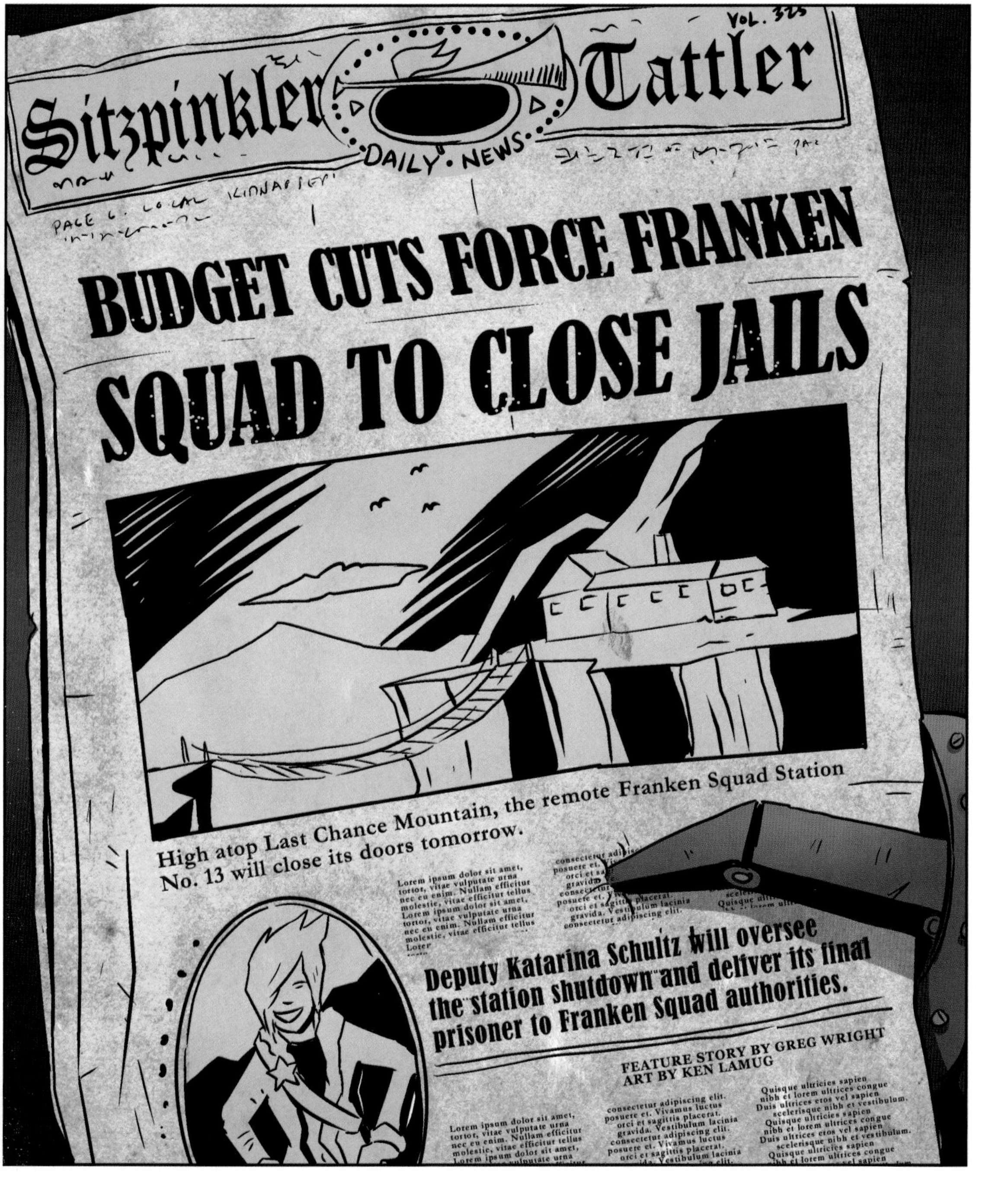
Sitzpinkler Tattler
DAILY NEWS
BUDGET CUTS FORCE FRANKEN SQUAD TO CLOSE JAILS
High atop Last Chance Mountain, the remote Franken Squad Station No. 13 will close its doors tomorrow.
Deputy Katarina Schultz will oversee the station shutdown and deliver its final prisoner to Franken Squad authorities.
FEATURE STORY BY GREG WRIGHT
ART BY KEN LAMUG

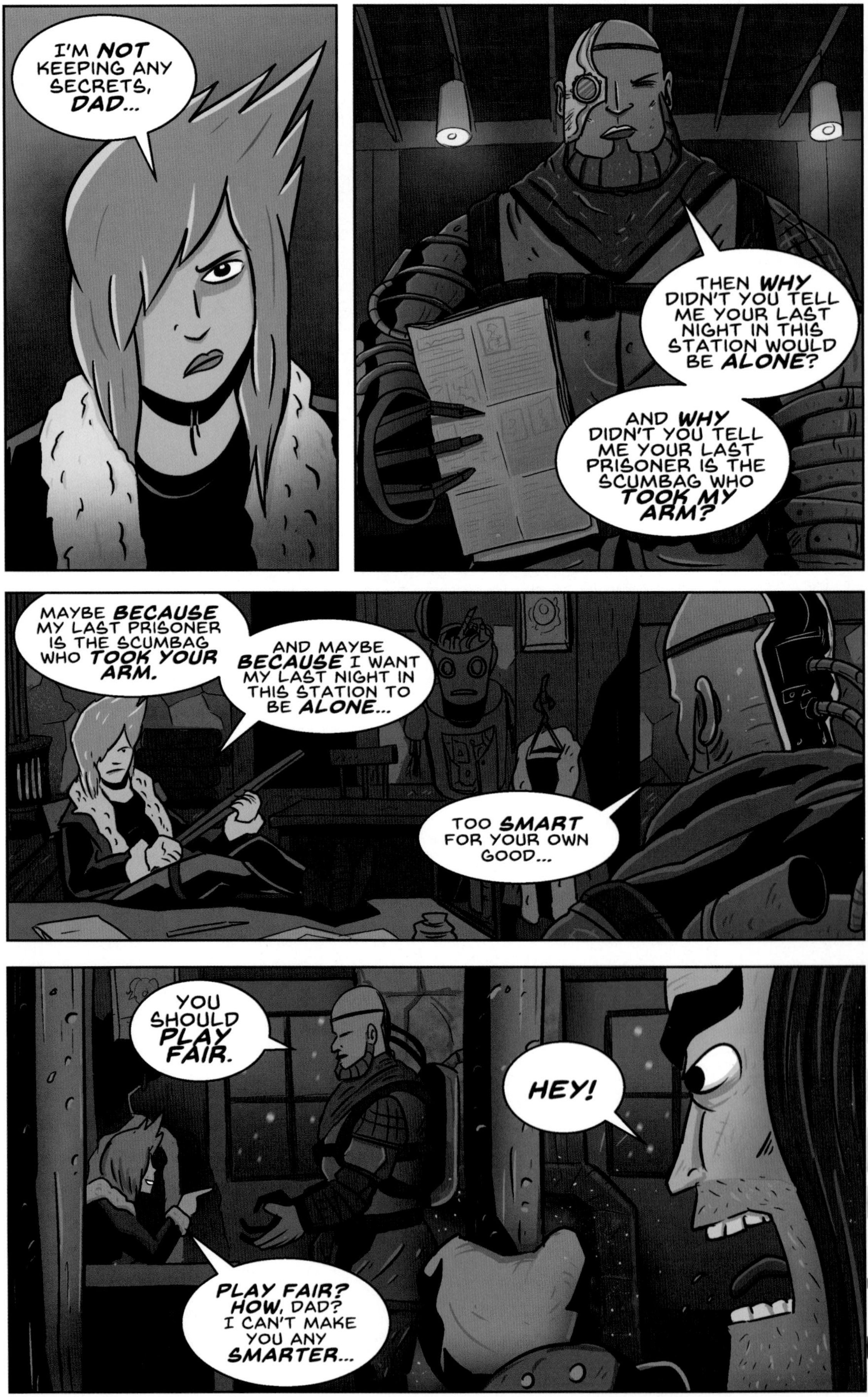
I'M NOT KEEPING ANY SECRETS, DAD...
THEN WHY DIDN'T YOU TELL ME YOUR LAST NIGHT IN THIS STATION WOULD BE ALONE?
AND WHY DIDN'T YOU TELL ME YOUR LAST PRISONER IS THE SCUMBAG WHO TOOK MY ARM?
MAYBE BECAUSE MY LAST PRISONER IS THE SCUMBAG WHO TOOK YOUR ARM.
AND MAYBE BECAUSE I WANT MY LAST NIGHT IN THIS STATION TO BE ALONE...
TOO SMART FOR YOUR OWN GOOD...
YOU SHOULD PLAY FAIR.
HEY!
PLAY FAIR? HOW, DAD? I CAN'T MAKE YOU ANY SMARTER...

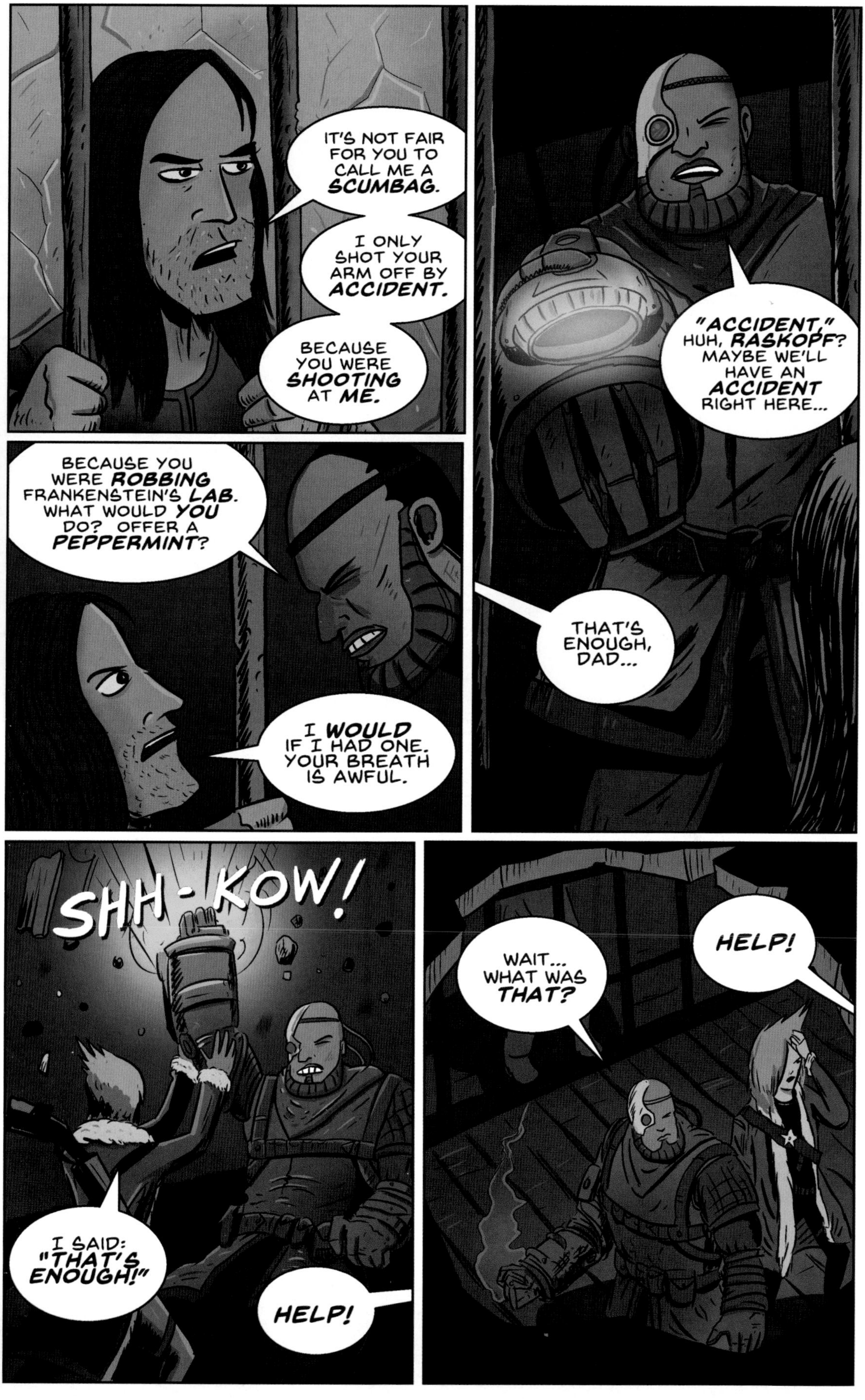
IT'S NOT FAIR FOR YOU TO CALL ME A SCUMBAG.
I ONLY SHOT YOUR ARM OFF BY ACCIDENT.
BECAUSE YOU WERE SHOOTING AT ME.
"ACCIDENT," HUH, RASKOPF? MAYBE WE'LL HAVE AN ACCIDENT RIGHT HERE...
BECAUSE YOU WERE ROBBING FRANKENSTEIN'S LAB. WHAT WOULD YOU DO? OFFER A PEPPERMINT?
I WOULD IF I HAD ONE. YOUR BREATH IS AWFUL.
THAT'S ENOUGH, DAD...
SHH-KOW!
I SAID: "THAT'S ENOUGH!"
HELP!
HELP!
WAIT... WHAT WAS THAT?

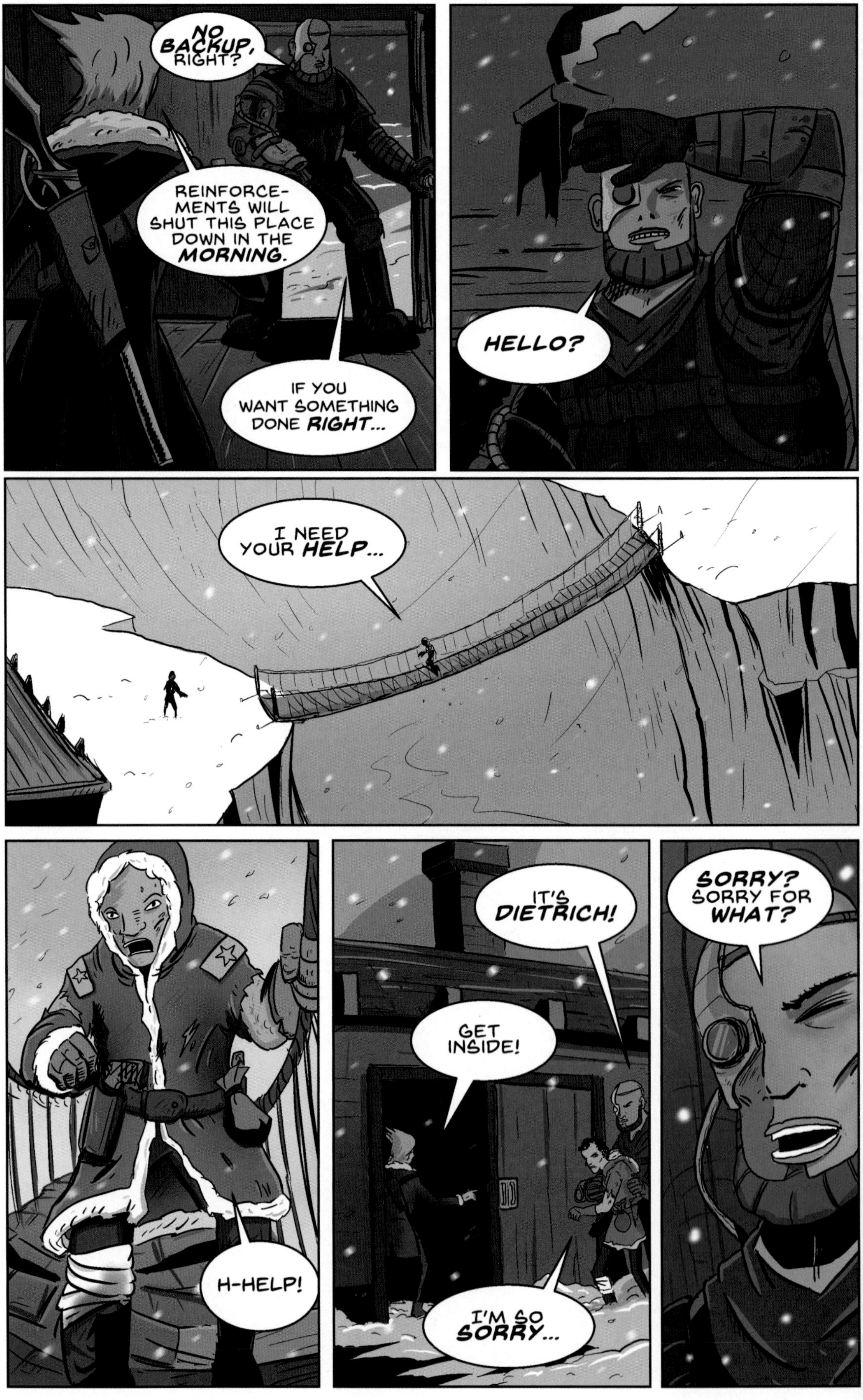
NO BACKUP, RIGHT?
REINFORCE-MENTS WILL SHUT THIS PLACE DOWN IN THE MORNING.
IF YOU WANT SOMETHING DONE RIGHT...
HELLO?
I NEED YOUR HELP...
H-HELP!
IT'S DIETRICH!
GET INSIDE!
I'M SO SORRY...
SORRY? SORRY FOR WHAT?

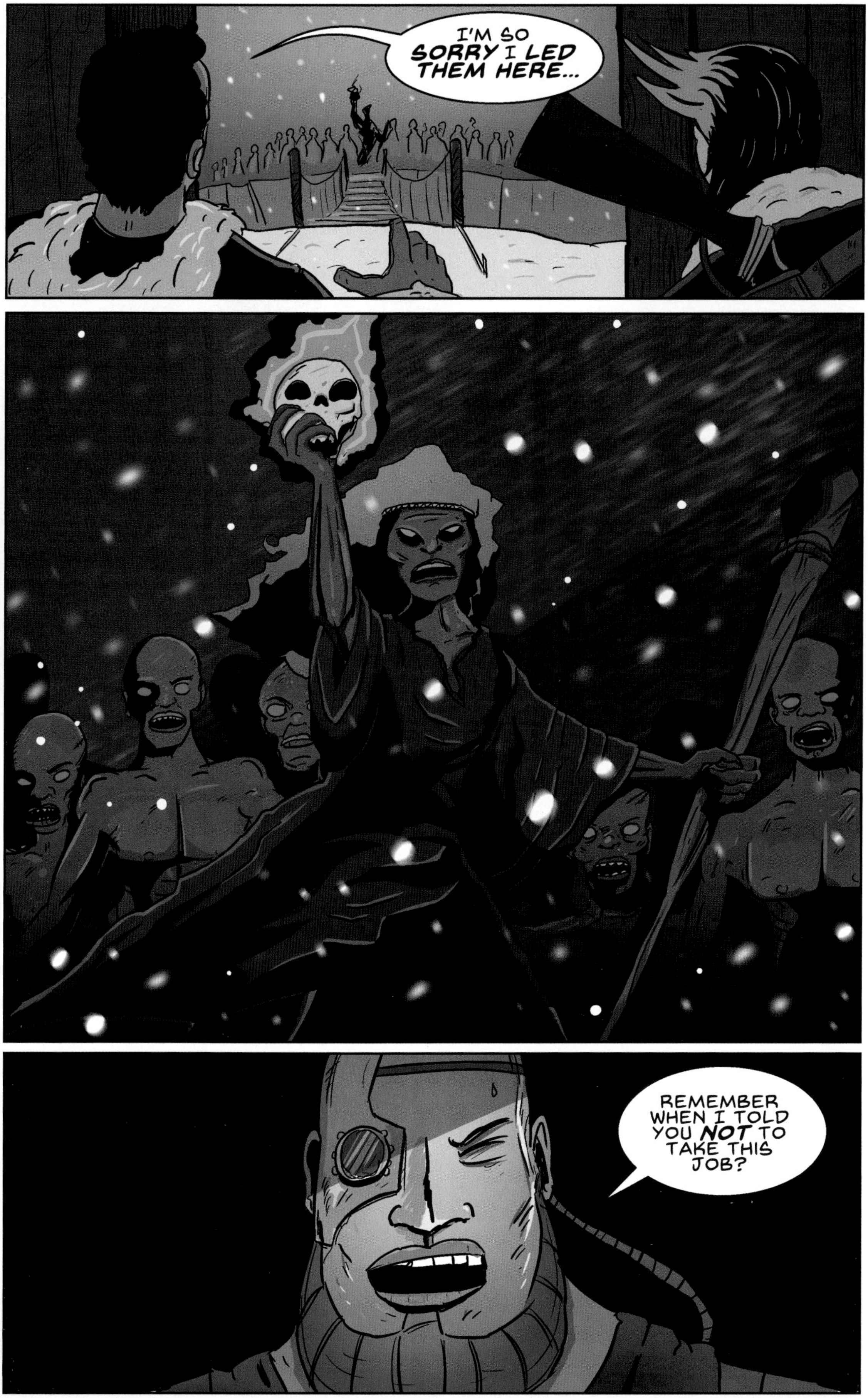
I'M SO SORRY I LED THEM HERE...
REMEMBER WHEN I TOLD YOU NOT TO TAKE THIS JOB?

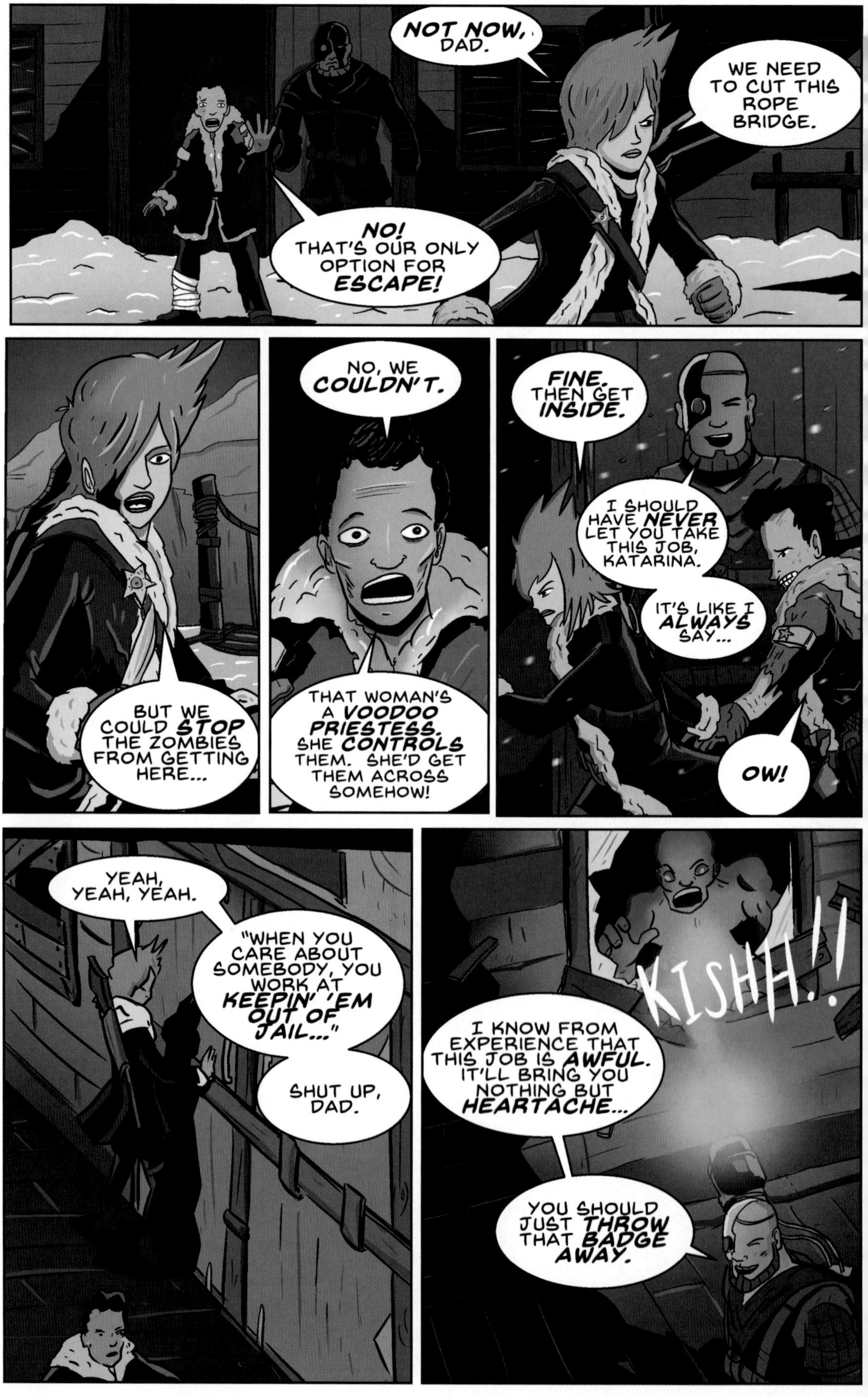
NOT NOW, DAD.
WE NEED TO CUT THIS ROPE BRIDGE.
NO! THAT'S OUR ONLY OPTION FOR ESCAPE!
BUT WE COULD STOP THE ZOMBIES FROM GETTING HERE...
NO, WE COULDN'T.
THAT WOMAN'S A VOODOO PRIESTESS. SHE CONTROLS THEM. SHE'D GET THEM ACROSS SOMEHOW!
FINE. THEN GET INSIDE.
I SHOULD HAVE NEVER LET YOU TAKE THIS JOB, KATARINA.
IT'S LIKE I ALWAYS SAY...
OW!
YEAH, YEAH, YEAH.
"WHEN YOU CARE ABOUT SOMEBODY, YOU WORK AT KEEPIN' 'EM OUT OF JAIL..."
SHUT UP, DAD.
KISHH!!
I KNOW FROM EXPERIENCE THAT THIS JOB IS AWFUL. IT'LL BRING YOU NOTHING BUT HEARTACHE...
YOU SHOULD JUST THROW THAT BADGE AWAY.

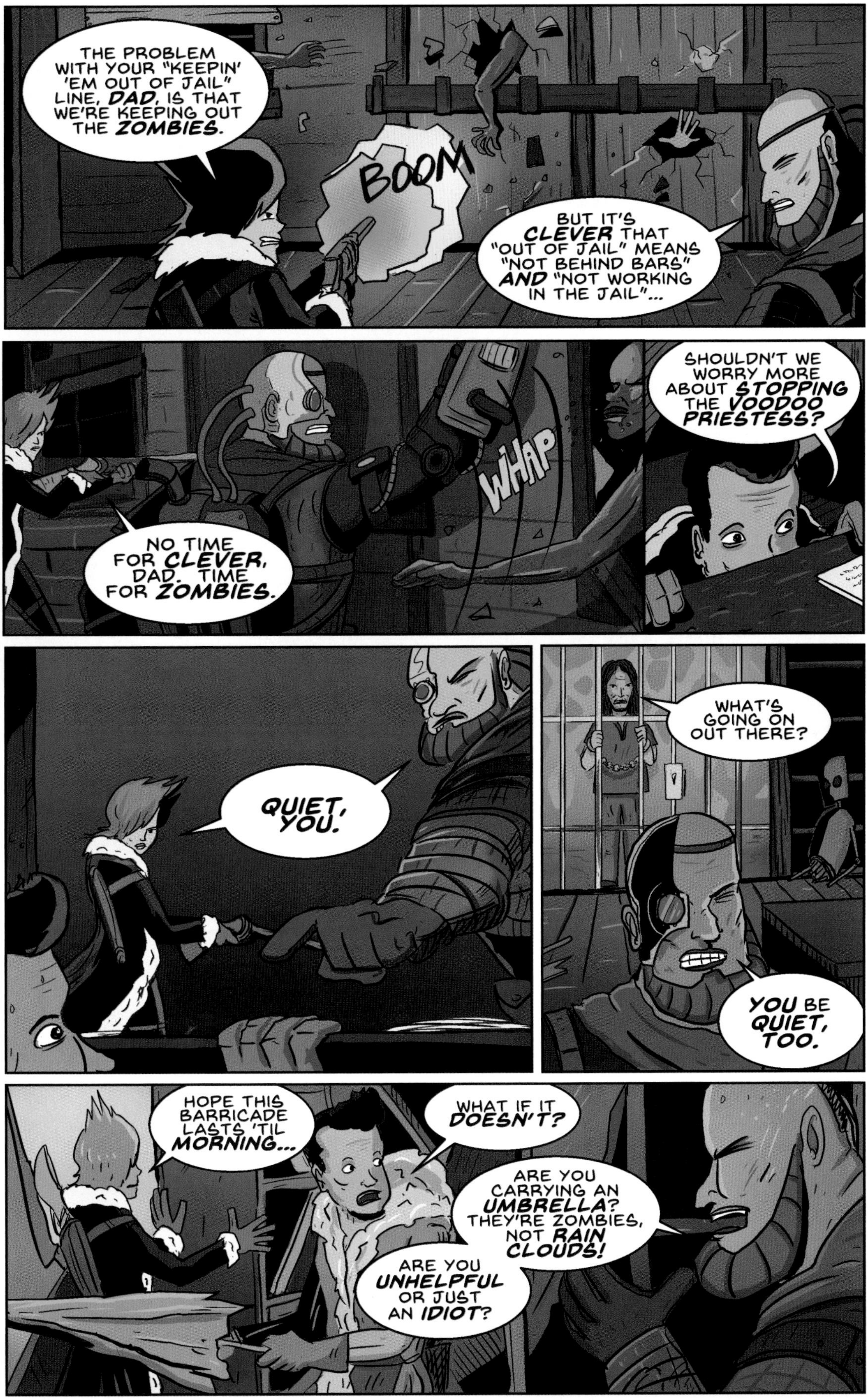
THE PROBLEM WITH YOUR "KEEPIN' 'EM OUT OF JAIL" LINE, DAD, IS THAT WE'RE KEEPING OUT THE ZOMBIES.
BOOM
BUT IT'S CLEVER THAT "OUT OF JAIL" MEANS "NOT BEHIND BARS" AND "NOT WORKING IN THE JAIL"...
WHAP
NO TIME FOR CLEVER, DAD. TIME FOR ZOMBIES.
SHOULDN'T WE WORRY MORE ABOUT STOPPING THE VOODOO PRIESTESS?
QUIET, YOU.
WHAT'S GOING ON OUT THERE?
YOU BE QUIET, TOO.
HOPE THIS BARRICADE LASTS 'TIL MORNING...
WHAT IF IT DOESN'T?
ARE YOU CARRYING AN UMBRELLA? THEY'RE ZOMBIES, NOT RAIN CLOUDS!
ARE YOU UNHELPFUL OR JUST AN IDIOT?

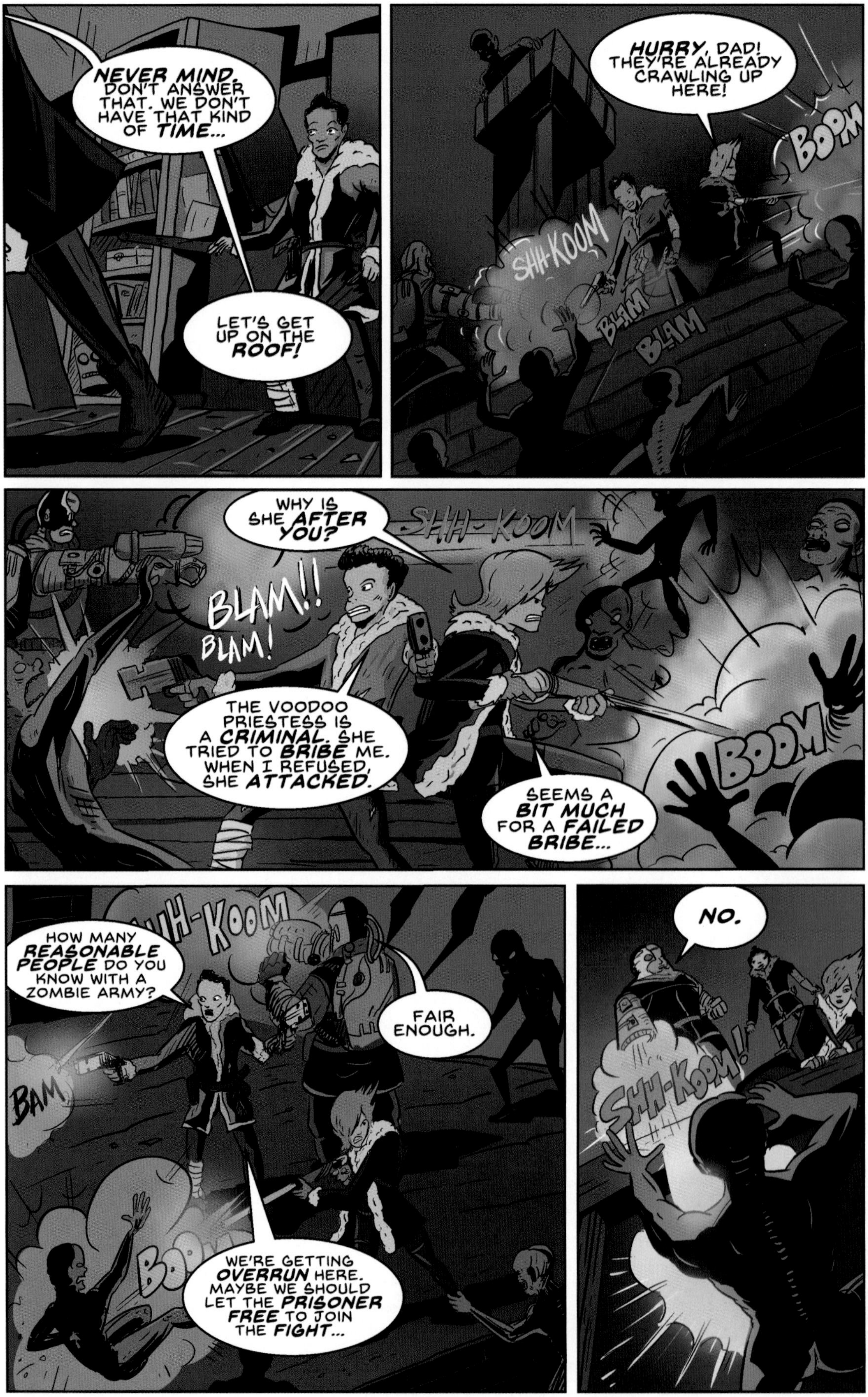
NEVER MIND. DON'T ANSWER THAT. WE DON'T HAVE THAT KIND OF TIME...
LET'S GET UP ON THE ROOF!
HURRY, DAD! THEY'RE ALREADY CRAWLING UP HERE!
BOOM
SHH-KOOM
BLAM
BLAM
WHY IS SHE AFTER YOU?
SHH-KOOM
BLAM!!
BLAM!
THE VOODOO PRIESTESS IS A CRIMINAL. SHE TRIED TO BRIBE ME. WHEN I REFUSED, SHE ATTACKED.
BOOM
SEEMS A BIT MUCH FOR A FAILED BRIBE...
HOW MANY REASONABLE PEOPLE DO YOU KNOW WITH A ZOMBIE ARMY?
FAIR ENOUGH.
BAM
WE'RE GETTING OVERRUN HERE. MAYBE WE SHOULD LET THE PRISONER FREE TO JOIN THE FIGHT...
NO.
SHH-KOOM!

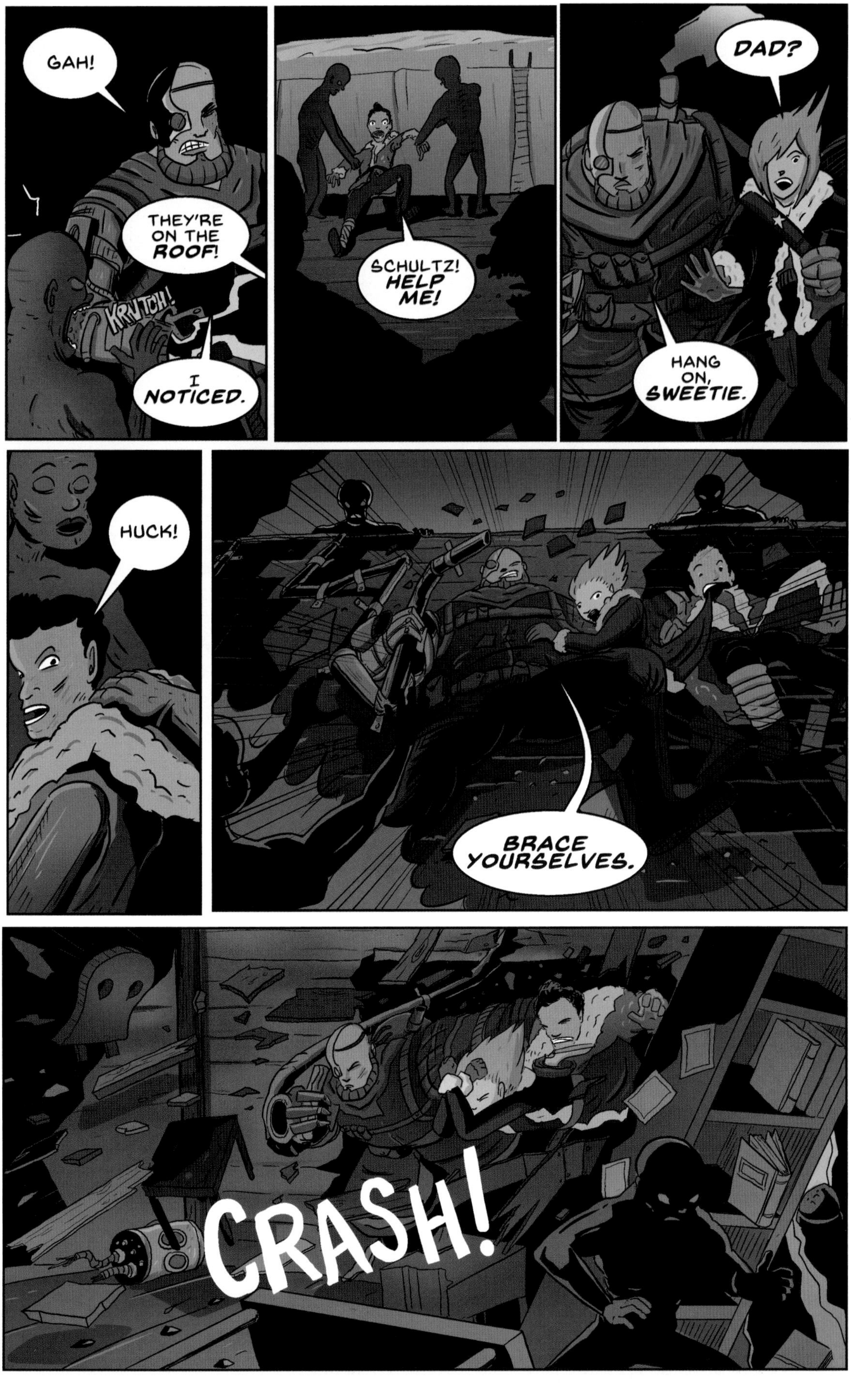
GAH!
THEY'RE ON THE ROOF!
KRNTCH!
I NOTICED.
SCHULTZ! HELP ME!
DAD?
HANG ON, SWEETIE.
HUCK!
BRACE YOURSELVES.
CRASH!

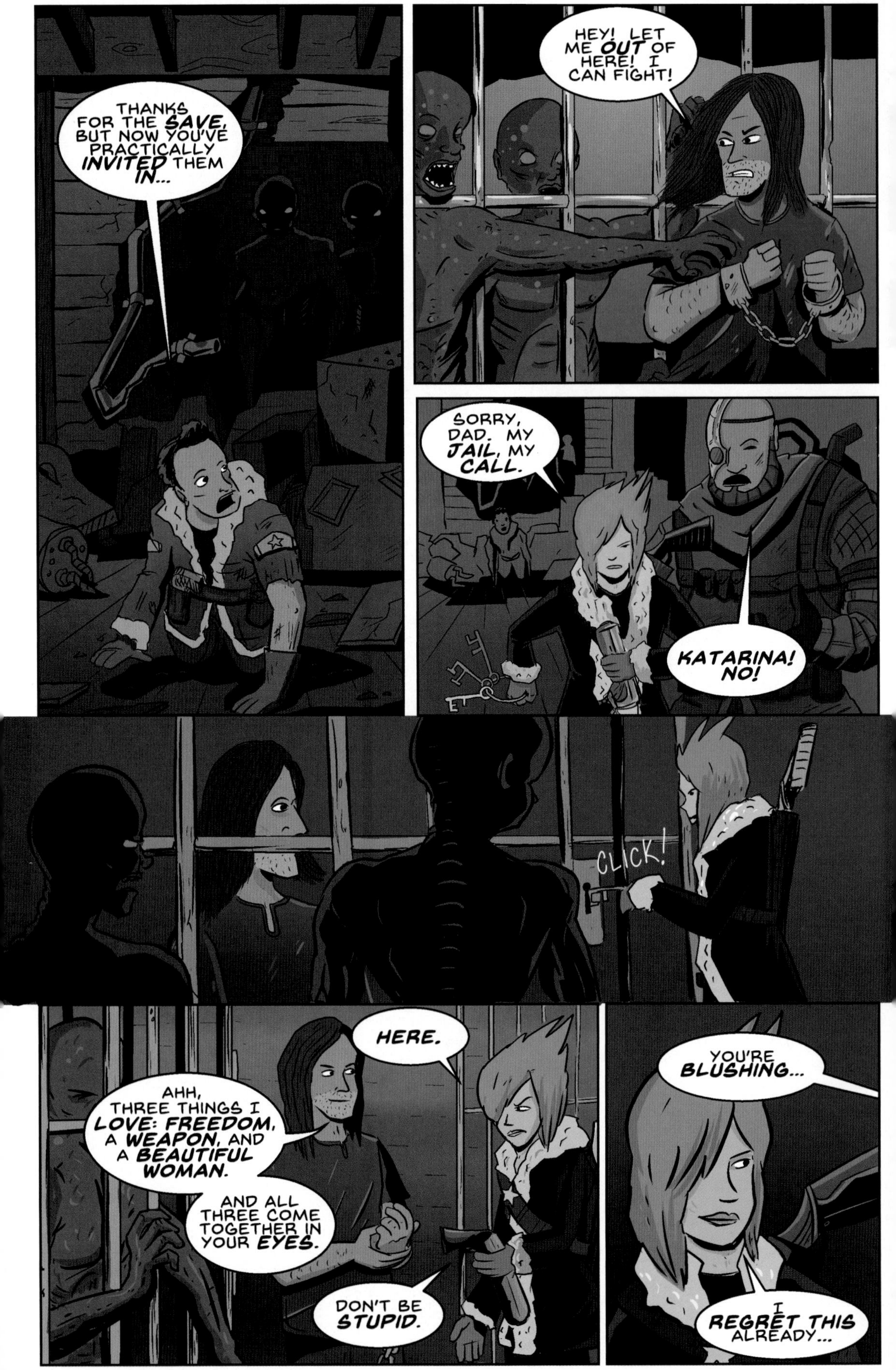
THANKS FOR THE SAVE, BUT NOW YOU'VE PRACTICALLY INVITED THEM IN...
HEY! LET ME OUT OF HERE! I CAN FIGHT!
SORRY, DAD. MY JAIL, MY CALL.
KATARINA! NO!
CLICK!
HERE.
AHH, THREE THINGS I LOVE: FREEDOM, A WEAPON, AND A BEAUTIFUL WOMAN.
AND ALL THREE COME TOGETHER IN YOUR EYES.
DON'T BE STUPID.
YOU'RE BLUSHING...
I REGRET THIS ALREADY...

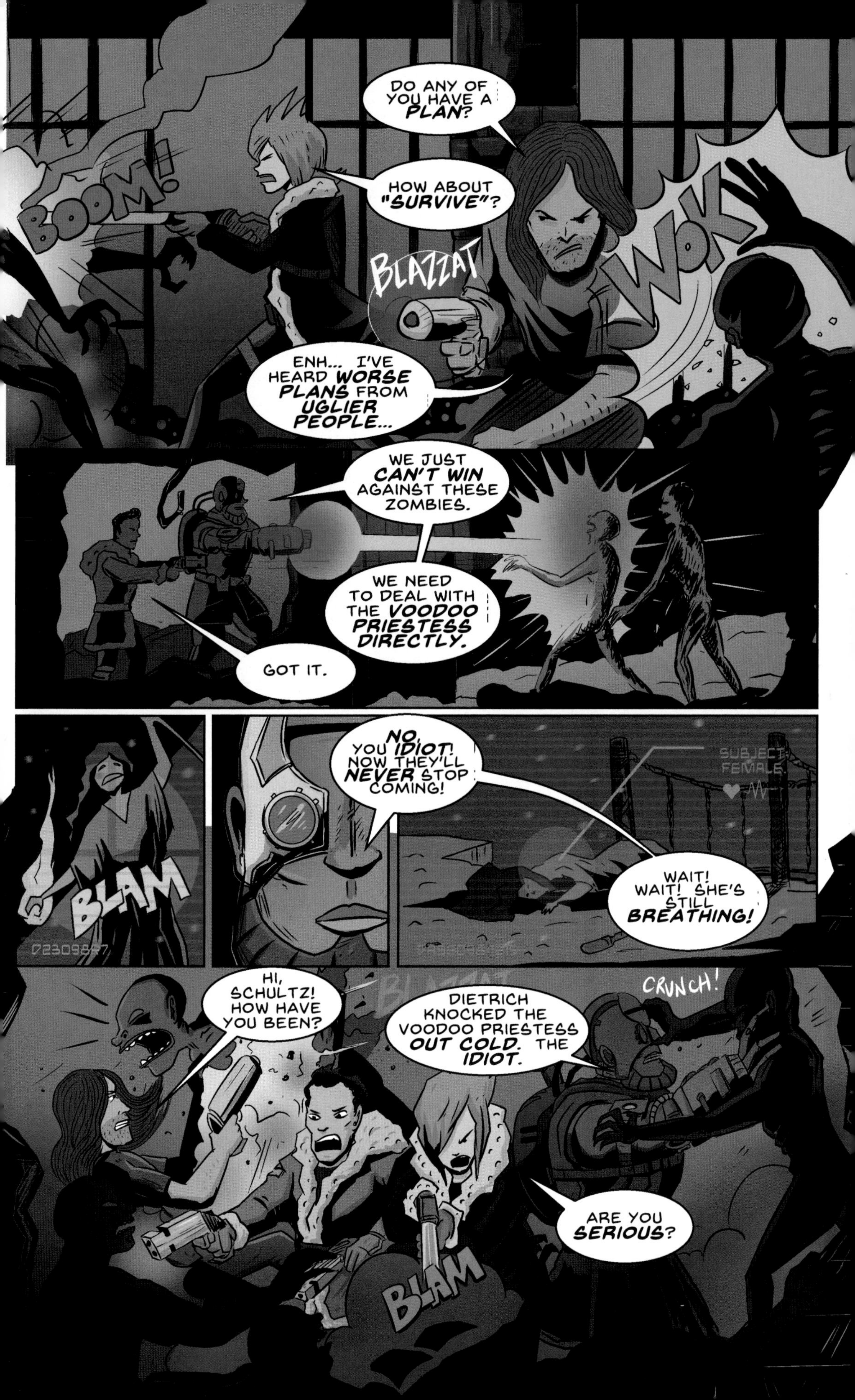
DO ANY OF YOU HAVE A PLAN?
BOOM!
HOW ABOUT "SURVIVE"?
BLAZZAT
WOK
ENH... I'VE HEARD WORSE PLANS FROM UGLIER PEOPLE...
WE JUST CAN'T WIN AGAINST THESE ZOMBIES.
WE NEED TO DEAL WITH THE VOODOO PRIESTESS DIRECTLY.
GOT IT.
BLAM
D23098R7
NO, YOU IDIOT! NOW THEY'LL NEVER STOP COMING!
SUBJECT: FEMALE.
WAIT! WAIT! SHE'S STILL BREATHING!
HI, SCHULTZ! HOW HAVE YOU BEEN?
BLAZZAT
DIETRICH KNOCKED THE VOODOO PRIESTESS OUT COLD. THE IDIOT.
CRUNCH!
ARE YOU SERIOUS?
BLAM

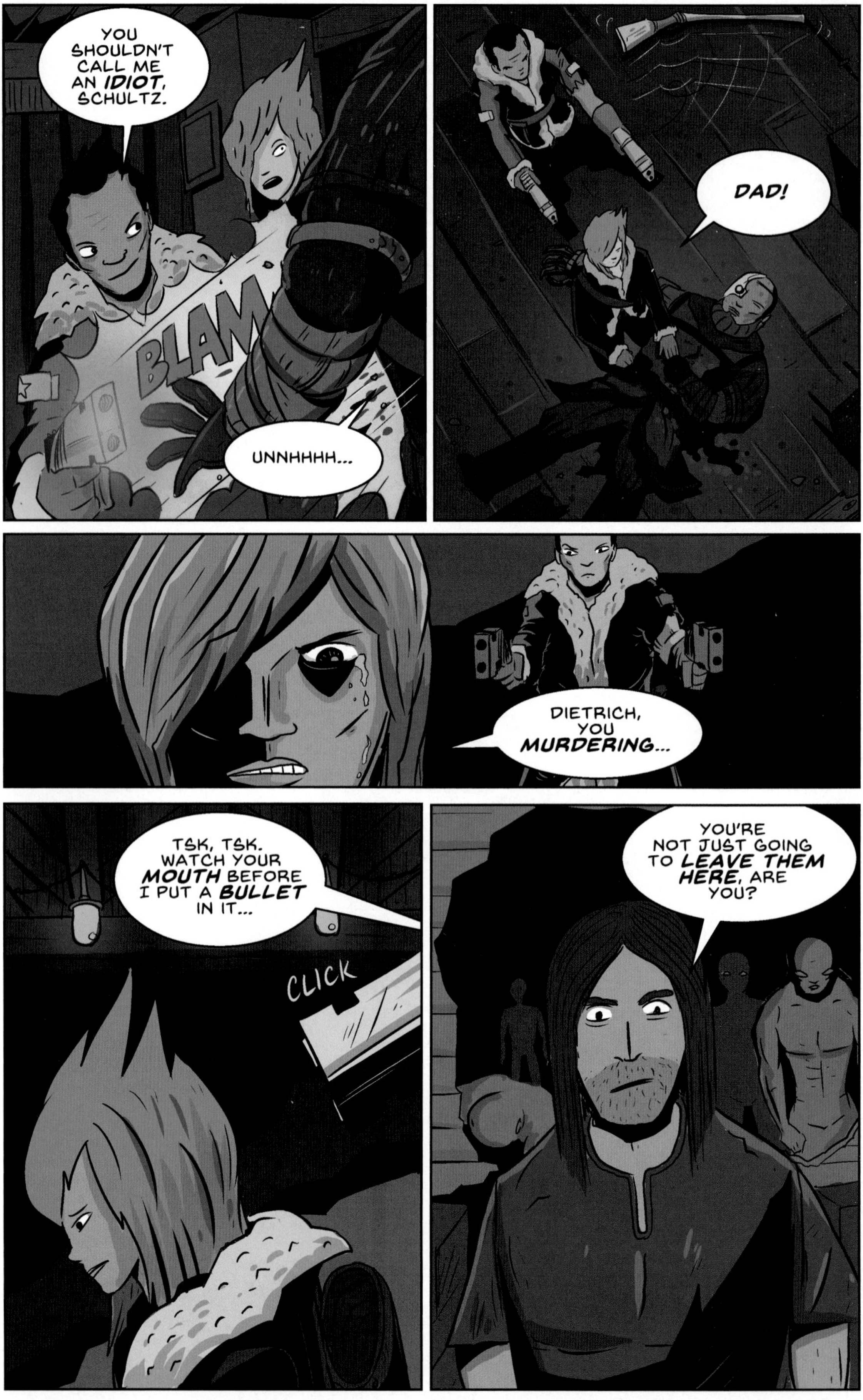
YOU SHOULDN'T CALL ME AN *IDIOT*, SCHULTZ.
BLAM
UNNHHHH...
DAD!
DIETRICH, YOU *MURDERING*...
TSK, TSK. WATCH YOUR *MOUTH* BEFORE I PUT A *BULLET* IN IT...
CLICK
YOU'RE NOT JUST GOING TO *LEAVE THEM HERE*, ARE YOU?

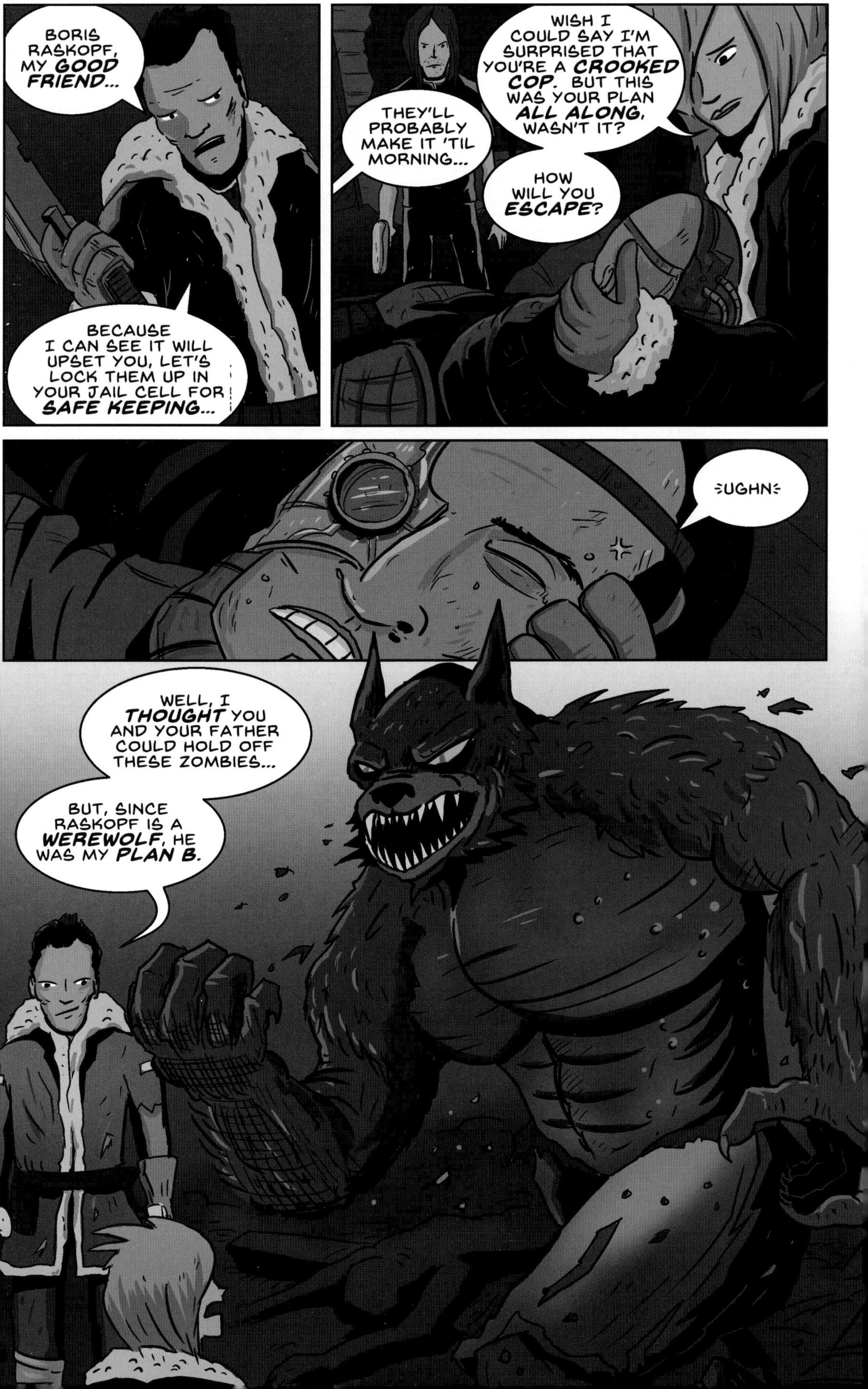
BORIS RASKOPF, MY GOOD FRIEND...
BECAUSE I CAN SEE IT WILL UPSET YOU, LET'S LOCK THEM UP IN YOUR JAIL CELL FOR SAFE KEEPING...
THEY'LL PROBABLY MAKE IT 'TIL MORNING...
WISH I COULD SAY I'M SURPRISED THAT YOU'RE A CROOKED COP. BUT THIS WAS YOUR PLAN ALL ALONG, WASN'T IT?
HOW WILL YOU ESCAPE?
UGHN
WELL, I THOUGHT YOU AND YOUR FATHER COULD HOLD OFF THESE ZOMBIES...
BUT, SINCE RASKOPF IS A WEREWOLF, HE WAS MY PLAN B.

I'M **SORRY** IT HAD TO BE THIS WAY, **BEAUTIFUL.**

AT LEAST YOU'LL BE **SAFE** IN THIS **CELL...**

HOW COULD YOU **PARTNER** WITH SOMEONE SO **HORRIBLE?**

HOW **COULD YOU?**

I NEEDED **MONEY.** MY **MOTHER--**

NOBODY **CARES** ABOUT YOUR LAME STORY, RASKOPF.

GO CLEAR US A **PATH OUT OF HERE.**

THAT **HEIST** FROM FRANKENSTEIN'S LAB WILL MAKE ME **RICH.**

MARIA, THE VOODOO PRIESTESS, WANTED A **CUT.** I REFUSED AND... **HURT** SOMEONE CLOSE TO HER...

NOW I'LL TAKE HER OUT. AND I'LL TAKE **YOU TWO** OUT.

RASKOPF DOESN'T EVEN **NEED TO KNOW...**

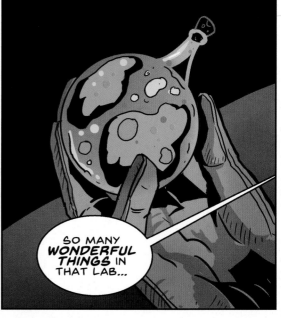

SO MANY **WONDERFUL THINGS** IN THAT LAB...

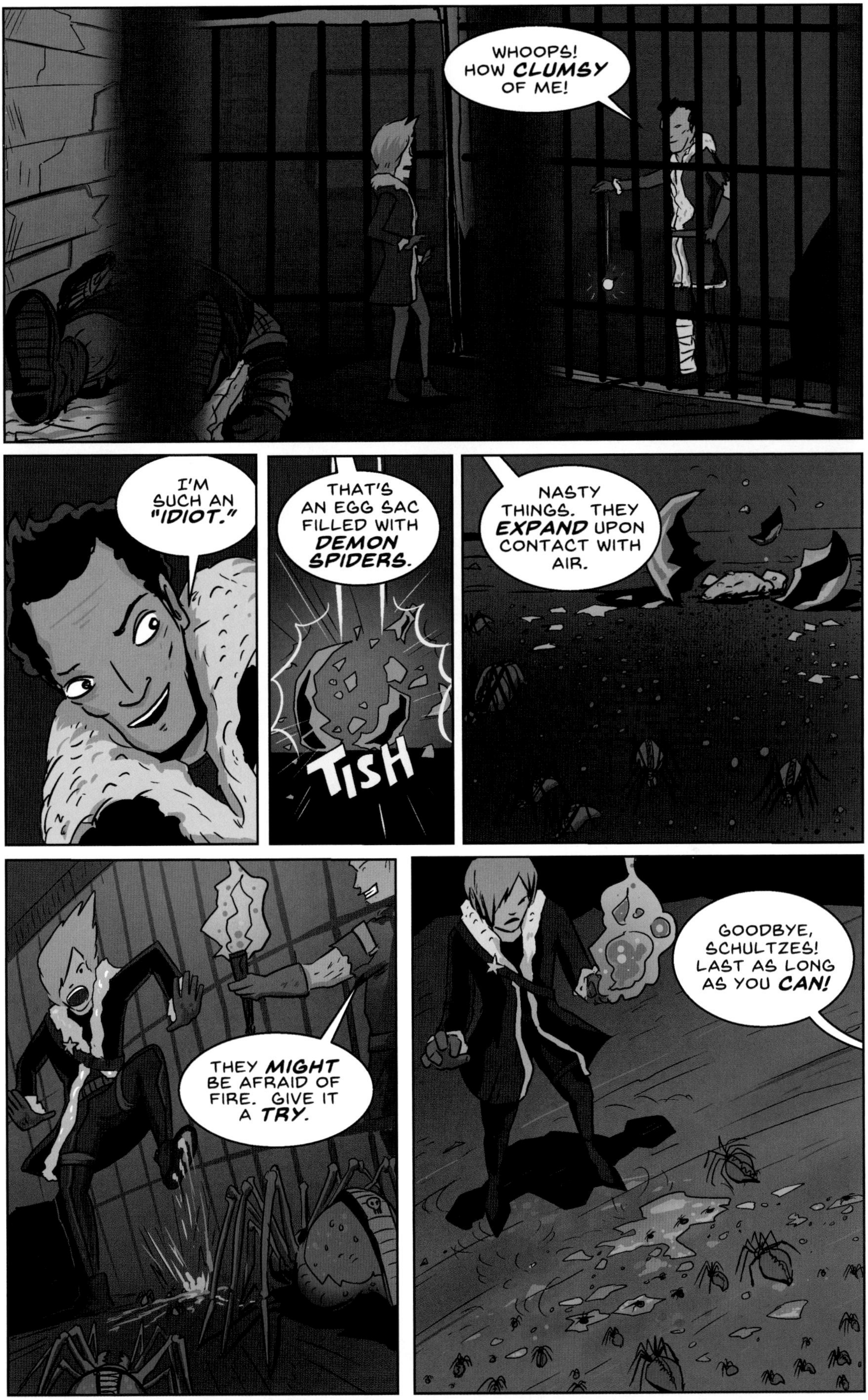
WHOOPS! HOW CLUMSY OF ME!
I'M SUCH AN "IDIOT."
THAT'S AN EGG SAC FILLED WITH DEMON SPIDERS.
TISH
NASTY THINGS. THEY EXPAND UPON CONTACT WITH AIR.
THEY MIGHT BE AFRAID OF FIRE. GIVE IT A TRY.
GOODBYE, SCHULTZES! LAST AS LONG AS YOU CAN!

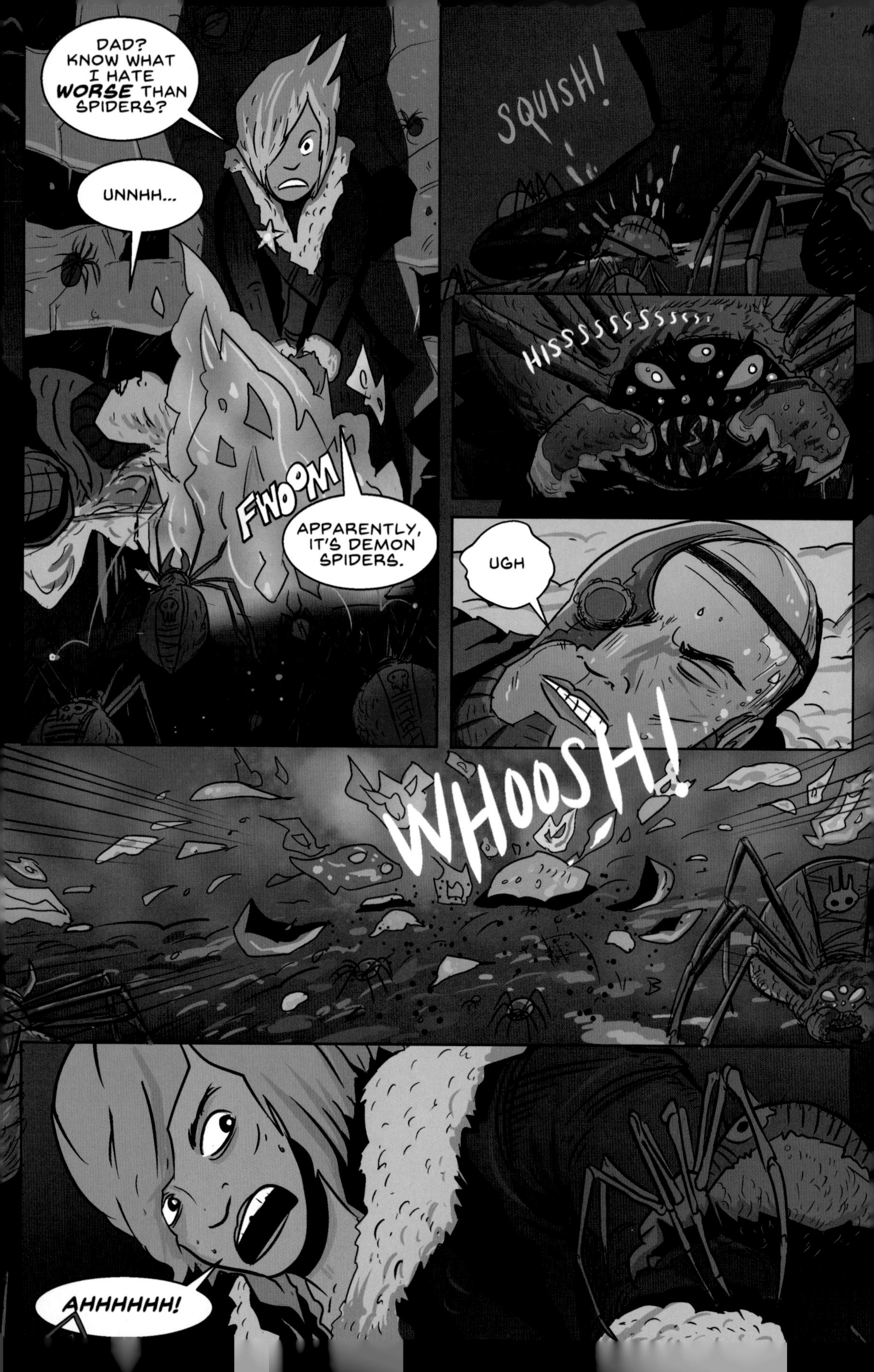
DAD? KNOW WHAT I HATE WORSE THAN SPIDERS?
UNNHH...
FWOOM
APPARENTLY, IT'S DEMON SPIDERS.
SQUISH!
HISSSSSSSSSS
UGH
WHOOSH!
AHHHHHH!

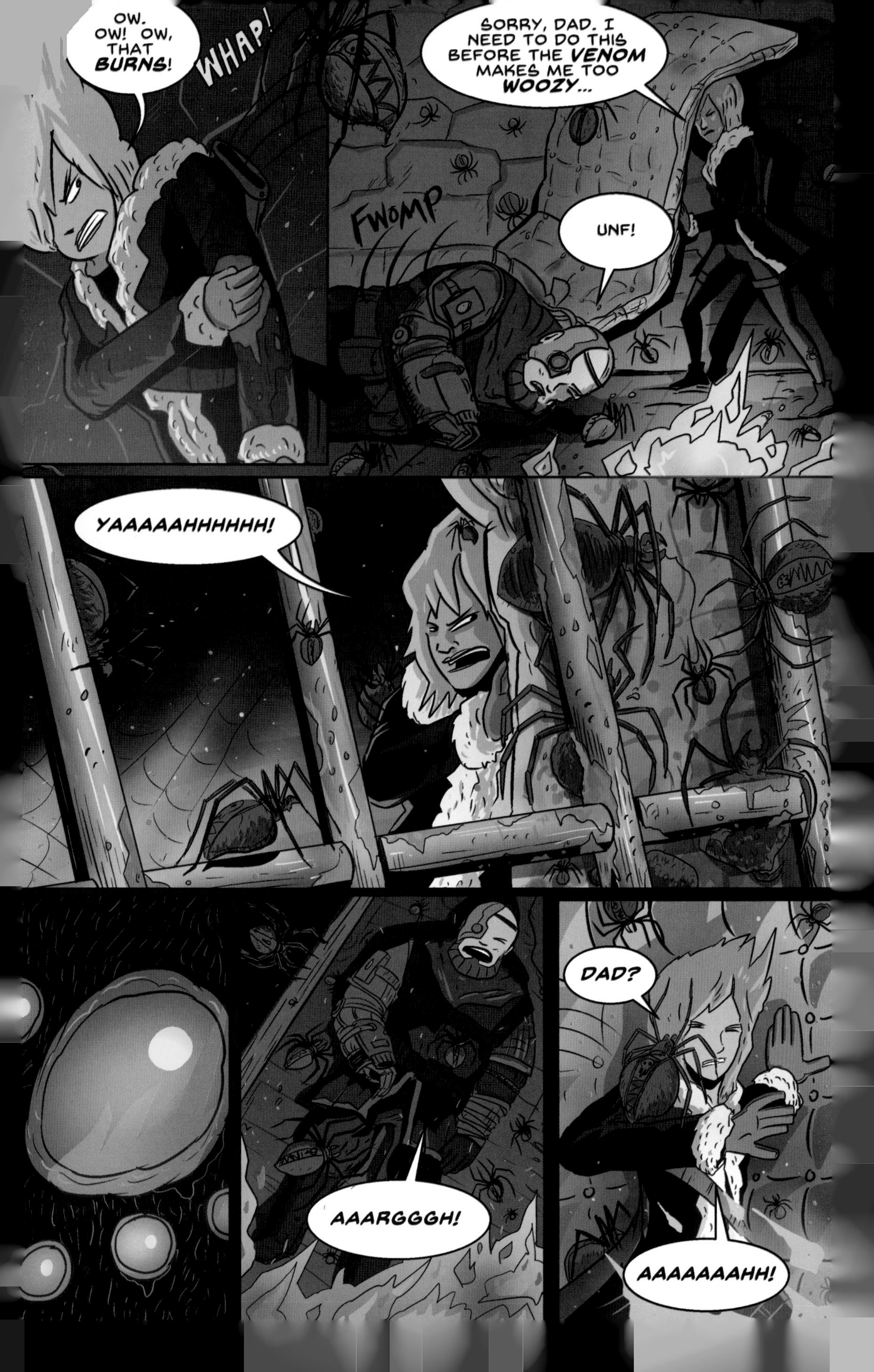
OW. OW! OW, THAT BURNS!
WHAP!
SORRY, DAD. I NEED TO DO THIS BEFORE THE VENOM MAKES ME TOO WOOZY...
FWOMP
UNF!
YAAAAAHHHHHH!
AAARGGGH!
DAD?
AAAAAAAHH!

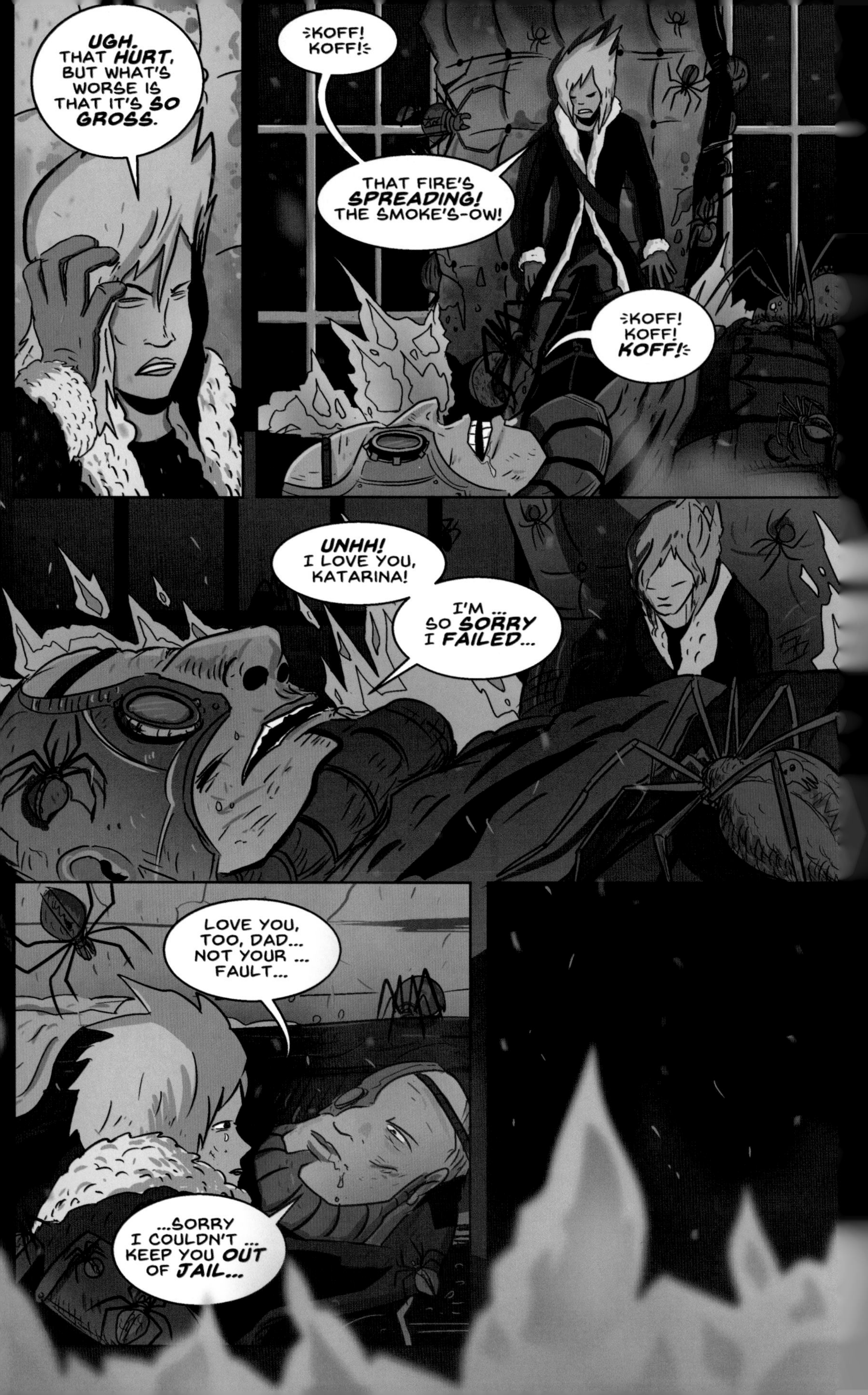
UGH. THAT HURT, BUT WHAT'S WORSE IS THAT IT'S SO GROSS.
KOFF! KOFF!
THAT FIRE'S SPREADING! THE SMOKE'S-OW!
KOFF! KOFF! KOFF!
UNHH! I LOVE YOU, KATARINA!
I'M ... SO SORRY I FAILED...
LOVE YOU, TOO, DAD... NOT YOUR ... FAULT...
...SORRY I COULDN'T ... KEEP YOU OUT OF JAIL...

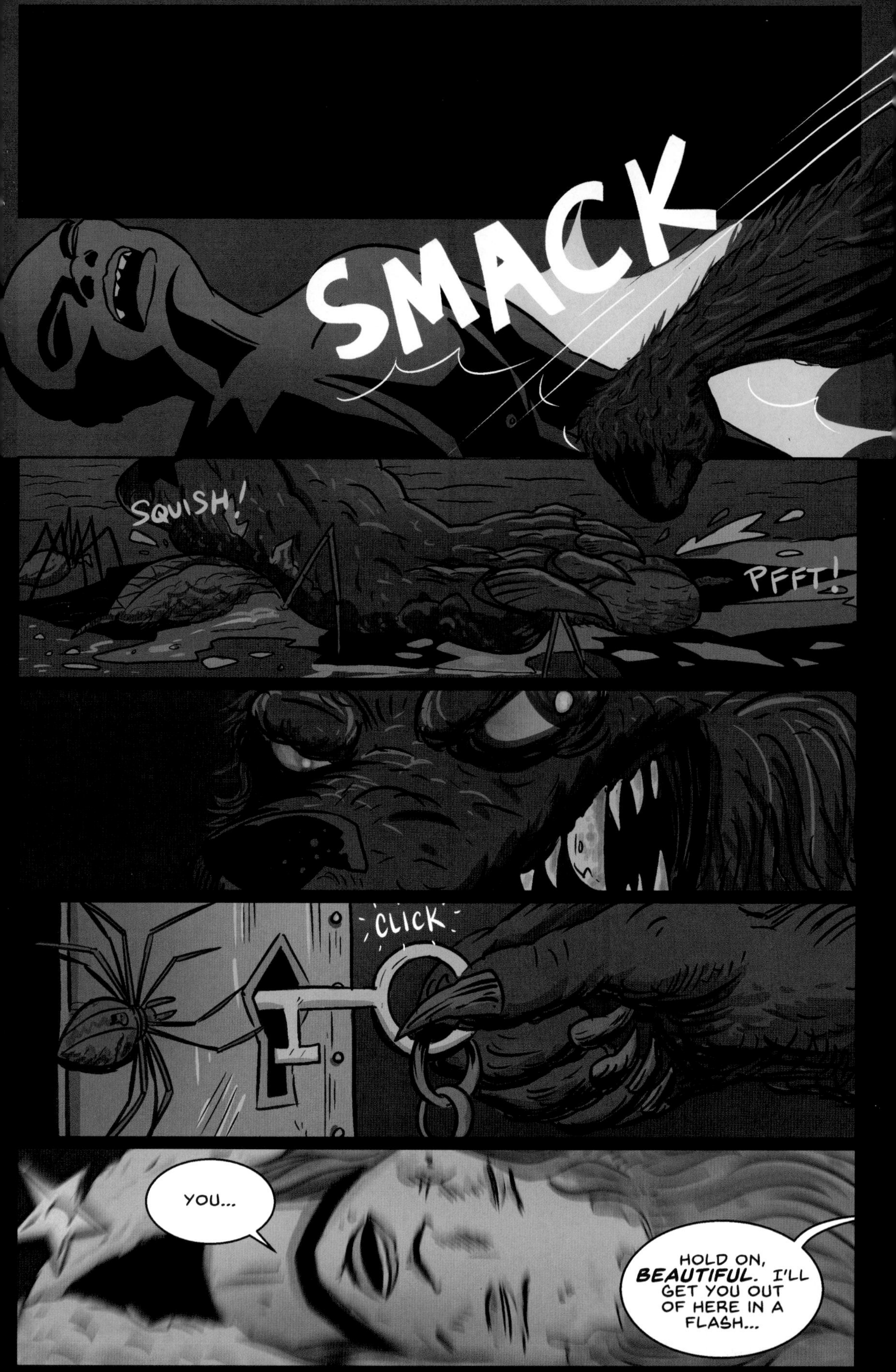
SMACK
SQUISH!
PFFT!
CLICK
YOU...
HOLD ON, **BEAUTIFUL.** I'LL GET YOU OUT OF HERE IN A FLASH...

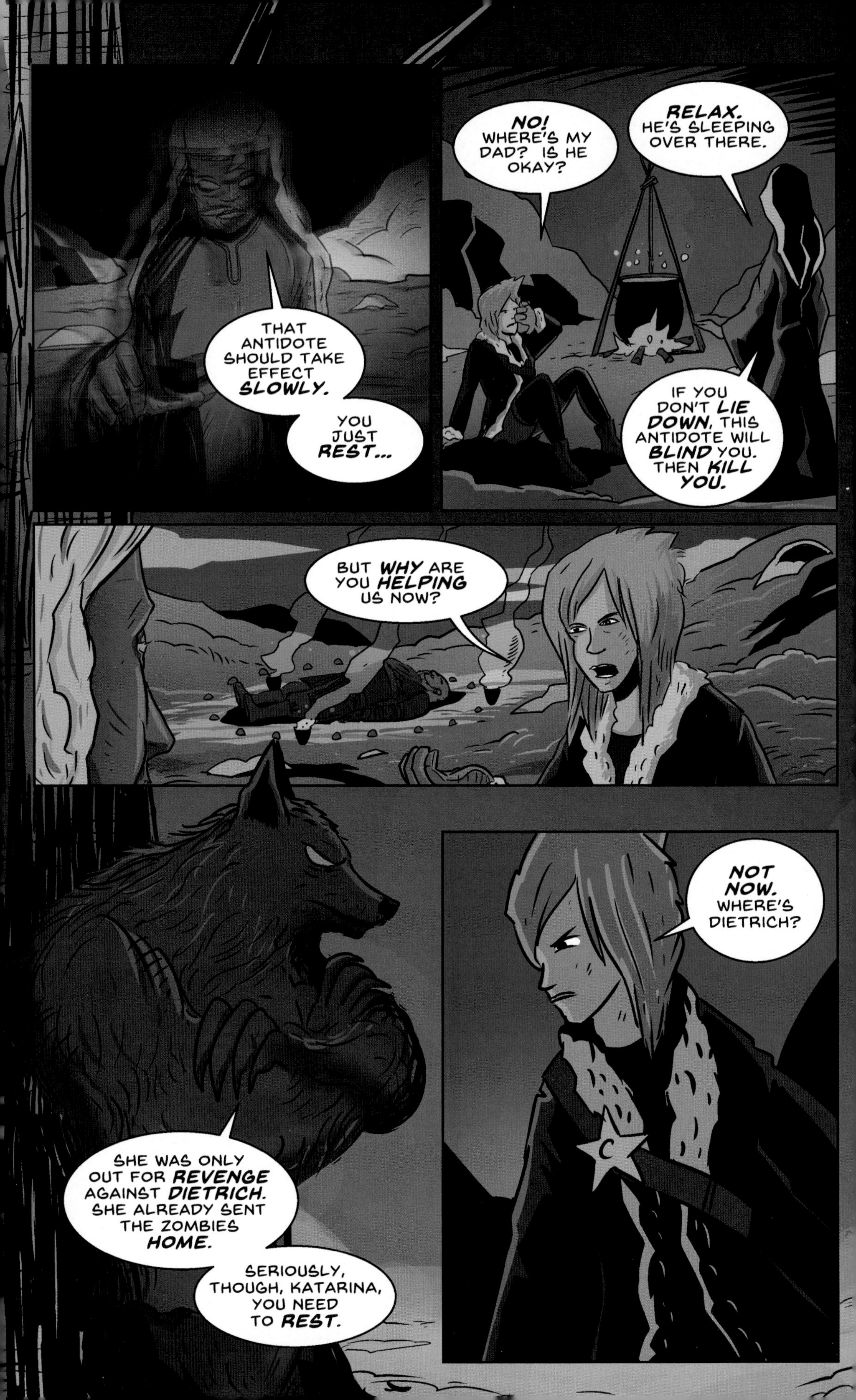
THAT ANTIDOTE SHOULD TAKE EFFECT SLOWLY.
YOU JUST REST...
NO! WHERE'S MY DAD? IS HE OKAY?
RELAX. HE'S SLEEPING OVER THERE.
IF YOU DON'T LIE DOWN, THIS ANTIDOTE WILL BLIND YOU. THEN KILL YOU.
BUT WHY ARE YOU HELPING US NOW?
SHE WAS ONLY OUT FOR REVENGE AGAINST DIETRICH. SHE ALREADY SENT THE ZOMBIES HOME.
SERIOUSLY, THOUGH, KATARINA, YOU NEED TO REST.
NOT NOW. WHERE'S DIETRICH?

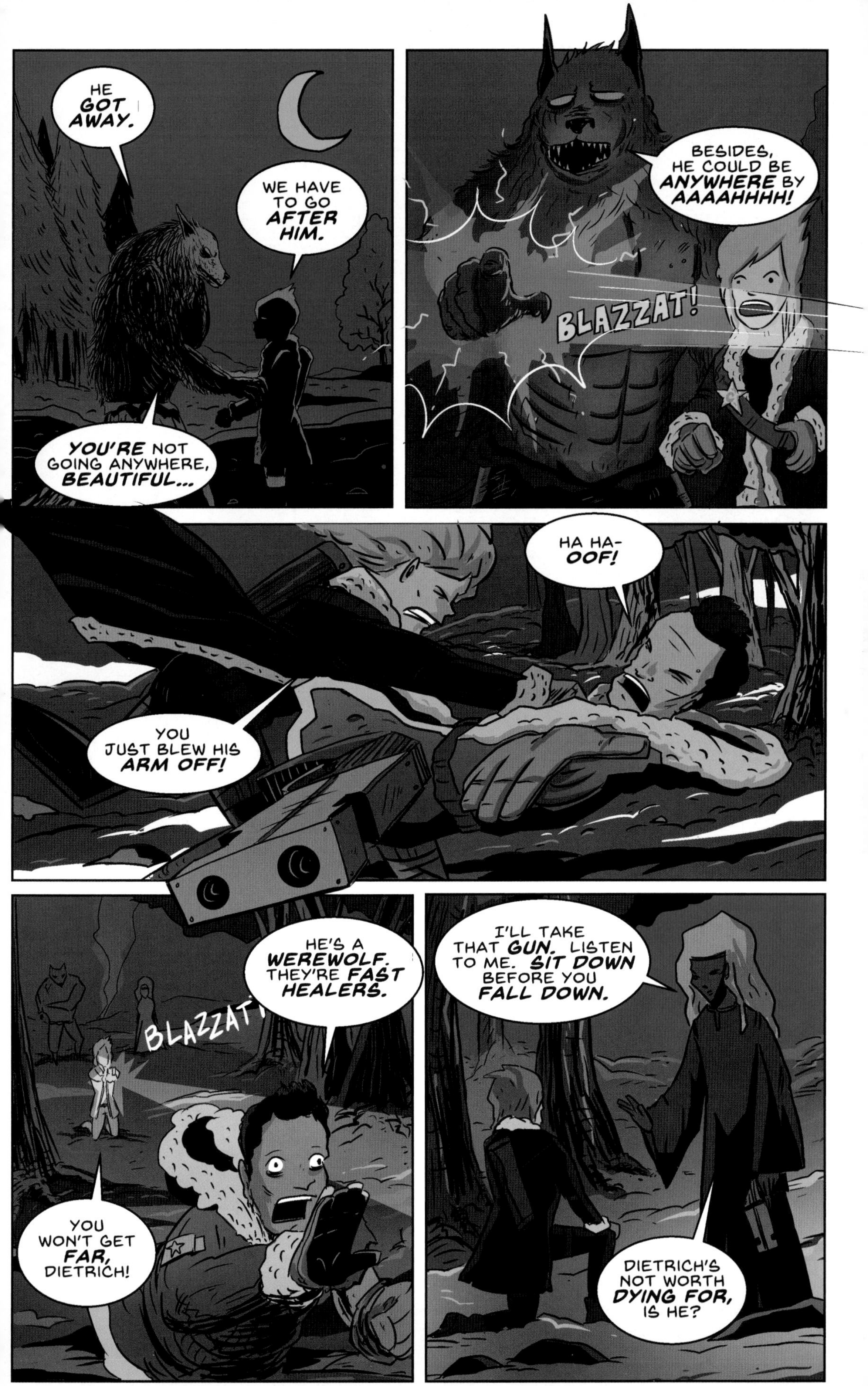
HE GOT AWAY.
WE HAVE TO GO AFTER HIM.
YOU'RE NOT GOING ANYWHERE, BEAUTIFUL...
BESIDES, HE COULD BE ANYWHERE BY AAAAHHHH!
BLAZZAT!
HA HA- OOF!
YOU JUST BLEW HIS ARM OFF!
HE'S A WEREWOLF. THEY'RE FAST HEALERS.
BLAZZAT!
YOU WON'T GET FAR, DIETRICH!
I'LL TAKE THAT GUN. LISTEN TO ME. SIT DOWN BEFORE YOU FALL DOWN.
DIETRICH'S NOT WORTH DYING FOR, IS HE?

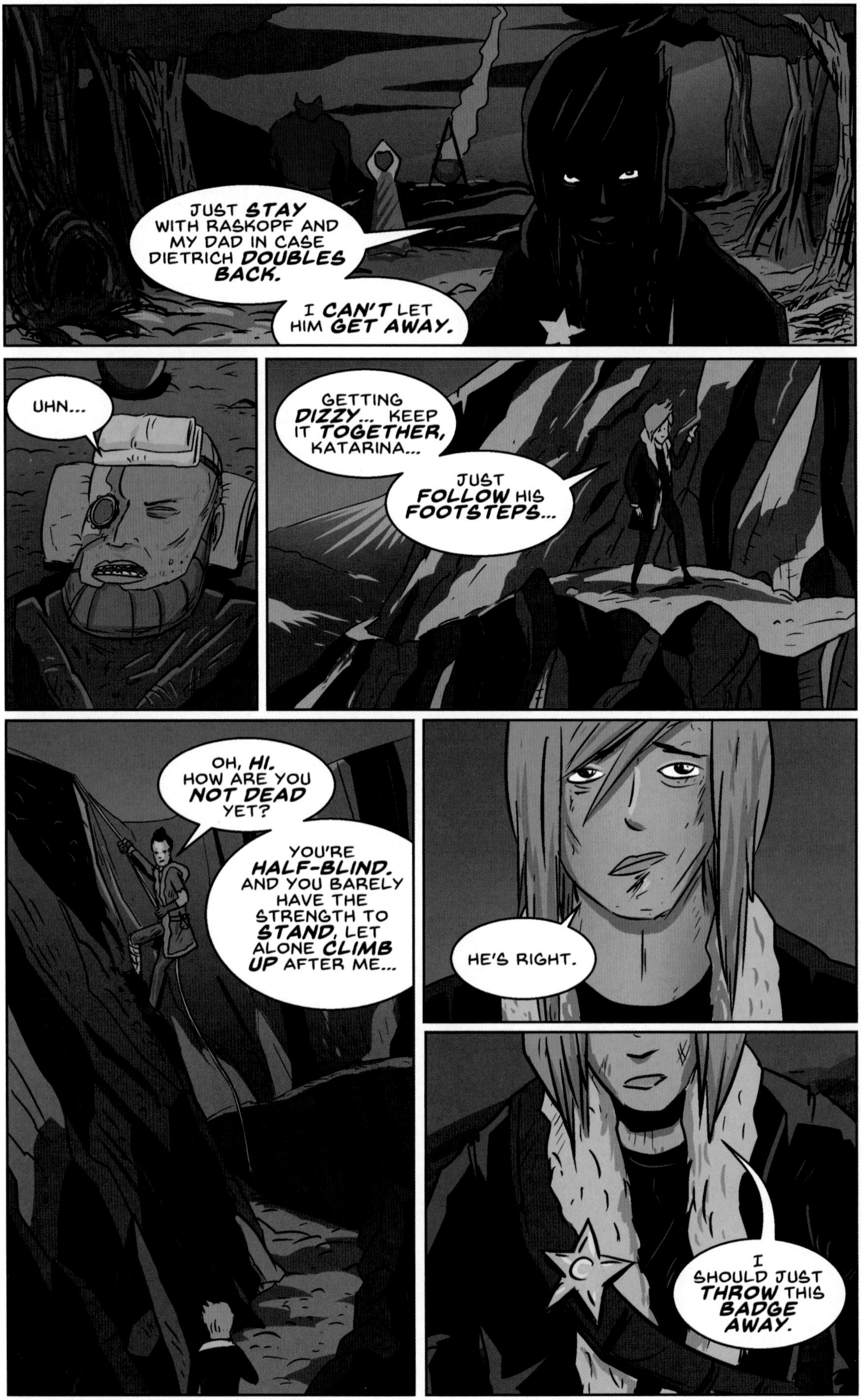
JUST STAY WITH RASKOPF AND MY DAD IN CASE DIETRICH DOUBLES BACK.
I CAN'T LET HIM GET AWAY.
UHN...
GETTING DIZZY... KEEP IT TOGETHER, KATARINA...
JUST FOLLOW HIS FOOTSTEPS...
OH, HI. HOW ARE YOU NOT DEAD YET?
YOU'RE HALF-BLIND. AND YOU BARELY HAVE THE STRENGTH TO STAND, LET ALONE CLIMB UP AFTER ME...
HE'S RIGHT.
I SHOULD JUST THROW THIS BADGE AWAY.

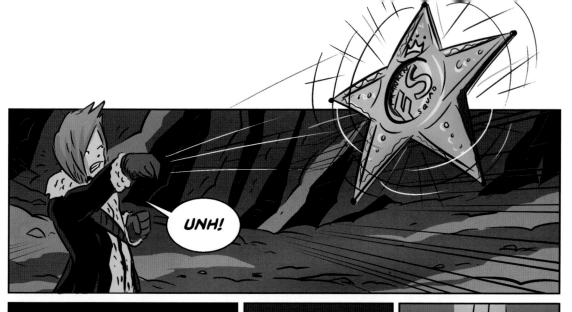

UNH!

WHAT?

SNAP!

AAAAAHHHHHHH!

SMACK!

IT'S BEEN A *LONG NIGHT*, DIETRICH...

BUT NOW IT'S *OVER.*

YOU'RE GOING TO *JAIL.*

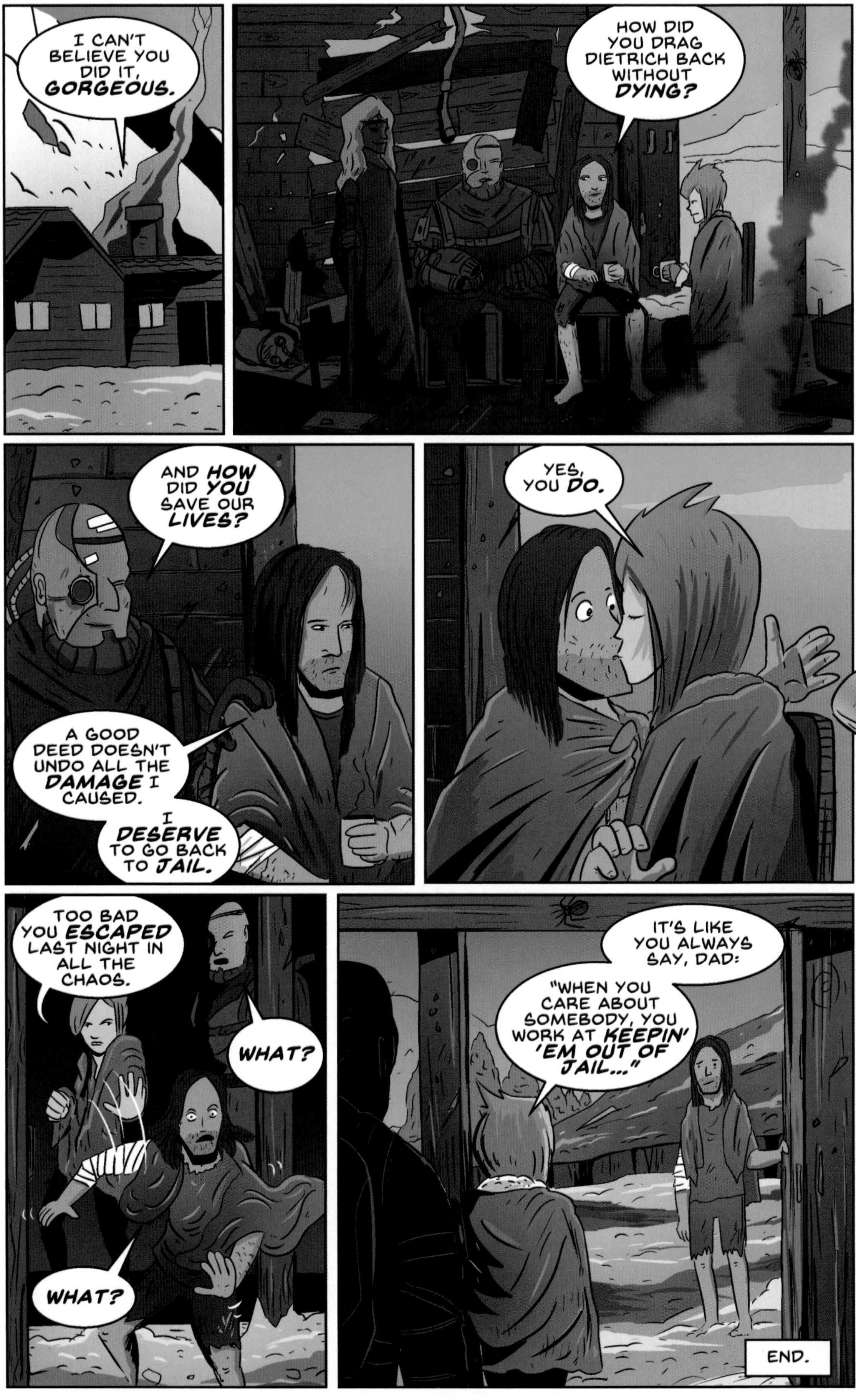
I CAN'T BELIEVE YOU DID IT, GORGEOUS.
HOW DID YOU DRAG DIETRICH BACK WITHOUT DYING?
AND HOW DID YOU SAVE OUR LIVES?
A GOOD DEED DOESN'T UNDO ALL THE DAMAGE I CAUSED.
I DESERVE TO GO BACK TO JAIL.
YES, YOU DO.
TOO BAD YOU ESCAPED LAST NIGHT IN ALL THE CHAOS.
WHAT?
WHAT?
IT'S LIKE YOU ALWAYS SAY, DAD:
"WHEN YOU CARE ABOUT SOMEBODY, YOU WORK AT KEEPIN' 'EM OUT OF JAIL..."
END.

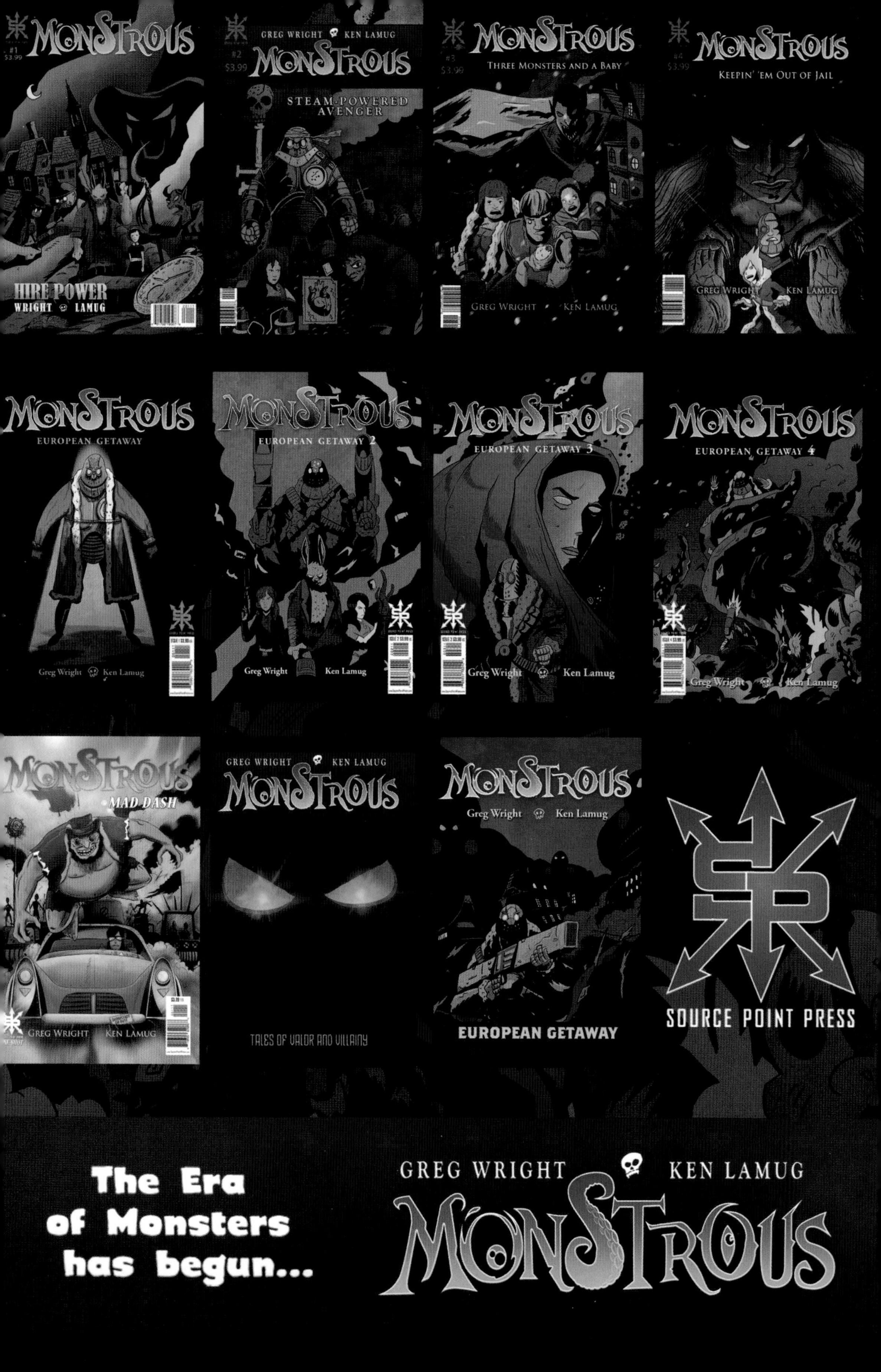
MONSTROUS
#1
$3.99
HIRE POWER
WRIGHT LAMUG
GREG WRIGHT KEN LAMUG
MONSTROUS
#2
$3.99
STEAM-POWERED AVENGER
MONSTROUS
#3
$3.99
THREE MONSTERS AND A BABY
GREG WRIGHT KEN LAMUG
MONSTROUS
#4
$3.99
KEEPIN' 'EM OUT OF JAIL
GREG WRIGHT KEN LAMUG
MONSTROUS
EUROPEAN GETAWAY
Greg Wright Ken Lamug
MONSTROUS
EUROPEAN GETAWAY 2
Greg Wright Ken Lamug
MONSTROUS
EUROPEAN GETAWAY 3
Greg Wright Ken Lamug
MONSTROUS
EUROPEAN GETAWAY 4
Greg Wright Ken Lamug
MONSTROUS
MAD DASH
GREG WRIGHT KEN LAMUG
GREG WRIGHT KEN LAMUG
MONSTROUS
TALES OF VALOR AND VILLAINY
MONSTROUS
Greg Wright Ken Lamug
EUROPEAN GETAWAY
SOURCE POINT PRESS
The Era of Monsters has begun...
GREG WRIGHT KEN LAMUG
MONSTROUS

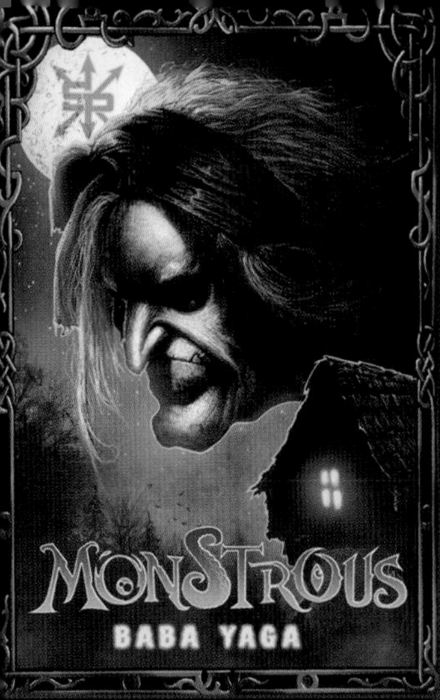
MONSTROUS
BABA YAGA
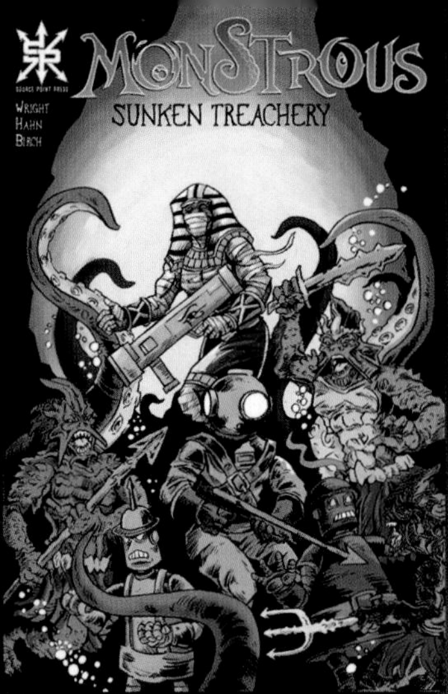
MONSTROUS
WRIGHT
HAHN
BIRCH
SUNKEN TREACHERY
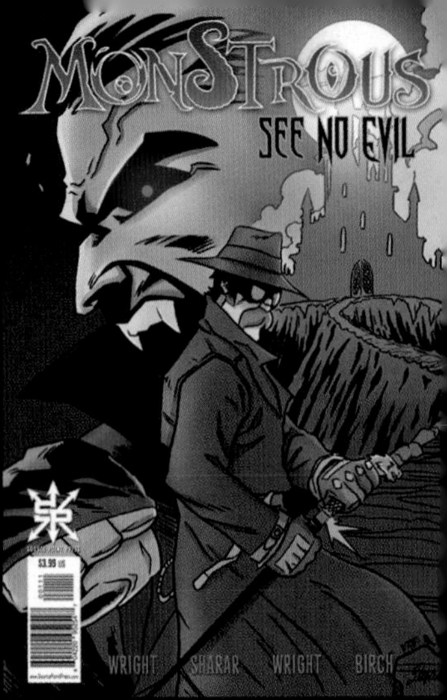
MONSTROUS
SEE NO EVIL
$3.99 US
WRIGHT SHARAR WRIGHT BIRCH
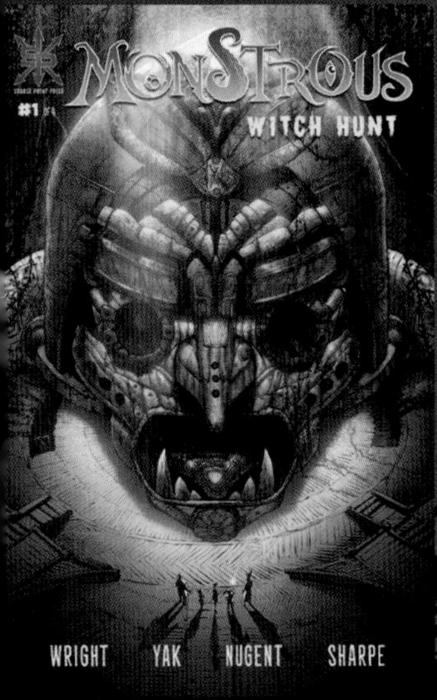
MONSTROUS
#1
WITCH HUNT
WRIGHT YAK NUGENT SHARPE
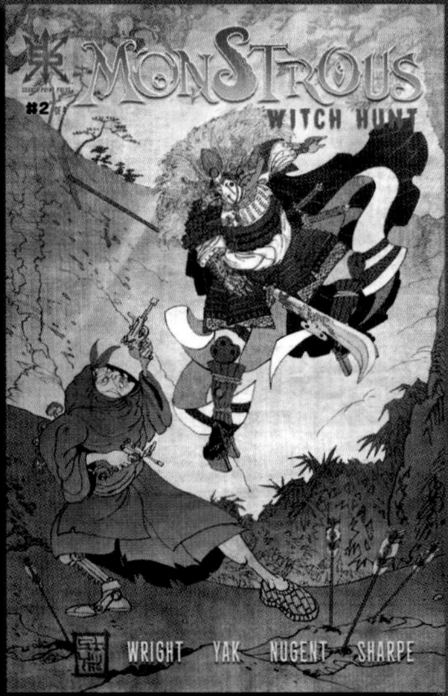
MONSTROUS
#2
WITCH HUNT
WRIGHT YAK NUGENT SHARPE
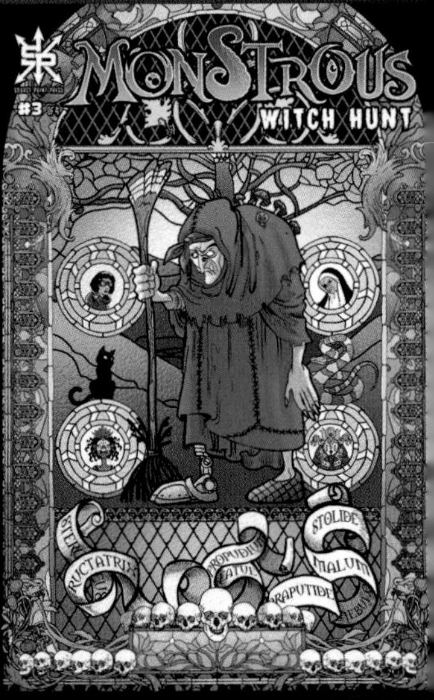
MONSTROUS
#3
WITCH HUNT
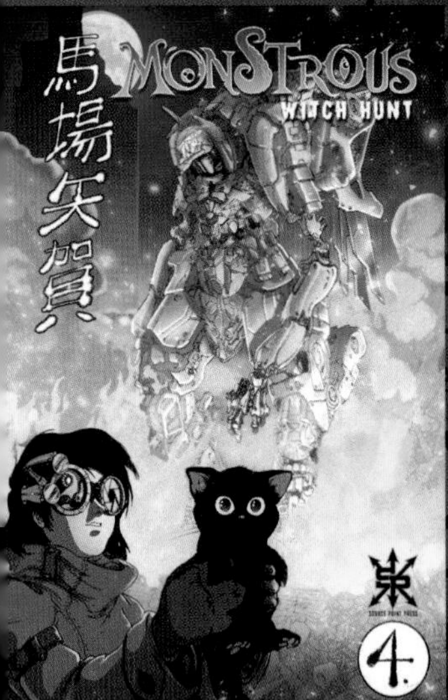
馬場矢賀
MONSTROUS
WITCH HUNT
4.

WITCH HUNT

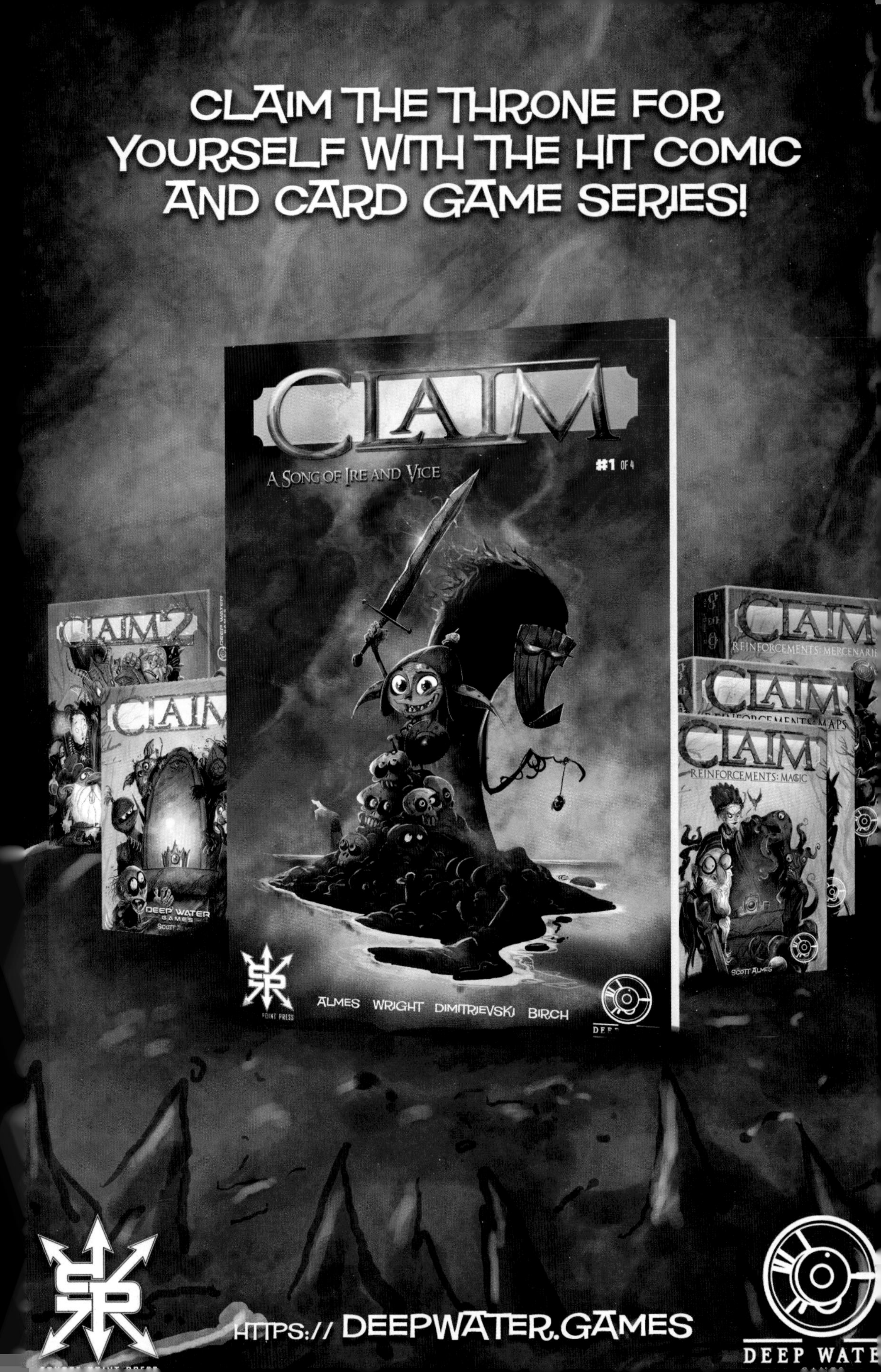
CLAIM THE THRONE FOR YOURSELF WITH THE HIT COMIC AND CARD GAME SERIES!
CLAIM
A SONG OF IRE AND VICE
#1 OF 4
ALMES WRIGHT DIMITRIEVSKI BIRCH
POINT PRESS
CLAIM 2
CLAIM
DEEP WATER GAMES
CLAIM
REINFORCEMENTS: MAGIC
SCOTT ALMES
HTTPS:// DEEPWATER.GAMES